Microsoft Office 365 |

The Ultimate Crash Course to Maximize Productivity with Step-by-Step Illustrated Instructions for Word, Excel, PowerPoint, Outlook, OneDrive, Publisher, Teams and More

Ethan Redcliffe

Table Of Contents

Book 1: Microsoft Word Mastery

Embarking on the journey to master Microsoft Word is a path filled with discoveries and opportunities to enhance your document creation skills. This comprehensive guide is designed to take you from the fundamental aspects of Word to the more intricate and powerful features, equipping you with the knowledge to transform how you interact with this essential tool. Whether you are a beginner seeking to build a solid foundation or an experienced user aiming to refine your expertise, this guide offers valuable insights and practical advice.

We begin by exploring the basics, ensuring a strong understanding of the interface and core functionalities of Word. This foundation is crucial as it sets the stage for more advanced learning. As you progress, you will delve into the art of crafting professional documents, where you'll learn to leverage formatting, styles, and templates to create visually appealing and coherent work.

The guide also addresses the integration of advanced text features, enhancing your documents beyond basic text to include SmartArt, graphics, and images, turning simple documents into engaging and informative presentations. You'll also discover the efficiency of using tools like Mail Merge for mass communication, a vital skill in today's fast-paced world.

Moreover, effective collaboration in document creation is more important than ever. You'll learn how to utilize Word's collaborative tools to work seamlessly with colleagues, enhancing productivity and creativity. Finally, the guide covers troubleshooting common challenges, ensuring that you're equipped to overcome any obstacles in your Word journey.

Whether for professional advancement, academic success, or personal projects, mastering Microsoft Word opens a world of possibilities in document creation. This guide is your companion on this journey, providing you with the skills and confidence to utilize Word to its fullest potential.

1. Word Basics: Starting with Confidence

Embarking on the journey of mastering Microsoft Word is akin to unlocking a treasure chest of possibilities in document creation and design. This versatile tool, a cornerstone of the Office 365 suite, opens up a world where your ideas can transform into professional, visually engaging documents.

As we delve into the basics of Word, remember that each step taken is a building block towards becoming proficient in this powerful word processor.

When you first launch Microsoft Word, you're greeted by a clean, inviting interface. It might seem a bit overwhelming at first glance, but it's designed to be intuitive and user-friendly. The ribbon at the top houses an array of tools and features, neatly organized into tabs. These are your instruments for crafting and molding your document. The beauty of Word lies in its ability to cater to both first-time users and seasoned professionals. As you familiarize yourself with the layout, you'll find that creating, editing, and formatting documents becomes a more fluid and natural process.

Starting a new document in Word is like turning to a blank page in a notebook, full of potential and ready for your ideas. Clicking 'New' brings up a fresh page, a canvas awaiting your input. As you begin typing, you'll notice the ease with which text flows on the page. Here, your words start to take shape, forming the basis of your communication, whether it's a simple letter, a complex report, or anything in between.

One of the first steps in making your document stand out is text formatting. This is where you give your words personality and emphasis. The 'Home' tab on the ribbon is where you'll spend a lot of your time. It's here that you can change the font style, adjust the size, and alter the color of your text. Each font has its own character; a font like Arial gives a modern, clean look, while Times New Roman carries a more traditional tone. Playing with font sizes and colors adds depth and emphasis to your text, helping you to highlight key points and organize information effectively.

The structure and layout of your document play a crucial role in how it's perceived. Formatting paragraphs, adjusting alignment, and using lists are essential skills. Word offers several alignment options – left, center, right, and justify – each lending a different aesthetic and flow to your text. Left alignment is standard and easy on the eyes, making it ideal for most documents. Center alignment works well for titles and headers, adding a focal point to your page. Right alignment and justification offer alternative ways to style your document, useful for specific types of formatting.

Lists, both bulleted and numbered, are integral to organizing information. They break down content into manageable chunks, making it easier for your reader to digest and follow. The 'Home' tab provides easy access to creating these lists. Bullets are perfect for non-sequential items, offering a clear way to present various points. Numbered lists are ideal when order and sequence matter, such as in instructions or ranked information.

Saving your work is an essential habit to develop. Word's versatility shines through in its variety of saving options. You can save your documents in the classic Word format (.docx) or as a PDF, among other formats. This flexibility allows you to share your work across different platforms and ensures that your documents are accessible and viewable in the intended format. Regularly saving your work also safeguards against data loss, ensuring that your effort and creativity are preserved.

As you become more comfortable with these foundational aspects of Word, your confidence in using the software will naturally grow. Exploration and practice are key to mastering any tool, and Word is no exception. Try adding a unique header to your document, or experiment with inserting a hyperlink to relevant information. Each document you create is an opportunity to explore new features and refine your skills.

In conclusion, beginning your journey with Microsoft Word is about embracing its capabilities and letting your creativity flourish. With each feature you learn, a new realm of possibilities opens up.

Your documents become more than just text on a page; they transform into powerful tools of communication and expression. As you continue to explore and master the intricacies of Word, you'll find that it becomes an invaluable companion in your professional, academic, and personal endeavors. The path ahead in Word is filled with opportunities for growth and innovation. Embrace it with enthusiasm and confidence.

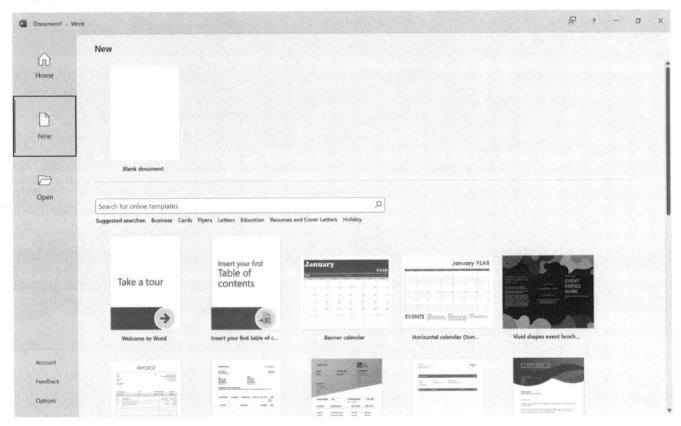

2. Navigating the Interface: A Beginner's Guide

Mastering the interface of Microsoft Word is a fundamental step towards leveraging its full capabilities. The interface might initially appear complex, but it's designed to be intuitive and user-centric, allowing seamless navigation even for beginners. Let's embark on a detailed exploration of Word's interface, focusing on each element's role and how it can enhance your document creation experience.

The Ribbon is the core of Word's interface, featuring a series of tabs like 'Home', 'Insert', 'Design', and more, each focusing on specific types of tasks. For instance, while the 'Home' tab offers basic text formatting tools, the 'Insert' tab allows you to add diverse elements to your document. This organizational structure ensures that tools are logically grouped and easy to find. Familiarizing yourself with the Ribbon is crucial, as it houses the majority of Word's features. Take your time to explore each tab, understanding the purpose of the tools. Remember, becoming proficient with these tools is a gradual process that will develop naturally as you use the program more.

Above the Ribbon, you'll find the Quick Access Toolbar. This small, customizable toolbar allows you to pin shortcuts to your most frequently used features. This is incredibly useful for enhancing your efficiency, as it keeps essential tools readily accessible. You can easily modify this toolbar to suit your specific workflow needs, making your interaction with Word more personalized and efficient.

The main area where you'll be spending most of your time is the document area. This is the blank canvas where your text and ideas take shape. Word offers various view modes for this area, such as 'Read Mode', 'Print Layout', and 'Web Layout', each offering a different perspective of your document. The ability to switch between these views enables you to work in an environment that best suits the task at hand, whether you are drafting, reviewing, or finalizing your document.

An often-overlooked yet important feature is the status bar at the bottom of the Word window. This bar provides essential information like page number, word count, and zoom controls. For those working on lengthy documents, the status bar is a valuable tool for keeping track of your progress and quickly adjusting the view of your document.

Word's interface is also characterized by its intelligent use of contextual tabs. These tabs appear on the Ribbon only when they are relevant to the task you are performing. For example, if you insert a table, a 'Table Tools' tab appears, providing specific features for table customization. This dynamic feature helps keep the Ribbon uncluttered, presenting you with the right tools at the right moment.

In addition to the mouse-based navigation, knowing some keyboard shortcuts can greatly enhance your productivity. Common shortcuts like Ctrl+C (Copy), Ctrl+V (Paste), and Ctrl+Z (Undo) are just the beginning. Word offers a comprehensive list of shortcuts that can speed up many tasks, from basic text editing to more complex formatting and navigation. Utilizing these shortcuts can significantly streamline your workflow, making your interactions with Word more efficient.

Another aspect of the interface that you can tailor to your needs is the customization of the workspace. Word allows you to modify the Ribbon, Quick Access Toolbar, and the application's overall theme to better suit your working style. This level of customization ensures that the interface aligns with your preferences and work habits, making your experience with Word more comfortable and intuitive.

Navigating through Microsoft Word's interface is like embarking on an exciting journey where each element and tool you discover adds to your proficiency in document creation. The Ribbon, Quick Access Toolbar, document area, status bar, contextual tabs, keyboard shortcuts, and customization options all work together to create a user-friendly environment.

Each component has been thoughtfully designed to enhance your productivity and make the process of creating, editing, and formatting documents as seamless as possible.

As you become more familiar with these elements, you'll find that navigating Word's interface becomes an intuitive part of your workflow. With practice and exploration, you'll be able to harness the full potential of Word, transforming it from a simple word processor into a powerful tool for your professional, academic, or personal projects.

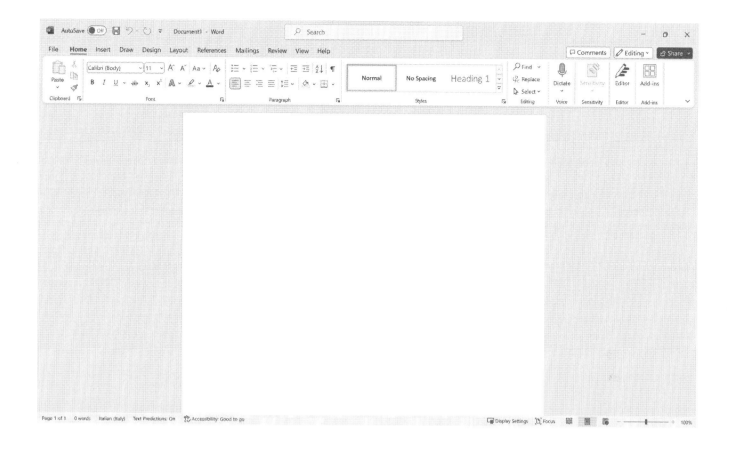

3. Crafting Professional Documents: Tips and Tricks

Creating professional documents in Microsoft Word is an art that blends technical know-how with an understanding of design aesthetics and audience engagement. To craft a document that not only conveys information effectively but also captures the reader's attention and interest, a combination of various elements must be thoughtfully employed.

The first step in this creative process is understanding the purpose and audience of your document. This initial consideration shapes the entire approach to the document - from its tone and style to its level of detail. For instance, a business proposal should embody a formal and persuasive tone, whereas an instructional manual may take on a more explanatory and casual demeanor.

Consistency in formatting is a cornerstone of professional documentation. This includes a uniform application of fonts, heading styles, and spacing. Word's built-in styles are instrumental in maintaining a coherent look throughout your document. These styles not only enhance readability but also lend an organized and polished appearance.

The strategic use of headers and footers adds a layer of professionalism. Typically housing the document title, chapter headings, page numbers, and dates, they frame the content and aid in its navigation. Word's functionality allows for the easy insertion and customization of these elements, thereby enhancing both the aesthetics and the functionality of the document.

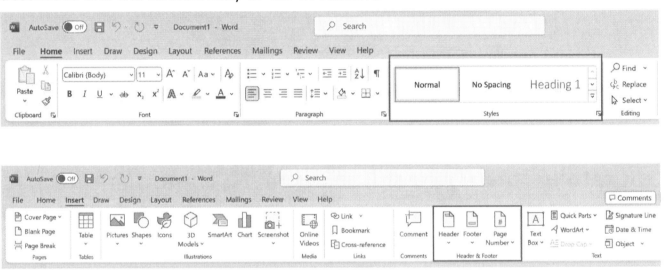

Data presentation through tables and charts is a powerful way to convey information. Word's capabilities in this regard allow for the integration of complex data in a visually digestible format. However, the key lies in simplicity; overly complex tables or visually dense charts can detract from the document's readability. Incorporating bullet points and numbered lists is an effective way to organize information. They break down content into easily consumable segments and facilitate quick comprehension. Word's customization options enable these elements to be tailored to fit the overall style and tone of the document.

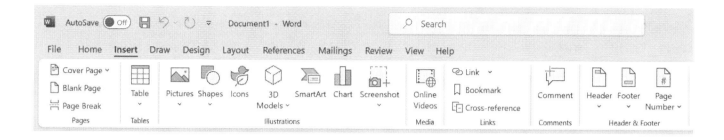

The layout of the document, particularly the balance between text and white space, plays a significant role in its readability and visual appeal. Crowded pages can overwhelm the reader, so it's important to utilize margins, spacing, and breaks thoughtfully to create a document that's inviting and easy to navigate.

Images can significantly enhance the visual impact of a document but must be used judiciously. Word allows for the insertion and formatting of images, enabling them to complement rather than overpower the textual content. High-quality, relevant images, properly formatted, can elevate the professional standard of the document.

The introduction and conclusion of a document are its bookends and should be crafted with care. A compelling introduction sets the tone and purpose, engaging the reader right from the start, while a well-articulated conclusion provides closure, summarizing the content and, if necessary, prompting the reader to action.

No document is complete without rigorous proofreading and review. While Word's spell check and grammar tools are helpful, they are not infallible. A thorough review for errors, inconsistencies, and clarity is indispensable. External review, if possible, can provide valuable insights and a different perspective.

Finally, leveraging Word's array of templates can be a great starting point, especially when time constraints are a factor. These templates offer pre-formatted layouts and styles, providing a foundation that can be customized to suit the specific needs of your document.

In summary, the creation of professional documents in Word is a nuanced process that requires more than just writing skills. It demands an understanding of design principles, audience expectations, and the purposeful use of Word's extensive features. By skillfully combining these elements, you can transform your document from a mere compilation of text into an impactful, professional, and engaging piece of communication. Remember, each document is a representation of your professional identity; investing time and effort into its creation reflects your commitment to quality and excellence.

4. Formatting Text for Impact

The art of formatting text in Microsoft Word transcends mere aesthetic appeal; it's a strategic approach to communication, enhancing the reader's experience and effectively delivering your message. In the nuanced world of document creation, understanding the power of typography and the interplay of various formatting elements is essential to create an impact.

Typography in Word is not just a choice; it's a statement. The fonts you choose set the tone for your document. Serif fonts, such as Times New Roman, bring a formal, traditional feel, ideal for academic or official documents. Sans-serif fonts like Arial, on the other hand, offer a modern touch, suitable for business or casual documents. The size of your font is equally crucial. Larger fonts draw attention and are best used for headings and titles, creating a clear hierarchical structure that guides the reader through the document. This structural clarity is not only visually appealing but also simplifies the navigation of your content.

Color in text formatting is like seasoning in cooking – a little can go a long way. Standard black text is readable and professional, but introducing color can highlight significant points, differentiate sections, or align with a brand's palette. The key is to use color with a purpose and restraint to maintain legibility and avoid visual overload.

The use of bold and italics offers subtle yet effective ways to add emphasis. Bold text stands out and is perfect for headings or key points, while italics, often used for quotes or technical terms, add a stylistic flair. These text styles, when used strategically, enhance the reader's focus on important aspects of your content.

Alignment and spacing are the unsung heroes of text formatting. While left alignment is standard for its readability, center or right alignments can be used for specific purposes, such as titles or captions. Proper spacing – between lines, paragraphs, and different sections – creates a breathable, organized layout that invites the reader in. This organizational clarity is not just about aesthetics; it's about making your document user-friendly and accessible.

Bullet points and numbered lists are essential tools for clarity and organization.

They distill information into digestible, easy-to-follow points, facilitating quick comprehension. Word's versatility allows you to choose from various styles to best match your document's tone and style, whether it's a formal report or a creative project.

Consistency in your formatting choices is crucial to maintaining professionalism. Uniformity in fonts, styles, sizes, and colors not only looks polished but also unifies the various elements of your content. A document with haphazard formatting can distract and detract from the message you're trying to convey.

Word's Styles feature is a boon for applying consistent formatting across your document. By designing a set of styles for different text elements and applying them consistently, you ensure uniformity and save valuable time. This feature is particularly useful in longer documents where maintaining consistent formatting can be challenging.

Beyond the basics, Word offers advanced customization options like text effects, character spacing, and borders. These features, when used judiciously, can add a creative touch or draw attention to certain parts of your document. However, the overuse of these elements can overshadow the content, so they should be used sparingly and with a clear purpose.

In summary, formatting text for impact in Word is about more than just making words look pretty; it's about using text as a tool to communicate effectively. It involves a careful blend of typography, color, emphasis, alignment, spacing, and consistency. By mastering these elements, you turn your document into a powerful communication tool that is not only visually appealing but also resonates with your audience. Well-formatted text reflects your attention to detail and your commitment to quality, making it an indispensable skill in professional document creation.

5. Advanced Text Features: Beyond Basics

Venturing into the advanced text features of Microsoft Word opens up a dynamic world of document design and presentation, allowing you to infuse your projects with a level of sophistication and professionalism. These advanced features go beyond the basic text formatting, enabling you to create documents that are not just functional but visually compelling and engaging.

In the realm of advanced typography, Word offers options like kerning and ligatures. Kerning adjusts the space between characters, enhancing the overall look of the text, making it appear more uniform and aesthetically pleasing. Ligatures, on the other hand, are typographic designs that combine two or more letters into a single, fluid form. These typography tools are subtle yet powerful, capable of transforming the appearance of your text from ordinary to professional-grade.

Text effects such as shadows, reflections, glow, bevel, and 3D rotation add creative dimensions to your documents. When used with a discerning eye, these effects can significantly elevate key elements like titles and important quotes. However, the key to using these effects effectively lies in their judicious application; overuse can detract from the document's readability and professional appearance.

The functionality of linking text boxes is a standout feature, particularly useful in multi-column layouts like newsletters or magazines. This feature allows for a seamless flow of text from one box to another, enabling you to craft a visually engaging layout. The control it offers over content distribution enhances not just the aesthetics but the readability of your document.

Pull quotes are an excellent tool for emphasizing key points or quotes. They serve to break the monotony of continuous text, drawing the reader's attention and adding an element of interest. With Word, you can format these pull quotes distinctively, using unique fonts, borders, and shading to make them stand out.

Drop caps are a classic design element used to add an artistic touch to the beginning of a paragraph. They capture the reader's attention, making the entry point into your text more engaging. Word's functionality allows for the easy insertion of drop caps and customization of their appearance, aligning them with the overall design of your document.

Advanced paragraph formatting in Word goes beyond simple alignment and spacing. It encompasses control over line and paragraph spacing, indentation, and tab stops. These tools give you the power to fine-tune how your text is displayed, allowing you to create a layout that is not only visually appealing but also enhances the readability of your document.

For lengthy or complex documents, features like bookmarks and cross-references are invaluable. Bookmarks help you quickly navigate to specific parts of your document, while cross-references link to other sections, figures, or tables, enhancing the document's navigability and usefulness, particularly in academic and technical writing.

The Track Changes and Comments features in Word are essential for collaborative editing. They provide a platform for multiple reviewers to suggest edits and leave comments, which can then be accepted or rejected by the document owner. This feature ensures transparency in the editing process and is crucial for maintaining the integrity of the document during collaborative efforts.

Custom watermarks in Word allow you to add a personal or professional touch to your documents. Whether it's for branding purposes or to mark a document as confidential, the ability to create custom text or image-based watermarks adds a layer of customization and security to your documents.

In summary, the advanced text features in Microsoft Word equip you with a robust set of tools for enhancing your documents. From refined typography to creative text effects, from functional layouts to collaborative editing tools, these features enable you to produce documents that are not only rich in content but also superior in presentation and design. By harnessing these advanced capabilities, you can elevate your documents, making them more impactful, engaging, and professional.

6. Working with Styles: Consistency Made Easy

Harnessing the power of Styles in Microsoft Word significantly enhances the efficiency and consistency of document formatting. Styles, an often overlooked feature, are pre-set collections of formatting options that can be applied to text within a document with just a few clicks. They encompass various elements like font type, size, color, paragraph spacing, and alignment, enabling you to maintain a consistent appearance throughout your document.

Styles come in different forms, each serving unique purposes. Paragraph styles are applied to entire paragraphs, making them perfect for setting the appearance of body text, headings, and titles. Character styles focus on specific text selections, such as a word or phrase, allowing for more detailed formatting. Linked styles combine the attributes of both paragraph and character styles, offering a versatile solution for text formatting. These predefined styles can be effortlessly applied, significantly streamlining the formatting process.

Beyond the convenience of pre-defined styles, Word allows you to create and save custom styles. This functionality is particularly beneficial for branding purposes or adhering to specific formatting guidelines. Once created, these custom styles can be reused across various documents, ensuring uniformity and saving time in the long run.

The impact of Styles extends beyond mere aesthetics; they play a pivotal role in document navigation and management. For instance, applying heading styles enables the use of the Navigation Pane for quick access to different sections, a feature invaluable in managing longer documents. This structural organization, facilitated by Styles, is not just a visual aid but a functional tool enhancing the usability of the document.

Moreover, the use of Styles contributes significantly to the accessibility of documents. Screen readers and other assistive technologies rely on well-structured documents to effectively convey information. Heading styles, in particular, provide a clear, hierarchical structure that assistive technologies can navigate, making your documents accessible to a broader audience.

One of the most practical applications of Styles is in the automated generation of tables of contents. By applying heading styles throughout your document, Word can automatically create a table of contents that accurately reflects and links to each section. This not only streamlines the creation process but also ensures that your table of contents remains current with the document's content.

In collaborative settings, Styles are invaluable in ensuring consistency across a document, regardless of the number of contributors. By defining a standard set of styles to be used in a document, you can ensure that everyone adheres to the same formatting guidelines, maintaining the document's professional appearance and coherence.

In summary, mastering Styles in Microsoft Word is an essential skill for anyone looking to create well-structured, professional, and consistent documents. The efficient application of Styles not only enhances the visual appeal of your documents but also improves their functionality and accessibility. Whether working solo or collaboratively, on simple or complex documents, the effective use of Styles will elevate your document creation process, saving time and ensuring a high standard of quality in your work.

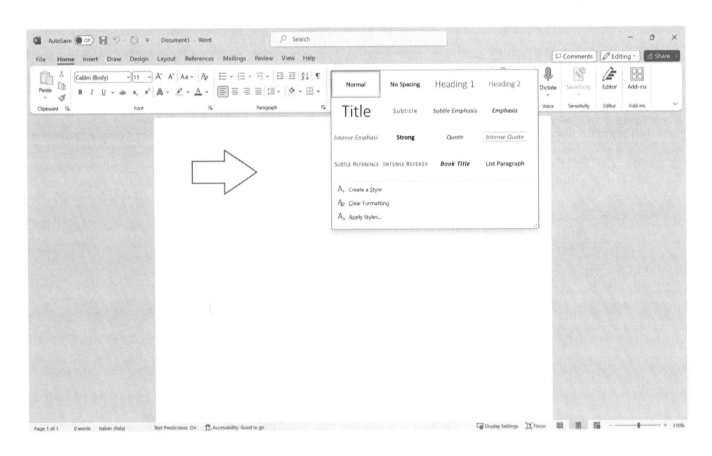

7. Mastering Templates: A Time-Saving Approach

Mastering the use of templates in Microsoft Word streamlines the document creation process, providing a time-saving approach that enhances efficiency and ensures consistency. In Word, templates act as a foundation for your documents, offering pre-designed layouts and styles that can be customized to suit specific needs. This feature is especially beneficial for creating professional documents quickly without having to start from scratch every time.

When you delve into the world of Word templates, you'll find a wide array of options suitable for various document types. Whether you're drafting a business report, designing a newsletter, or updating your resume, there's likely a template that fits the bill. These templates are not only practical but also serve as a source of inspiration, showcasing different design possibilities within Word.

Customizing templates is where you can really make them work for you. Almost every element of a Word template can be tailored to meet your specific requirements. You can modify colors, fonts, layouts, and add your own branding elements, such as logos or specific color schemes. This level of customization allows you to maintain brand consistency across all your documents or add a personal touch to your projects.

For those who frequently create documents with unique formats, the ability to create and save your own templates in Word is invaluable. If the existing templates don't quite meet your needs, you can design a document from scratch and save it as a custom template. This personalized template can then be reused, saving you time and effort in the long run, and ensuring a consistent look and feel across all your documents.

Templates are particularly beneficial in collaborative settings. By utilizing a common set of templates within a team or organization, you ensure that everyone is on the same page in terms of document formatting and style. This uniformity is key to maintaining a professional appearance and brand identity, especially when multiple people contribute to document creation.

In addition to their practical uses, templates can also be a powerful learning tool. For those who are not yet familiar with the more advanced aspects of Word formatting and design, dissecting and modifying existing templates can provide valuable insights into how certain styles and effects are achieved. This hands-on approach can enhance your understanding of Word's capabilities and inspire you to create more sophisticated document layouts.

In essence, mastering templates in Microsoft Word is about more than just saving time; it's about enhancing the quality and consistency of your documents. Whether you're choosing from existing templates, customizing them to fit your style, or creating your own from the ground up, understanding how to effectively utilize templates is a crucial skill. It elevates your productivity, ensures a professional standard across your work, and opens up more time for you to focus on the content rather than the format of your documents. With templates, you have a powerful tool at your disposal to create high-quality documents efficiently and consistently.

8. Inserting and Managing Images

In the digital age, where visual content plays a crucial role in communication, the ability to adeptly insert and manage images in Microsoft Word documents is indispensable. This skill elevates your documents, transforming them from simple text to visually engaging pieces that capture and retain the reader's attention.

When you begin inserting images into your Word document, you're not just adding visual elements; you're enhancing the narrative of your text. Adding images is a straightforward process in Word. Through the 'Insert' tab, you can choose pictures from your computer or directly from online sources. Once an image is in your document, you can freely move and resize it to suit your layout. This ease of insertion is the first step in bringing visual dynamism to your document.

However, merely inserting an image is not enough. The real art lies in how you format these images. Word offers an extensive range of formatting tools that let you customize images to suit your document's style and tone. You can apply artistic effects, adjust the brightness and contrast, or apply color filters to your images. The cropping tool is particularly useful, allowing you to focus on a specific part of the image or to fit an image into a certain area of your document. For images with busy backgrounds, the 'Remove Background' feature is invaluable, helping to highlight the main subject of your image.

Integrating images with text is a critical aspect of document design, and Word excels in this area with its text wrapping options. These options allow you to determine how text will flow around your image, ensuring that the readability of your document is not compromised. From in-line placement to square, tight, or through wrapping, each style offers a different aesthetic and functional impact on your document.

The positioning and alignment of images are crucial in achieving a balanced and aesthetically pleasing document layout. Word facilitates this with features that allow for precise alignment of images with text, margins, or other page elements. The 'Position' feature provides preset positioning options, aiding you in effortlessly finding a harmonious placement for your images.

Managing the size and quality of the images you insert is crucial. High-resolution images are perfect for printed documents but can make your file size unwieldy. Conversely, lower-resolution images are suitable for digital documents, where file size might be a concern. Being mindful of the resolution and file size of your images ensures that your document remains practical for its intended use.

It's also important to be conscientious about the images you choose. Copyright and usage rights are a serious consideration, especially for documents intended for public distribution. Ensuring you have the rights to use an image, or opting for royalty-free images, is critical in avoiding legal issues.

For more complex layouts, Word allows advanced techniques like grouping and layering images. This feature is invaluable for creating composite images or when you need to overlay text over an image. These advanced techniques can significantly enhance the visual appeal and professionalism of your documents.

In essence, effectively inserting and managing images in Microsoft Word is about more than just adding pictures to a document. It's about enhancing the storytelling of your text, ensuring that your document is not only informative but also visually compelling. By mastering these skills, you elevate your ability to communicate more effectively, making your documents more engaging and professional. This skillset is crucial in a world where visual content is increasingly important in both personal and professional communication.

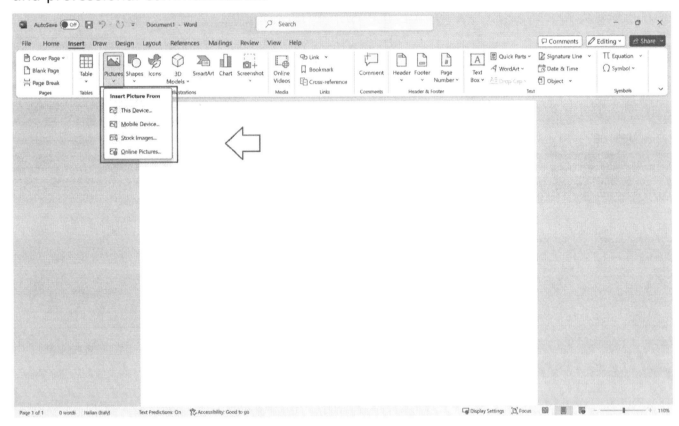

9. Creating Tables: Organization at its Best

Creating tables in Microsoft Word is an essential skill for organizing information clearly and efficiently. Tables are versatile tools in document creation, used for various purposes like displaying data, structuring content, and even enhancing layout design. In Word, the process of creating and formatting tables is intuitive yet powerful, allowing you to present information in a more digestible and visually appealing format.

The first step in creating a table in Word is to consider what the table will represent and how it will fit into your document. Tables are excellent for displaying numerical data, but they're also great for organizing text, such as in schedules, plans, or lists. Once you have a clear purpose for your table, you can begin creating it.

To create a table, you can use the 'Insert' tab and choose 'Table.' Word offers several methods to insert a table. You can select the number of rows and columns by using the grid or use the 'Insert Table' option for more specific dimensions. There's also the 'Draw Table' feature, which allows you to create a custom table by drawing it directly onto the document. This flexibility in table creation ensures that you can design a table that perfectly suits your needs.

Once your table is inserted, you can start to input data or text. Word allows you to easily add or delete rows and columns as needed, making the table adaptable as your content evolves. You can also merge cells to create custom layouts within your table, which is particularly useful for headers or categories.

Formatting a table in Word is where you can really make it stand out. You can choose from a variety of styles and designs in the 'Design' tab, from simple gridlines to colorful, professional designs. Formatting options include adjusting cell size, aligning text, and choosing different colors and styles for borders. Applying these formatting options enhances the readability and visual appeal of your table.

In addition to basic formatting, Word offers advanced features like sorting and formula functions. These features are particularly useful for tables with numerical data, as they allow you to sort data in ascending or descending order and perform calculations directly within the table.

For tables that contain a lot of data, the 'Header Row' feature is invaluable. By designating the first row of your table as a header, the text in this row remains visible when scrolling through a long table, making it easier to keep track of your data.

When it comes to integrating tables with the rest of your document, text wrapping and positioning are key considerations. Word allows you to position your table within the document and wrap text around it, ensuring that your table complements the overall layout of your document.

Tables in Word can also be converted to and from text. This feature is useful if you have data in paragraph form that would be better presented in a table, or vice versa. It provides flexibility in how you present your information, allowing you to choose the format that best conveys your message.

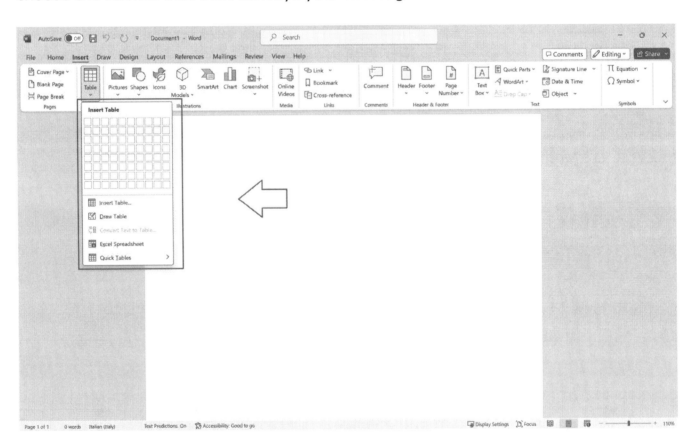

In conclusion, mastering the creation and management of tables in Microsoft Word enhances your ability to organize and present information effectively. Whether you're dealing with data, planning a project, or simply organizing content, tables are powerful tools in your document creation arsenal.

By utilizing the various features and formatting options available in Word, you can create tables that are not only functional but also add to the aesthetic appeal of your documents. Tables, when used effectively, can transform your documents from simple text pages to organized, professional presentations of information.

10. Smart Art and Graphics: Enhancing Visuals

In the realm of document design, the use of SmartArt and graphics in Microsoft Word is a transformative approach to enhancing visuals, turning simple documents into engaging presentations. SmartArt, a feature unique to Microsoft Office, allows the integration of complex information into visually appealing graphics. It's an invaluable tool for anyone looking to add a professional touch to reports, presentations, and other documents.

SmartArt graphics provide a dynamic way of displaying information, from basic lists to complex processes and relationships. It includes a variety of diagram types such as hierarchical, cyclical, and matrix structures, each serving a different purpose. This diversity makes SmartArt suitable for a wide range of applications, whether you're creating an organizational chart, a timeline, or illustrating a process flow.

The process of inserting SmartArt into your Word document is straightforward. It can be accessed from the 'Insert' tab, where you can browse through the different categories of SmartArt graphics. Once you've selected a suitable graphic, you can start adding your text directly into the predefined text boxes. This integration of text and visual design is what makes SmartArt an efficient tool for conveying complex information in an easily digestible format.

Customization is a key aspect of working with SmartArt. You can change the color scheme and style of your graphic to match the tone and look of your document. The SmartArt Tools Design tab offers various options for changing colors, applying styles, and switching the layout of the graphic. This flexibility allows you to tailor the graphic to fit seamlessly with the rest of your document.

In addition to SmartArt, incorporating standard graphics and images into your Word document can significantly enhance its visual appeal. Word offers a range of options for inserting and formatting images, shapes, icons, and 3D models. These elements can be used to complement text, break up large blocks of text, and add visual interest to your document.

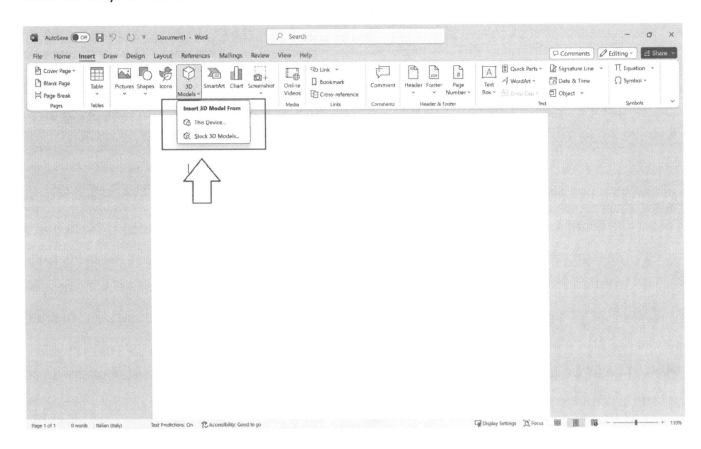

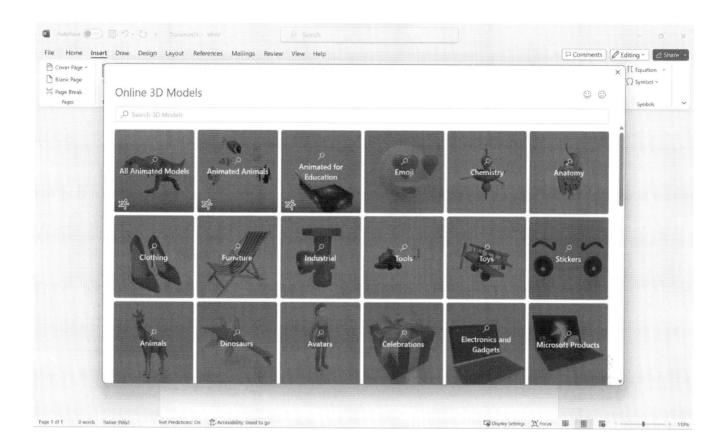

Positioning and layering these graphics is crucial for maintaining the readability and aesthetic balance of your document. Word provides tools for aligning, grouping, and ordering your graphics, ensuring that they are placed precisely where you want them. This level of control is essential for creating a polished and professional-looking document.

One of the advanced features of Word in terms of graphics is the ability to layer text over images or shapes. This can be used to create eye-catching headings or to emphasize important information. The text wrapping feature allows you to integrate text and images seamlessly, making sure that the layout remains clean and organized.

Another powerful aspect of using graphics in Word is the ability to link data from other Office applications. For example, you can insert a chart from Excel into your Word document, and it will update automatically when the data in the Excel file changes. This feature is particularly useful for reports and documents that rely on data analysis.

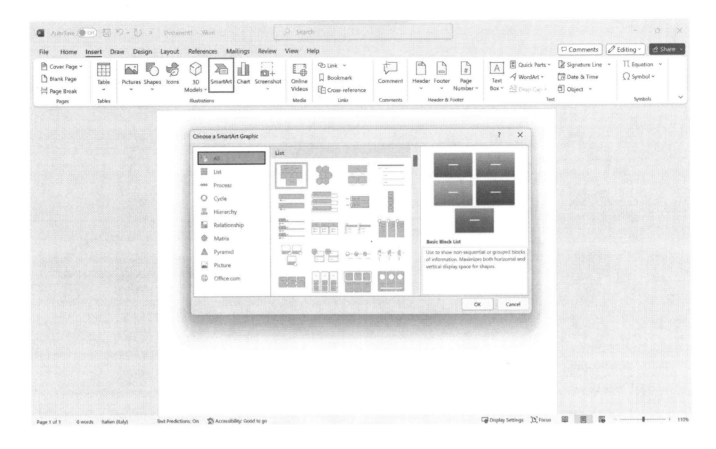

In conclusion, SmartArt and graphics are essential components of modern document design in Microsoft Word. They provide a means to present information not just as text but as visual stories.

By mastering these tools, you can transform your documents from simple text to engaging, informative, and visually appealing presentations. Whether you're creating a business report, an academic paper, or a project proposal, the effective use of SmartArt and graphics can enhance the overall impact of your document, making it more likely to capture and hold the attention of your audience.

11. Effective Document Collaboration

Effective document collaboration is a pivotal aspect of modern work environments, and mastering this skill in Microsoft Word is essential for professionals across various fields. With the advent of cloud-based technologies and real-time editing capabilities, Word has evolved into a powerful platform for collaborative document creation and editing.

This advancement in technology allows multiple users to work on a single document simultaneously, enhancing productivity and ensuring a seamless collaborative experience.

The cornerstone of effective document collaboration in Word is the utilization of cloud-based sharing and storage, such as OneDrive or SharePoint. These platforms enable you to store documents in a central location that can be accessed by all collaborators from anywhere, at any time. This accessibility is crucial for teams that are geographically dispersed or working remotely.

Sharing a document for collaboration in Word is straightforward. You can share a document directly from Word by using the 'Share' button. This allows you to invite collaborators by entering their email addresses and assigning them specific permissions, such as 'Can edit' or 'Can view.' This level of control ensures that each collaborator has the appropriate access rights, depending on their role in the document creation process.

Once shared, collaborators can work on the document simultaneously. This real-time collaboration is visibly marked in Word, where each user's cursor and the text they are editing are shown in different colors. This feature not only adds transparency to the collaboration process but also prevents overlapping edits and conflicts.

The commenting and reviewing features in Word further enhance the collaborative process. Collaborators can leave comments on specific parts of the text, making suggestions or asking questions. The 'Track Changes' feature is particularly useful during the review process, as it allows all changes to be tracked and reviewed before finalizing the document. This ensures that every edit is accounted for and that the final document is a product of collective input and agreement.

Effective collaboration also involves maintaining the consistency and integrity of the document. Word's styles and templates play a significant role in this regard. By using predefined or custom styles and templates, collaborators can ensure that the document remains consistent in terms of formatting and layout, regardless of the number of people working on it.

In addition to these features, Word also provides tools for managing access and version control. You can view the version history of a document to see past edits, who made them, and when. This is invaluable in keeping track of the evolution of the document and in understanding the contributions of each collaborator.

However, successful collaboration in Word is not just about technical skills; it's also about effective communication and coordination among team members. Establishing clear guidelines and expectations for document collaboration, such as timelines, sections of responsibility, and review processes, is crucial. This ensures that all collaborators are aligned in their efforts and that the collaboration process is efficient and productive.

In conclusion, mastering effective document collaboration in Microsoft Word involves a combination of leveraging the right tools and fostering good communication and coordination among team members. By utilizing cloud-based sharing, real-time editing, commenting, and reviewing features, along with maintaining consistency through styles and templates, teams can collaborate effectively, producing documents that are cohesive, well-constructed, and reflective of collective expertise. In today's fast-paced and often remote work environments, these skills are invaluable in ensuring that collaborative efforts are successful and that the final documents meet the highest standards of quality and professionalism.

12. Mail Merge: Simplifying Mass Communication

Mail Merge in Microsoft Word is a transformative feature that simplifies mass communication, making it an indispensable tool for personal and professional use.

This powerful functionality allows for the creation of multiple personalized documents from a single template, utilizing data from sources like Excel spreadsheets or databases. The magic of Mail Merge lies in its ability to customize each document with individual details, while keeping the core content consistent across all documents.

Embarking on a Mail Merge project begins with the creation of a main document in Word. This template contains the standard text that will appear in every document, interspersed with placeholders known as merge fields. These fields are linked to the columns in your data source and are crucial for personalizing each document. For instance, in a batch of customer letters, the body of the letter remains constant, but elements like customer names, addresses, and specific greetings vary and are pulled from the data file.

Linking your main document to a data source is a straightforward process guided by Word's Mail Merge Wizard. This crucial step involves selecting your data file and establishing a connection to your Word document. Once linked, inserting merge fields into your document is a simple task. These fields act as markers, instructing Word on where to insert corresponding data from your source file.

The finesse in a Mail Merge project lies in the seamless integration of these merge fields into your main document. It involves ensuring that the format and appearance of the merged data match the rest of your document. This might mean adjusting font sizes, aligning text, or applying specific formatting styles to the merge fields. The aim is to create a final product that appears as though it was individually tailored and manually composed for each recipient.

Previewing your merged documents is an essential step in the Mail Merge process. This allows you to check how your final documents will appear with the actual data inserted. Previewing is vital for spotting any inconsistencies or errors in formatting and ensuring that all data is correctly aligned and displayed. Once you are satisfied with the preview, completing the merge is a matter of a few clicks. Word offers the flexibility to either print your documents directly or create a new document where each page is a unique merged document.

For more complex communication needs, Word's Mail Merge extends its capabilities beyond simple letter merging. It includes features like conditional statements, which allow for the inclusion or exclusion of certain text based on specific conditions in your data. Additionally, integrating Mail Merge with email capabilities in Word lets you send out personalized emails directly, a feature immensely useful for email marketing campaigns or large-scale announcements.

The applications of Mail Merge are diverse and impactful. Businesses leverage it for efficient customer communication, marketing campaigns, and extensive reporting. Individuals find it useful for sending out personalized invitations, holiday greetings, or any communication that requires a personal touch at scale. The time-saving aspect of Mail Merge, coupled with its ability to maintain accuracy and consistency, makes it a valuable skill for anyone dealing with large-scale communication.

In essence, mastering Mail Merge in Microsoft Word equips you with the ability to handle mass communication efficiently and professionally. It not only streamlines the process of creating personalized documents but also ensures that each recipient receives a communication that feels uniquely addressed to them. In a digital age where personalized communication holds significant value, proficiency in Mail Merge is a powerful asset, allowing you to convey your message personally and effectively to a large audience.

13. Customizing Word: Tailoring to Your Needs

Customizing Microsoft Word to tailor it to your specific needs is a crucial skill that enhances both your efficiency and enjoyment in using the program. Microsoft Word is not just a one-size-fits-all tool; it offers a plethora of customization options that allow you to tweak the program according to your individual preferences and workflow requirements. From changing the visual layout to creating custom commands, the potential to personalize Word is extensive.

The first step in customizing Word is to adjust the overall visual layout of the program to suit your preferences and needs. This includes changing the theme of the interface, which can be especially helpful for those who prefer a darker or lighter workspace, or require specific color schemes for better visibility.

Adjusting the theme not only makes Word more comfortable to use for long periods but can also help reduce eye strain.

Customizing the Ribbon, the toolbar that houses Word's commands, is another powerful way to tailor Word to your needs. You can add, remove, or rearrange the tabs and commands on the Ribbon, ensuring that the tools you use most frequently are always easily accessible. For instance, if you often work with images, you can create a custom tab on the Ribbon dedicated to image editing tools. This level of customization saves time and streamlines your workflow, making your experience with Word more efficient and enjoyable.

Quick Access Toolbar customization is an essential aspect of tailoring Word. This small toolbar provides shortcuts to commands and can be customized to include the tools you use most often. Whether it's adding a shortcut to the 'Save As' command or having quick access to your favorite font style, customizing the Quick Access Toolbar can significantly speed up your document creation process.

Word also allows for the customization of keyboard shortcuts. This feature is particularly beneficial for power users who rely on keyboard navigation more than the mouse. You can assign shortcuts to commands that don't have them by default or change existing shortcuts to suit your typing habits better. Custom keyboard shortcuts can greatly enhance your productivity, especially when working on lengthy documents.

Another customization option in Word is the ability to create and use templates and styles. While Word provides a range of built-in templates and styles, creating your own can ensure that your documents consistently meet specific formatting requirements. This is especially useful in professional environments where documents need to adhere to certain branding guidelines.

For advanced users, Word offers macros – a powerful tool that can automate repetitive tasks. By recording a series of actions as a macro, you can execute these actions with a single command. This not only saves time but also ensures accuracy in performing complex or repetitive tasks.

Customizing the proofing and language settings is another aspect of tailoring Word to your needs. You can set the default language, adjust the settings for the spell checker and grammar checker, and even add words to the dictionary. These settings help ensure that your documents are always polished and error-free.

In conclusion, customizing Microsoft Word is about making the program work for you in the most efficient and comfortable way possible. By tailoring the visual layout, Ribbon, Quick Access Toolbar, keyboard shortcuts, templates, styles, macros, and proofing settings, you can create a personalized Word environment that suits your specific needs and preferences. These customizations not only enhance your productivity but also make the experience of using Word more enjoyable and aligned with your personal workflow. Whether you're a casual user or a professional, taking the time to customize Word can have a significant impact on your efficiency and effectiveness in document creation.

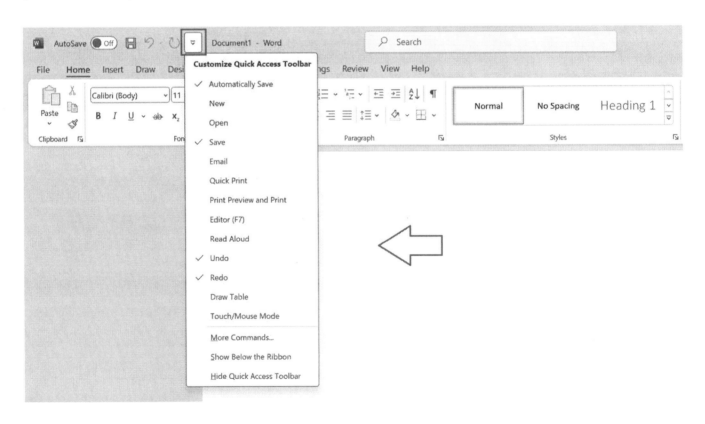

14. Troubleshooting Common Word Challenges

Navigating through the common challenges in Microsoft Word is crucial for maintaining productivity and efficiency. Users frequently encounter a range of issues, from formatting glitches to software crashes, which can disrupt the workflow. Developing the skills to troubleshoot these problems is essential for anyone relying on Word for daily tasks.

Formatting inconsistencies often arise, especially when importing text from different sources. This can lead to a document appearing disjointed and unprofessional. The 'Clear Formatting' tool is invaluable in these situations, removing unwanted formatting and providing a clean slate for applying new styles. Additionally, gaining a thorough understanding of Word's Styles feature can prevent many formatting issues before they occur, ensuring consistency throughout the document.

Software crashes and unresponsiveness are among the more severe challenges faced by Word users. These issues can stem from a variety of sources, such as conflicts with add-ins or the handling of large files. Regularly updating Word and the operating system can often resolve these issues. Disabling add-ins can help identify if they are causing conflicts, and enabling auto-save features or frequently saving your work can prevent data loss in case of a crash.

When working with images and graphics, problems may occur in integrating these elements seamlessly with the text. Issues often relate to the size, resolution, or placement of images. Adjusting these aspects, along with the text wrapping settings, can usually resolve such problems. Ensuring that images are of an appropriate size and resolution for the intended purpose of the document is key to maintaining a balance between visual appeal and practical functionality.

Tables are a powerful tool in Word but can be complex to manage. Common issues with tables include difficulties in aligning text and formatting cells. Utilizing the Table Tools - Design and Layout tabs allows for precise control over these aspects, enabling users to fine-tune tables to fit their needs.

Mail Merge problems are often data-related, arising from inconsistencies in the source file or errors in field placement. Carefully reviewing the data source for accuracy and conducting test runs with a few records can help prevent issues during the full merge process.

Collaboration features like track changes and comments enhance Word's functionality but can also be sources of confusion. Ensuring all collaborators are using a compatible version of Word and have appropriate access rights can alleviate many issues. Understanding how to navigate the Review tab and manage sharing settings is also crucial for effective collaboration.

Customizing Word, such as creating templates or macros, offers enhanced functionality but can lead to unique challenges. When issues arise with custom templates or macros, checking the setup or the macro code for errors is a good first step. Ensuring that macros are enabled in your Word settings is also important for those who rely on this feature.

Document recovery is a critical aspect of troubleshooting in Word. The Document Recovery feature can be a lifesaver in instances of crashes or unexpected shutdowns. Familiarizing yourself with this feature and adopting a habit of regular saving can minimize the impact of such incidents.

In summary, troubleshooting common challenges in Microsoft Word involves a combination of technical know-how and practical problem-solving skills. From addressing formatting issues to managing software crashes, each challenge requires a specific approach. Keeping the software updated, understanding the intricacies of formatting tools, and being prepared for data recovery are all key to navigating these challenges. With these skills, users can minimize disruptions and maintain a smooth, efficient document creation process in Microsoft Word.

15. Expert Tips: Taking Your Skills Further

Elevating your proficiency in Microsoft Word to an expert level involves exploring and mastering a range of advanced features and techniques. By delving deeper into Word's capabilities, you can unlock new possibilities in document creation, streamline your workflow, and produce professional-grade documents with efficiency and flair.

An advanced grasp of Find and Replace goes beyond simple text substitutions. This powerful feature can search and alter specific formatting and special elements like page breaks or tabs. Imagine quickly changing all instances of a specific font or color throughout a lengthy document – this is the kind of efficiency advanced Find and Replace offers.

For those working with extensive documents, the Navigation Pane becomes an invaluable tool. It's not just a way to quickly navigate through your document but also an organizational tool. You can restructure your document on the fly by dragging headings in the Navigation Pane, immediately reflecting changes in the content layout. This dynamic approach to organizing your document is a significant time-saver and increases your agility in editing.

Field codes in Word are often overlooked but offer dynamic content capabilities. These placeholders can automate elements in your document, such as inserting up-to-date references, page numbers, or linked content. For example, using field codes to insert a table of contents or an index can make managing large documents significantly more manageable.

Linking and embedding content from other applications like Excel enhances the interactivity and relevance of your Word documents. This is particularly beneficial for data-driven reports where real-time data is crucial. Embed a chart from Excel, and it updates automatically in your Word document – a feature that ensures your data is always current.

Macros in Word can be a game-changer for automating repetitive tasks. By recording a series of actions or writing custom macro scripts, you can automate complex or repetitive tasks, saving time and minimizing errors. Whether it's formatting, data entry, or regular document setup tasks, macros can handle it efficiently.

Understanding and using section breaks is essential for creating documents with varied layouts. Different sections of your document can have unique formatting, headers, footers, and page number styles. This capability is vital for creating complex documents like reports, proposals, or theses, where different sections require distinct formatting.

Quick Parts is a feature that allows you to store and reuse common document elements – a snippet of text, a logo, a signature block. This tool is perfect for those elements you frequently use but don't want to recreate each time. Quick Parts streamlines the process of adding these elements to your documents, ensuring consistency and saving time.

Going beyond basic styles, understanding Style Sets and Themes in Word lets you apply a cohesive design to your entire document. These features control the overall look of your document – from fonts and colors to paragraph spacing. Customizing Style Sets and Themes enables you to quickly give your document a polished, professional look.

In today's collaborative work environment, being adept at using collaborative editing features in Word is essential. Mastery of track changes, comments, and document sharing functionalities is crucial for smooth, effective team collaborations. Knowing how to efficiently navigate these features can significantly enhance your collaborative projects.

Lastly, continuously updating your Word skills is vital in an ever-evolving digital landscape. Stay abreast of the latest features and updates in Word. Leverage online resources, tutorials, forums, and webinars to continually expand your knowledge and stay ahead in your Word mastery.

In summary, taking your Microsoft Word skills to an expert level is about much more than just knowing the basic functionalities. It's about exploring and mastering the advanced features that enable efficiency, creativity, and professionalism. From advanced document management to automation and collaboration, these expert tips will equip you with the skills to take full advantage of everything Word has to offer, making you a proficient, versatile, and effective user.

As we conclude this comprehensive exploration into Microsoft Word, it's clear that the journey through its myriad features and capabilities is both enriching and empowering. From the foundational basics to the more advanced and nuanced aspects of Word, this guide has aimed to equip you with a robust set of skills and knowledge, enabling you to navigate and utilize this powerful tool with confidence and creativity.

Throughout this guide, we've delved into the essentials of formatting, the artistry of incorporating images and SmartArt, and the intricacies of creating tables and managing complex documents. These skills are fundamental in crafting professional and visually compelling documents. The exploration of advanced features like Mail Merge and document collaboration tools underlines the versatility and efficiency of Word in various professional and personal contexts.

The journey through Word also emphasized the importance of customizing the software to your individual needs, enhancing not just your productivity but also your overall user experience. The ability to troubleshoot common challenges further ensures that your workflow remains smooth and uninterrupted.

In essence, the mastery of Microsoft Word is more than just learning a software application; it's about harnessing a tool that can significantly elevate the quality and impact of your written communication. Whether you are a student, a professional, or someone who uses Word for personal projects, the skills and knowledge acquired here will undoubtedly contribute to your success and efficiency in numerous ways.

As you continue to use and explore Word, remember that each feature and function is designed to enhance your ability to communicate and organize information effectively. With the foundations laid in this guide, you're well-equipped to explore the full potential of what Microsoft Word has to offer.

Book 2: Excel for Excellence

Embarking on a journey with Excel is like unlocking a world brimming with potential for transforming data into powerful insights. This tool, renowned for its versatility and depth, serves not just as a medium for data entry and basic calculations, but as a robust platform for complex data analysis, visualization, and management. The path to Excel excellence is multifaceted, requiring a keen understanding of its vast array of features, a strategic approach to data manipulation, and an ongoing commitment to learning and adaptation.

From the fundamental steps of navigating spreadsheets and crafting basic formulas to the more intricate art of complex calculations, each aspect builds a foundation for more advanced Excel functionalities. The journey involves delving into sophisticated data analysis techniques, where proficiency in functions like VLOOKUP, INDEX, and MATCH becomes crucial. As expertise grows, so does the ability to create dynamic, interactive dashboards that bring data to life, allowing for intuitive data exploration and storytelling.

The realm of Excel extends into automation, where mastery in macros and VBA opens doors to efficiency and precision, transforming repetitive tasks into seamless operations. Understanding how to optimize Excel's performance, especially when dealing with large datasets, is another critical skill, ensuring smooth and effective data handling. Additionally, the importance of data integrity cannot be overstated, where expert skills in data validation and error checking are essential in maintaining the reliability of data analyses.

Integration with other applications and embracing Excel's evolving features signifies the adaptive nature of Excel proficiency. This journey through Excel is not just about mastering a tool; it's about harnessing a powerful ally in the world of data, continually evolving and adapting to unlock deeper insights and drive informed decisions.

16. Excel Essentials: First Steps

Beginning your journey into Microsoft Excel, a vital tool in the modern data-driven world, is an exciting step toward unlocking the power of data analysis and management. This chapter, "Excel Essentials: First Steps," is designed to introduce you to the fundamental aspects of Excel, setting a strong foundation for further exploration and mastery. Whether you are a complete novice or looking to refresh your basic skills, this section is your starting point in becoming proficient in Excel.

Excel, at its core, is a spreadsheet application, but its capabilities extend far beyond mere data entry. It's a powerful tool for analyzing data, making calculations, and presenting information in a way that is both accessible and insightful. The first step in harnessing this power is understanding the Excel interface. Familiarizing yourself with the Ribbon, the primary tool where you will find various tabs and commands, is crucial. The Ribbon is intuitively organized into tabs that group related features together, making it easier to navigate and find the tools you need.

Another fundamental aspect of Excel is understanding workbooks and worksheets. A workbook is an Excel file that contains one or more worksheets - the individual "pages" where you work with your data. Learning how to navigate between worksheets, how to add new ones, and how to organize them effectively is essential for efficient Excel use.

Cell referencing is a key concept in Excel. Each piece of data resides in a cell identified by a unique address made up of a column letter and a row number. Understanding how to reference these cells is critical when it comes to entering data, creating formulas, and analyzing data.

One of Excel's most basic yet powerful features is data entry and formatting. Inputting data accurately and formatting it for readability and clarity is foundational to all Excel tasks. This includes learning how to format text and numbers, adjust column width and row height, and use cell styles for consistency.

Creating basic formulas is where Excel begins to show its true power. Even simple formulas for addition, subtraction, multiplication, and division can significantly enhance your data analysis capabilities. Understanding how to create these formulas is the first step in leveraging Excel's computational power.

Sorting and filtering data are fundamental skills in Excel. These features allow you to organize your data efficiently and focus on specific information you need from a dataset. Whether it's sorting data alphabetically or numerically, or filtering out specific data based on criteria, these tools are essential for effective data analysis.

Charts are a vital part of Excel's ability to visualize data. Even at a basic level, creating simple charts like bar charts, line charts, or pie charts can transform columns of data into understandable and insightful visual representations. Learning the basics of chart creation and customization is an important step in your Excel education.

Printing your Excel sheets with the desired layout and settings is also a fundamental skill. This involves setting print areas, adjusting page orientation and size, and ensuring that the printout is both readable and professionally presented.

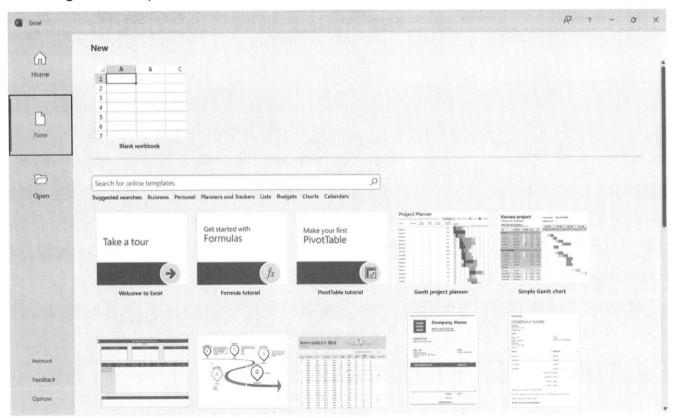

In conclusion, the first steps in Excel are about building a solid foundation in understanding the interface, navigating workbooks and worksheets, mastering basic data entry and formatting, and beginning to explore Excel's powerful features like formulas, sorting, filtering, and charting. As you grow comfortable with these essentials, you will be well-prepared to delve into more advanced features and techniques. Excel is not just a tool but a gateway to efficiency and insight in a wide array of professional and personal contexts. This chapter sets you on the path to Excel excellence, opening up a world where data becomes not just numbers but a canvas for insight and decision-making.

17. Building and Navigating Spreadsheets

Building and navigating spreadsheets in Excel is an art and science that forms the cornerstone of effective data management and analysis. Mastering this skill is not just about understanding how to input data but also about organizing and structuring your spreadsheets in a way that makes them intuitive, accessible, and efficient to use.

At the heart of building effective spreadsheets is the understanding of Excel's grid-like structure, comprised of rows and columns. Each cell, the intersection of a row and column, is where you enter your data. The first step in building a spreadsheet is planning its layout. Consider what kind of data you'll be entering and how it should be organized. A well-thought-out plan for how your spreadsheet is structured can save countless hours and reduce errors in data entry and analysis.

Entering data into Excel should be done with precision and intent. Consistency in data entry is key. This means being consistent in how you format dates, currencies, or any other type of data. This consistency is not just for aesthetic purposes; it also ensures that Excel can accurately interpret and process your data.

Effective navigation through your spreadsheet is just as important as how you build it. Learning keyboard shortcuts for navigation, such as 'Ctrl + Arrow keys' to move to the edge of data regions or 'Ctrl + Page Up/Page Down' to switch between worksheets, can significantly increase your efficiency. Familiarizing yourself with these shortcuts allows you to navigate your spreadsheet quickly, making your work faster and more productive.

In addition to data entry, understanding and using Excel's powerful organizational tools is crucial. This includes sorting and filtering data, which are fundamental for managing large datasets. Sorting can organize your data in ascending or descending order, while filtering allows you to display only the data that meets certain criteria. These tools are indispensable for analyzing large datasets and finding the information you need.

Another important aspect of building spreadsheets is the use of tables. Converting a range of data into a table format in Excel offers several benefits. Tables not only make the data visually appealing but also make managing and analyzing data easier. Tables support additional functionalities like automatic column filtering and the ability to quickly add total rows.

Naming ranges in Excel is a feature that often goes underutilized but can greatly enhance your ability to navigate and use your spreadsheet. By assigning a name to a specific range of cells, you can quickly navigate to that range or use the name in formulas and functions, making your spreadsheet more intuitive and easier to understand.

Data validation is another powerful tool in building spreadsheets. It controls what type of data can be entered into a cell, helping to prevent data entry errors and ensuring data integrity. For example, you can set a cell to only accept dates, numbers within a certain range, or a list of predefined items.

Finally, setting up print layouts is an essential skill for when you need a physical copy of your spreadsheet. Understanding how to adjust page orientation, margins, scaling, and print areas ensures that your printed spreadsheet is as clear and useful as the digital version.

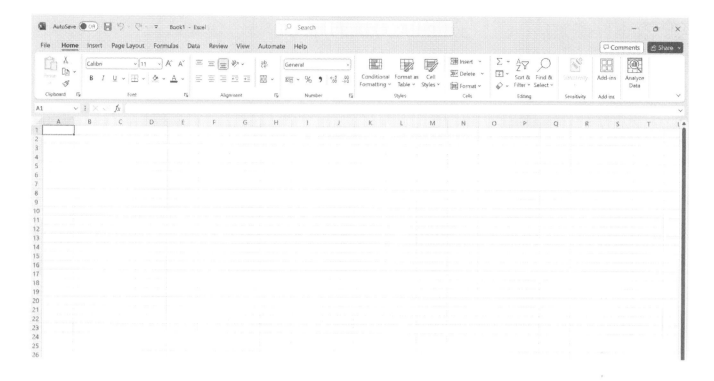

In conclusion, building and navigating spreadsheets in Excel is a foundational skill that requires both careful planning and attention to detail. From the initial layout planning to the final print setup, each step is crucial in creating a spreadsheet that is not only functional but also efficient to use. Whether you are managing personal finances, analyzing business data, or organizing large datasets, the ability to effectively build and navigate spreadsheets in Excel is an invaluable skill in today's data-driven environment.

18. Basic Formulas: The Foundation

Understanding and utilizing basic formulas in Excel is the bedrock of efficient and effective spreadsheet management. Formulas are the tools that allow you to make calculations, analyze data, and automate tasks within your Excel workbook. Mastering these basics is not just about learning a set of commands; it's about developing a mindset that looks at data analytically and understands how to manipulate it to get the desired results.

The first step in mastering Excel formulas is understanding the anatomy of a formula. At its simplest, a formula in Excel starts with an equal sign (=), followed by a combination of cell references, operators, values, and functions. Cell references point to the cells containing the data you want to use, operators define the type of calculation (such as +, -, *, / for addition, subtraction, multiplication, and division), and functions are predefined formulas in Excel that perform complex calculations.

One of the foundational skills in using formulas is cell referencing. There are two main types of cell references in Excel: relative and absolute. A relative cell reference changes when the formula is copied to another cell because it is relative to its position. An absolute cell reference, denoted by a dollar sign ($), remains constant, no matter where the formula is copied. Understanding when to use each type of reference is key to building effective formulas.

Basic arithmetic operations are the most straightforward formulas in Excel. These include addition, subtraction, multiplication, and division, which can be used for simple calculations such as totaling sales figures, calculating differences in data, or determining average values. Even these basic operations can provide significant insights into your data when used correctly.

Beyond basic arithmetic, Excel offers a range of basic functions that are essential for data analysis. Functions like SUM(), AVERAGE(), MIN(), and MAX() are some of the commonly used formulas that can be used to quickly perform calculations that would otherwise be time-consuming. For instance, the SUM() function can be used to add up a range of cells, while the AVERAGE() function can be used to find the average value of a series of numbers.

Another fundamental aspect of formulas in Excel is understanding how to combine multiple functions and operations in a single formula. This is known as nesting, where you place one function inside another. This can be incredibly powerful, allowing you to perform complex calculations within a single cell. However, it's important to ensure that the functions are correctly nested and that the formula is structured properly to avoid errors.

Error checking is an integral part of working with formulas in Excel. Excel provides several tools to help identify and fix errors in formulas. Understanding common error values like #DIV/0!, #NAME?, and #VALUE! can help you troubleshoot and correct mistakes in your formulas. Excel's Formula Auditing tools can also be used to trace and evaluate formulas, making it easier to understand how they work and to spot potential errors.

Printing and sharing formulas is another important aspect of working with Excel. When printing a spreadsheet, you might want to print the formulas themselves, rather than the results of the calculations. This can be done through the 'Formulas' tab in the Ribbon. When sharing an Excel file, it's important to ensure that the formulas work correctly on another user's computer and that the data references remain intact.

In conclusion, mastering basic formulas in Excel is a crucial step towards becoming proficient in data analysis and spreadsheet management. It's about understanding the logic behind how formulas work and applying this knowledge to manipulate and analyze data effectively. As you become more comfortable with basic formulas, you'll be well-prepared to tackle more advanced calculations and functions, further enhancing your capabilities in Excel. Whether for personal use, academic needs, or professional data analysis, a solid foundation in Excel formulas is an indispensable skill in today's data-driven world.

19. Complex Calculations: Advanced Formulas

Delving into the realm of complex calculations and advanced formulas in Excel is akin to unlocking a secret garden of data analysis capabilities. This journey takes you beyond the realm of simple arithmetic into a world where data is not just crunched but woven into insightful narratives. Advanced formulas in Excel are your tools to unravel complex data puzzles, making sense of numbers in ways that are both sophisticated and impactful.

At the core of advanced Excel use is a deep understanding of logical functions such as IF, AND, OR, and NOT. These functions are the building blocks of decision-making within your spreadsheets, enabling you to set conditions and responses that reflect real-world scenarios. For instance, the IF function becomes a pivotal tool in scenarios where decisions hinge on certain criteria being met, allowing you to automate responses based on specific data points.

Excel's prowess in handling complex datasets is further exemplified in its lookup functions like VLOOKUP, HLOOKUP, INDEX, and MATCH. These are not just functions but gateways to efficient data retrieval and management. Picture a vast dataset where you need to find specific information – these functions are your compass, guiding you to the exact data point you need without the hassle of manual search.

The world of array formulas, though initially daunting, offers a wealth of possibilities. These formulas are capable of performing multiple calculations on extensive data ranges and can yield results that would otherwise require cumbersome manual intervention. Array formulas are particularly beneficial when dealing with data that requires simultaneous calculations across multiple cells or ranges.

For those in finance or needing to perform financial analysis, Excel's financial functions like PMT, RATE, and NPER are indispensable. These functions allow you to delve into complex financial scenarios, computing loans, investments, and more with precision and ease. They transform Excel into not just a data processing tool but a sophisticated financial calculator.

Excel is equally adept at statistical analysis, thanks to its comprehensive range of statistical functions. Whether it's calculating averages with conditions using AVERAGEIFS or summing data based on specific criteria with SUMIFS, these functions allow for detailed and nuanced statistical analysis. They enable you to sift through large datasets, extracting meaningful insights from the numbers.

In managing date and time data, Excel's functions like NOW, DATE, and DATEDIF are essential. They provide the ability to perform intricate date and time calculations, crucial in project planning, scheduling, and tracking.

Dynamic range names in Excel add a layer of flexibility and clarity to your spreadsheets. By creating named ranges, you can reference these in your formulas, making your spreadsheets more intuitive and easier to navigate. This feature is especially useful in complex spreadsheets where referring to specific data ranges can become confusing.

Navigating the maze of complex formulas also requires a keen eye for error checking. Excel's error-checking tools are vital in ensuring the accuracy of your calculations. Familiarizing yourself with common error values and understanding how to use Excel's auditing features can save you from potential data analysis pitfalls.

Combining multiple functions in a single formula is where the magic of Excel truly lies. This ability to nest functions, to have multiple layers of calculations and conditions within a single cell, is what transforms a basic spreadsheet into a powerful data analysis tool. It's the difference between seeing data in black and white and viewing it in vibrant color.

In conclusion, the journey through complex calculations and advanced formulas in Excel is about transforming how you view and handle data. It's a journey from seeing Excel as a mere spreadsheet application to understanding it as a powerful tool for analysis, decision-making, and storytelling. This expertise in Excel's advanced capabilities empowers you to turn data into insights, driving informed decisions in business, research, and beyond. With these skills, Excel becomes more than a tool; it becomes an extension of your analytical thought process, capable of handling the complexities of today's data-driven world.

20. Data Analysis Techniques

In the world of Excel, data analysis is not just a function; it's an art. It's about weaving through vast arrays of data and extracting meaningful patterns, insights, and conclusions. This involves a range of techniques, each playing a pivotal role in transforming raw data into understandable and actionable information.

The journey into data analysis starts with descriptive statistics, the backbone of data interpretation in Excel. This step is all about summarizing your data, which includes calculating averages, medians, modes, standard deviations, and variances. These statistics provide an initial glimpse into your data, offering insights into trends and patterns, and often, they are the first step in any data analysis process.

Conditional formatting stands out as a visually intuitive way to analyze data. It brings your data to life, using colors, bars, and icons to differentiate and highlight key data points. Imagine a sheet of numbers where higher values glow warmer and lower values cool down with different shades. This immediate visual cue helps in quickly identifying trends and outliers, making your data analysis both efficient and effective.

Pivot tables take your data analysis to a multidimensional level. They are the powerhouse of Excel, allowing you to dissect and view your data from different angles and perspectives. Pivot tables enable you to summarize large datasets in comprehensible formats, making complex data sets manageable and understandable.

The ease of dragging and dropping fields to reorganize data breaks down complex analysis into simple, manageable steps.

What-If Analysis tools in Excel, including Scenario Manager, Goal Seek, and Data Tables, are like having a crystal ball. They allow you to speculate, project, and predict outcomes based on varying inputs. These tools are indispensable when you want to forecast future trends based on existing data, giving you a peek into the different outcomes of your business decisions.

When it comes to analyzing trends, Excel offers trendlines in charts and the Data Analysis Toolpak. Adding a trendline to a chart can illuminate patterns in your data, such as an upward sales trend or a downward expenditure trend. The Data Analysis Toolpak further complements this by providing advanced tools like regression and correlation, perfect for a deep dive into your data.

Solver, an Excel add-in, is your ally in problem-solving. It helps you determine the optimal value for a formula, respecting the constraints you set on other cells. This is especially useful in resource allocation, budget planning, or any scenario where you need to maximize or minimize a particular value within constraints.

Data validation is a guardian of data integrity. By controlling the type of data or the values that users can enter into a cell, data validation ensures accuracy and consistency. This feature is crucial, particularly in work environments where multiple stakeholders input data into the same Excel sheet.

Finally, charts and graphs in Excel translate numbers into visual narratives. Choosing the right type of chart for your data and customizing it effectively can greatly amplify the impact of your data presentation. Whether it's a pie chart illustrating market share or a line graph depicting revenue growth, a well-crafted chart can communicate complex data in an easily digestible format.

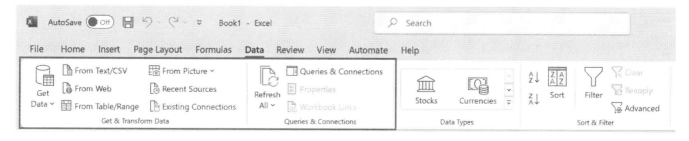

In essence, data analysis in Excel is about using the right combination of techniques to unlock the stories hidden within your data. It's about turning columns of numbers into insights that drive decision-making. Whether you are in business, academia, or any data-reliant field, these data analysis techniques are essential tools in your analytical toolbox, enabling you to derive meaningful information from the sea of data and make informed decisions.

21. Charting and Graphing for Clarity

In Excel, charting and graphing transform numerical data into visual stories, enhancing understanding and providing clarity. This visual representation is not just an aesthetic addition to data analysis; it's a crucial aspect of data communication. The right chart or graph can bring out hidden patterns, trends, and insights in a way that rows of numbers cannot.

Choosing the correct chart type is fundamental to effective data visualization. Excel's variety of chart options, each suited to different types of data, allows for a tailored approach to data presentation. Bar and column charts are perfect for comparing quantities, line charts excel in showing trends, pie charts are ideal for proportions, and scatter plots reveal relationships between variables. A well-chosen chart can not only represent your data accurately but also highlight the key insights you wish to convey.

Customization plays a significant role in chart clarity. Excel's flexibility in altering chart elements – from colors and labels to axes and trendlines – enables you to craft a chart that is both visually appealing and informative. For instance, applying a trendline to a scatter plot can emphasize the relationship direction between variables, adding depth to the analysis.

Graphs in Excel are powerful storytelling tools. They can narrate the story behind the data, guiding viewers to not just see what the data is, but understand why it matters. For this narrative to be effective, focus on simplicity and avoid over-cluttering. Every element in your graph should serve a purpose in communicating the data story.

Manipulating data series and chart elements is key to effective graphing. Whether it's adding or removing data series in a composite chart or using primary and secondary axes for comparison, understanding these elements can significantly enhance your chart's effectiveness.

PivotCharts bring a dynamic element to Excel charts, marrying PivotTable's versatility with graphical representation. They are especially useful for large, complex datasets, allowing you to create dynamic, easily updated visual representations of your PivotTable data.

Trend visualization is a common and vital use of charts in Excel. Line and area charts are particularly suited for illustrating data trends over time. Enhancing these charts with markers or annotations can provide additional context, making trends and patterns more apparent.

Comparative analysis benefits greatly from charting. By juxtaposing different datasets in bar, column, or stacked area charts, you can provide a clear visual comparison, making it easier to draw conclusions about the relative performance or status of different data sets.

Interactive charts with data filters take charting a step further, adding an element of engagement. By incorporating slicers and interactive controls, you create a dynamic charting experience that allows viewers to filter and explore the data that interests them most.

In essence, charting and graphing in Excel is about translating complex data into clear, compelling visual narratives. It's about choosing the right chart type, customizing it for clarity, and using it to tell a story that makes your data accessible and understandable.

Whether for professional presentations, academic research, or personal data analysis, effective charting and graphing skills are essential for anyone looking to unlock the full storytelling potential of their data in Excel. With these skills, your charts and graphs can become powerful tools, illuminating the insights hidden within numbers and making data-driven decision-making more intuitive and impactful.

22. Pivot Tables: Simplifying Data Analysis

Pivot Tables in Excel are a transformative tool for anyone delving into the world of data analysis. They offer a seamless, intuitive way to break down complex datasets into manageable, insightful summaries. The essence of Pivot Tables lies in their ability to take extensive, unwieldy data and distill it into a format that's not only comprehensible but also versatile in its analytical capabilities.

At the core of Pivot Table functionality is the ease of data organization. Consider a dataset sprawling with thousands of entries. The mere thought of sifting through this manually is daunting. Pivot Tables come to the rescue, allowing you to organize and categorize this sea of data into a coherent structure that highlights the most pertinent aspects for your analysis. This reorganization is not just about making the data look neater; it's about bringing forward the elements you need to focus on for your specific analytical goals.

The beauty of Pivot Tables lies in their simplicity of use coupled with profound flexibility. Creating a Pivot Table is a straightforward process – a few clicks, and you've laid the groundwork for your analysis. This simplicity, however, doesn't hamper their adaptability. Pivot Tables are immensely customizable, letting you dynamically choose and alter the data you wish to include, how it's grouped, and what specific segments you want to focus on through filters.

Dynamic data analysis is a standout feature of Pivot Tables. As your dataset grows or changes, the Pivot Table adapts, reflecting these updates instantaneously. This feature is particularly beneficial for projects with ongoing data inputs, ensuring your analysis remains current without the need for continual manual adjustments.

When it comes to summarizing data, Pivot Tables excel with their aggregation functions. Whether you're calculating totals, averages, counts, or identifying minimums and maximums, Pivot Tables make these computations almost effortless. This ability transforms them into a powerful tool for quick, comprehensive data summaries – for instance, summing up regional sales or averaging product prices with ease.

Enhancing Pivot Tables with Pivot Charts takes your data visualization to another level. This integration allows you to graphically represent the data you've summarized in your Pivot Table, making it not just analyzable but also visually engaging. These charts inherit Pivot Tables' dynamic nature, offering a visual complement that is as flexible and insightful as the tables themselves.

Slicers add an interactive dimension to Pivot Tables, simplifying the process of segmenting data for specific analyses. These visual tools act as intuitive filters, enhancing your ability to concentrate on particular data slices without getting lost in the entirety of the dataset.

Pivot Tables also play a pivotal role in crafting interactive dashboards in Excel. By orchestrating multiple Pivot Tables and Charts, you can construct a comprehensive, interactive dashboard that offers a panoramic view of your data, accommodating diverse analytical needs through interactive elements like slicers and filters.

For those delving deeper, Pivot Tables offer advanced functionalities such as calculated fields and items, allowing for custom computations within the tables. Additionally, the ability to group data within Pivot Tables – be it by dates, numbers, or custom groupings – opens up further avenues for layered, nuanced analysis.

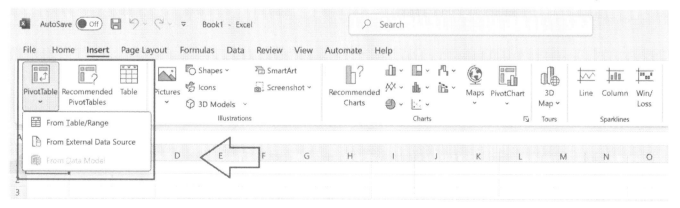

In sum, Pivot Tables are an indispensable element in Excel's data analysis arsenal. They simplify the complex, transforming the daunting into the manageable, and elevating data analysis from a task of endurance to one of insight. From generating quick data summaries to building comprehensive, interactive dashboards, Pivot Tables equip you with a tool that is as powerful in its analytical capacity as it is accessible in its usability. They encapsulate the essence of Excel's promise – to make data analysis not just possible but also practical and insightful for users at every level of expertise.

23. Excel Macros: Automating Tasks

In the realm of Excel, macros emerge as a transformative tool, revolutionizing the way repetitive tasks are approached. These powerful sequences of commands, created through Excel's macro feature, automate routine actions, drastically reducing manual input and enhancing both efficiency and accuracy. This is not merely a feature for expediency; it's about reshaping how you interact with data in Excel.

Creating a macro is remarkably straightforward, especially with Excel's macro recorder. This feature allows you to record a series of actions in Excel—be it data formatting, regular report generation, or routine data entry—and then automatically converts these actions into a VBA (Visual Basic for Applications) script. This script, when executed, replicates the recorded actions precisely. This process democratizes automation in Excel, making it accessible even to those who are not versed in programming.

For users with a more technical bent, the recorded macro can serve as a starting point for more advanced customization. The VBA Editor in Excel allows you to delve into the script, fine-tuning and expanding it to meet more complex requirements. This might involve integrating loops, adding conditional logic, or tweaking the macro to handle more diverse scenarios, offering an expansive playground for those looking to push the boundaries of what Excel can automate.

The consistent application of tasks is another standout benefit of macros. In environments where precision and regularity are paramount, macros ensure that each step of a process is executed uniformly, significantly reducing the risk of human error. This is particularly crucial in tasks where a single mistake can have significant repercussions.

Embedding macros into daily Excel workflows can lead to a remarkable surge in productivity. Processes that traditionally consumed hours can be condensed into moments, all with a click of a button. Imagine a macro that readies your data for analysis, performs the analysis, and formats the results, all executed swiftly and seamlessly.

This not only saves time but also allows you to focus on more complex, analytical tasks.

However, with great power comes great responsibility, particularly regarding security. Macros can be used to execute harmful code, so it's vital to exercise caution, enabling them only from trusted sources. Excel's security settings help manage this risk, letting you control macro execution to maintain a balance between safety and functionality.

Sharing Excel files with embedded macros can be a powerful way to collaborate, but it requires mindfulness. Ensuring that the recipients of your macro-enabled files are aware of how to enable and use the macros is crucial. Additionally, bear in mind compatibility – the macros you create should be functional on the Excel versions used by your colleagues to avoid any hiccups in collaborative work.

Embarking on a journey to master Excel macros can be both exciting and rewarding. For beginners, the macro recorder offers a gentle introduction to automation. As comfort grows, venturing into writing and editing macros in VBA opens up a new world of possibilities, advancing from simple automations to intricate, customized solutions. The learning curve is supported by a plethora of resources – from detailed online tutorials to active user forums, all contributing to your journey from a novice to an Excel macro expert.

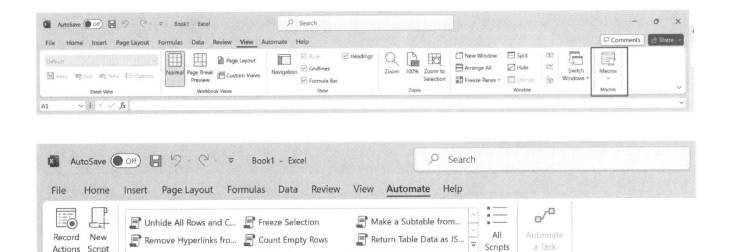

In essence, Excel macros represent a paradigm shift in data management and analysis. They streamline repetitive tasks, reduce error margins, and free up valuable time for more strategic work. Whether you're taking your first steps with the macro recorder or crafting complex custom scripts in VBA, harnessing the power of Excel macros can significantly elevate your data management capabilities, turning Excel from a mere tool into a powerful ally in your data journey.

24. Data Validation and Conditional Formatting

Excel's features of Data Validation and Conditional Formatting synergize to not only maintain the integrity of data input but also enhance its visual comprehension and analysis. These features are pivotal in any data-driven environment, offering a dual advantage: ensuring data accuracy and making it more intuitive to decipher complex data patterns.

Data Validation is a cornerstone of maintaining data accuracy in Excel. It allows you to set specific criteria for what can be entered into a cell, ensuring consistency and correctness in data entry. This is particularly invaluable in collaborative environments or in spreadsheets that require strict data entry guidelines.

The ability to create dropdown lists in Data Validation simplifies data entry, providing a set of predefined options to choose from, thereby streamlining data consistency and reducing input errors. The dropdown lists are not just about limiting options; they also speed up the data entry process, making it more efficient. Beyond the basic validation criteria, Excel enables the setting up of sophisticated rules using custom formulas, adding another layer of precision to your data control mechanisms. This advanced aspect of Data Validation allows for dynamic and responsive data entry rules, where the validation can depend on other cells' data or a set of complex conditions.

On the other hand, Conditional Formatting in Excel is about bringing a visual dimension to your data. It automatically applies formatting to cells based on set criteria, such as color-coding cells depending on their values, making it exceedingly efficient to spot trends, outliers, or critical data points at a glance. This feature becomes indispensable in large datasets where manually scanning through numbers would be cumbersome and error-prone. Conditional Formatting is not limited to simple color changes; it includes data bars, color scales, and icon sets that visually represent data magnitude, variations, or categories. Data bars provide a quick visual indicator, making it easy to compare values in a range, while color scales can represent a spectrum of values, such as from high to low, and icon sets can classify data into different categories based on specified conditions.

What makes Conditional Formatting particularly powerful is the ability to use formulas to define the conditions, offering limitless customization in how you want your data to be visually represented. This flexibility means that Conditional Formatting can be as straightforward or as complex as needed, tailored to the specific requirements of your data analysis.

When Data Validation and Conditional Formatting are used in tandem, they transform Excel from a mere data storage tool into an interactive, smart data management system. This combination not only safeguards data accuracy but also turns data into a visually interactive map. For example, you can use Data Validation to ensure that only specific types of data are entered into a cell and then use

Conditional Formatting to highlight cells that meet certain criteria, such as flagging overdue dates or values that are above or below a certain threshold.

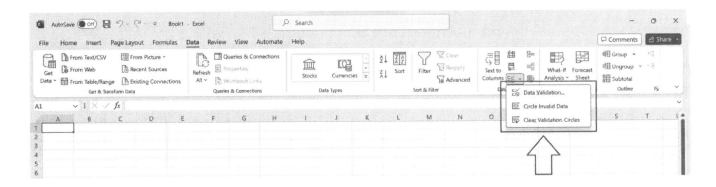

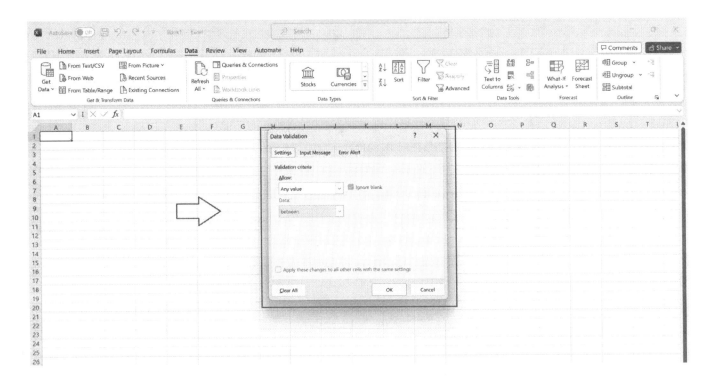

In essence, Data Validation and Conditional Formatting are about making your data work effectively and efficiently for you. They are tools that not only guard against data entry errors but also transform your data into a visually engaging and easy-to-analyze format.

Whether it's through ensuring the consistency and accuracy of data input or through visually mapping out data for quick analysis, these features of Excel enhance both the reliability and usability of your data.

They epitomize Excel's capability to be not just a passive data recording tool, but an active participant in data management and analysis, making your workflow more streamlined, accurate, and insightful.

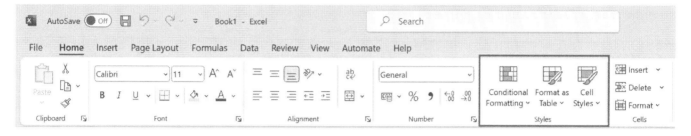

25. Securing and Protecting Your Data

Securing and protecting data in Excel is a multifaceted approach that combines robust built-in features with disciplined best practices. In a landscape where data breaches are increasingly common, safeguarding sensitive information is crucial. Excel's suite of security tools is designed to shield your data from unauthorized access and potential threats, ensuring that your valuable information remains confidential and intact.

Password protection in Excel is a primary defense mechanism. It enables you to restrict access to your entire workbook or specific sheets. This layer of security is pivotal in controlling who can view or modify your data. Creating strong, unique passwords and keeping them confidential is essential to maintain the integrity of this security feature.

Excel extends its security features to include file encryption, adding an extra layer of protection. This encryption is particularly vital when handling sensitive data, as it makes it nearly impossible for unauthorized individuals to access your information, even if they somehow acquire the file.

Managing user permissions is especially important in collaborative environments. Excel allows you to define different access levels for different users, ensuring that each person only has the level of access necessary for their role. This way, the risk of accidental or intentional data manipulation is minimized.

Backing up your Excel files regularly is a crucial practice in protecting your data against loss. Regular backups to secure locations, like external drives or cloud storage, ensure that your data is safe and retrievable in case of hardware failure, accidental deletion, or other unexpected events.

Keeping your Excel software updated is equally important. Software updates often include critical security patches and bug fixes, safeguarding your data against newly identified vulnerabilities.

While Excel macros are powerful tools, they also pose potential security risks. Being cautious with macros, particularly those from unknown or untrusted sources, is important. Excel's security settings allow you to manage macro execution effectively, reducing the risk of malicious code.

Data validation contributes to the security of your data by ensuring accuracy and integrity. By controlling the type of data entered into your cells, you prevent erroneous data entry, which could lead to data corruption or inaccurate analyses.

When sharing Excel files, especially via the internet, securing data in transit is vital. Using encrypted email services or secure file transfer methods can protect your data from being intercepted by unauthorized parties.

Educating yourself and your team on data security best practices is a critical component of protecting your data. Understanding the potential risks and knowing how to mitigate them is crucial in a world where digital threats are ever-present.

In summary, securing and protecting your data in Excel requires a comprehensive approach that encompasses both the use of Excel's security features and adherence to best practices in data management. From password protection and file encryption to regular backups and cautious sharing, each aspect plays a crucial role in ensuring the safety and privacy of your data.

Educating yourself and your team about these practices and the importance of data security further fortifies your defense against potential breaches. In today's digital age, being proactive in securing your Excel files is not just a recommendation but a necessity for anyone who handles sensitive data.

26. Collaborating in Excel: A Team Approach

Excel has transformed from a tool primarily used by individuals into a dynamic platform that fosters effective team collaboration. The evolution of Excel's features now allows teams to work together seamlessly, sharing, editing, and analyzing data in real-time. This collective approach to data management, powered by Excel's robust collaboration tools, is reshaping how teams interact with data, enhancing productivity and ensuring more accurate outcomes.

The introduction of shared workbooks is a game-changer in Excel's collaborative functionality. It allows multiple team members to access and work on the same workbook simultaneously, regardless of their physical locations. This simultaneous access, facilitated by cloud-based solutions like Excel Online or through integration with platforms like SharePoint or OneDrive, ensures that everyone is always on the same page, quite literally. Real-time collaboration not only boosts productivity but also minimizes the risk of data conflicts or errors that can arise from multiple versions of a document.

Tracking changes in Excel is a critical feature for collaboration, providing an audit trail of who changed what and when. This transparency is essential in collaborative projects where understanding the history and evolution of a document is as crucial as the final output. It adds a layer of accountability and aids in tracking the development of the data over time.

Effective collaboration in Excel is not just about sharing data; it's also about communicating within the tool. Excel's commenting feature serves as an efficient medium for this, allowing team members to leave context-specific notes, queries, or feedback directly on the data cells. This direct line of communication within Excel itself reduces misunderstandings and streamlines the collaborative process.

Data validation is another significant aspect of team collaboration in Excel. It ensures uniform data entry standards across the team, reducing discrepancies and errors. This consistency is crucial for the reliability of subsequent data analysis. By setting predefined criteria for data entry, teams can maintain uniformity in their data, enhancing the quality and reliability of their collective work.

Collaboration also demands a balance between openness and data security. Excel addresses this by allowing different access levels for users. This feature enables project leads to control who can view or edit specific data within the workbook, protecting sensitive information from unauthorized access while still promoting a collaborative environment.

Excel's integration with other tools and applications further augments its collaborative potential. By connecting with various data sources and business intelligence tools, Excel serves as a hub for data analysis and reporting. This integration enables a seamless flow of information across platforms, enriching the collaborative efforts of the team.

The heart of collaboration in Excel lies in enabling collective problem-solving and decision-making. Features like Pivot Tables simplify shared data analysis, allowing team members to dissect data in numerous ways, share insights, and make informed, data-driven decisions together. This collaborative approach to problem-solving harnesses the collective expertise and perspectives of the team, leading to more comprehensive and well-rounded analyses.

However, effective collaboration in Excel requires more than just functional knowledge; it necessitates a culture of continuous learning and skill development. Regular training, sharing of best practices, and fostering an environment that encourages exploration and mastery of Excel's features are vital for maximizing the collaborative potential of a team.

In conclusion, "Collaborating in Excel: A Team Approach" is about leveraging Excel's capabilities to foster a collaborative and productive work environment. It's about utilizing shared workbooks, tracking changes, and communicating effectively within Excel to enhance teamwork.

By ensuring consistent data entry through validation, maintaining data security, integrating with other tools, and encouraging a culture of continuous learning, Excel becomes not just a tool for individual use but a powerful platform for team collaboration. In the modern data-driven workplace, Excel's collaborative features are invaluable for any team looking to enhance its data management, analysis, and decision-making processes.

27. Excel Shortcuts: Efficiency Boosters

Excel shortcuts are the secret weapons that significantly enhance efficiency and productivity in navigating and manipulating data. These keystroke combinations allow you to bypass multiple mouse clicks, streamlining your workflow and reducing task completion time. Mastering these shortcuts is crucial for anyone looking to work more effectively in Excel, as they are not just about executing tasks quickly; they are about transforming the way you interact with this powerful tool.

The essence of using keyboard shortcuts in Excel is to minimize the constant back-and-forth between the keyboard and the mouse. Familiar shortcuts like Ctrl+C for copy, Ctrl+V for paste, and Ctrl+Z for undo are just the tip of the iceberg. Excel's extensive range of shortcuts includes Ctrl+Arrow keys for jumping to data edges, Alt+E+S+V for special paste options like values only, or Ctrl+Shift+L to toggle filters. These shortcuts make navigating large datasets and managing complex formulas much more efficient.

Data entry and formatting, often tedious tasks, can be expedited with shortcuts. For example, Ctrl+D and Ctrl+R are invaluable for copying data down or across cells, while Ctrl+1 quickly brings up the format cells dialog. These shortcuts help maintain a smooth and rapid flow of data entry and formatting, vital in handling extensive datasets.

In data analysis, shortcuts are indispensable. Quick summing with Alt+=, inserting new cells with Ctrl+Shift+"+", or editing a cell with F2, are examples of how shortcuts can streamline the analytical process.

These keystroke commands can drastically reduce the time and effort required for data manipulation, enabling you to focus more on analysis rather than the mechanics of data handling.

Efficient management of worksheets and workbooks is another area where shortcuts prove beneficial. Navigating between sheets using Ctrl+Page Up/Page Down or managing multiple workbooks with Ctrl+N for new workbook or Ctrl+Tab to switch between open files enhances your ability to multitask and manage data across different documents seamlessly.

Shortcuts extend their utility to the realm of data visualization in Excel. Quick chart creation from selected data using Alt+F1 or managing groups in a PivotTable with Ctrl+Shift+G illustrate how shortcuts can expedite the transformation of raw data into insightful visual formats.

Customization adds another layer of efficiency. Excel allows you to tailor the Quick Access Toolbar and create your own set of shortcuts, aligning Excel's functionality with your specific workflow needs. This personalization means that the most frequently used commands are just a keystroke away, perfectly suited to your unique work style.

Incorporating these shortcuts into your daily routine requires consistent practice. The initial effort to memorize and use these shortcuts consistently pays off in the long run, as they become an integral part of your workflow. Over time, these keystroke commands become instinctive, greatly speeding up your work and enhancing your overall productivity in Excel.

Excel shortcuts, therefore, are much more than quick fixes or cool tricks; they are essential components of efficient Excel usage. They empower you to work smarter, not harder, transforming lengthy procedures into swift, effortless actions. Whether you are a novice eager to increase your working speed or an experienced user looking to optimize your data management, mastering these shortcuts is a pivotal step in achieving Excel excellence. In today's fast-paced work environment, where time is a precious commodity, being proficient in Excel shortcuts is not just an advantage; it's a necessity.

28. Solving Common Excel Problems

Understanding and resolving common Excel problems is essential for anyone seeking to use this powerful tool efficiently. Excel, with its wide array of functionalities, can present various challenges. However, these challenges offer opportunities to deepen your understanding and enhance your problem-solving skills in Excel.

Error messages are among the most frequent issues users encounter. Rather than being a hindrance, these messages are clues pointing to the root of the problem. For example, "#DIV/0!" indicates division by zero, while "#VALUE!" suggests a mismatch in data types within a formula. Deciphering these messages is key to rectifying errors, often involving formula adjustments or data type corrections.

Formula-related problems often arise due to Excel's default use of relative cell references. When formulas are copied to different cells, these references change, which can lead to unexpected results. Switching to absolute references (using $ symbols, like in A1) or double-checking the formula syntax and function appropriateness can mitigate these issues.

Formatting inconsistencies, especially with dates or text alignment, are common and can be rectified in the Format Cells dialog box (Ctrl+1). This feature offers various options to standardize and enhance your data's appearance. Understanding and utilizing Excel's full range of formatting tools, including conditional formatting, is vital in presenting your data compellingly and accurately.

Handling large datasets can lead to performance slowdowns or crashes. To improve performance, simplify formulas where possible, reduce the usage of volatile functions, and consider organizing your data across multiple sheets or using Excel tables for more efficient data management.

Importing data from different sources into Excel can introduce compatibility issues or incorrect data displays. Using Excel's specialized data import tools, like Get & Transform Data, can help ensure that your data is correctly formatted and compatible with Excel's features.

PivotTables, powerful for data analysis, can sometimes display data incorrectly or not reflect updates. Refreshing the PivotTable, ensuring the data range is comprehensive, and proper data formatting can resolve most PivotTable issues.

In collaborative scenarios or when linking between different workbooks, broken links or outdated data can pose problems. Maintaining consistent file locations and regularly updating links can help, as can using collaborative tools like Excel Online for a more integrated teamwork experience.

For users working with macros and VBA, issues like non-functioning macros or code errors can occur. Ensuring your macro security settings allow macro execution and carefully debugging your VBA code are essential steps in solving these issues.

Becoming adept at troubleshooting in Excel often involves a combination of understanding Excel's functionalities and a systematic approach to identifying and resolving issues. Excel's extensive help resources, including online forums and tutorials, can also offer invaluable assistance.

In summary, being proficient in Excel isn't just about mastering its features; it's also about developing the ability to troubleshoot and resolve common problems. This skill set enhances your overall efficiency and effectiveness in Excel, allowing for smoother workflows and a more in-depth understanding of this multifaceted tool. Through practice and exploration, you can transform these challenges into opportunities for learning and development, further solidifying your expertise in Excel.

29. Expert Excel Strategies

Excel, as a versatile tool, offers an expansive range of functionalities that, when fully harnessed, can significantly enhance data analysis and management. Achieving expertise in Excel involves a deep dive into not only its advanced features but also developing strategic approaches to optimize your work.

Advanced data analysis lies at the core of Excel expertise. This includes mastering complex functions and knowing when and how to apply them effectively. Array formulas, for example, allow simultaneous calculations on multiple data items and are essential for complex analyses. Functions like VLOOKUP, INDEX, and MATCH, when used adeptly, can handle large datasets with ease, improving both accuracy and efficiency.

Creating dynamic and interactive dashboards represents a significant aspect of Excel mastery. These dashboards transform static data into a visually engaging and interactive experience. Effective use of PivotTables and PivotCharts, integrating interactive elements like slicers, and employing conditional formatting to visualize data changes are crucial skills for crafting these insightful dashboards.

Automation in Excel, primarily through macros and Visual Basic for Applications (VBA), is a game-changer in efficiency. Automating repetitive tasks not only conserves time but also minimizes errors. Writing custom VBA scripts to automate tasks or create specific functions tailored to unique requirements can significantly enhance productivity.

Optimizing spreadsheet performance becomes vital as data complexity increases. Expert users employ strategies to maintain smooth workbook operation, including minimizing the use of volatile functions, optimizing formula calculations, and managing data effectively. Techniques like using Excel's Power Query and Power Pivot features are also essential for handling extensive datasets without compromising performance.

Data validation and error checking are integral to Excel proficiency. Beyond setting up data validation rules, using auditing tools to trace cell relationships and employing error-checking functions are key to ensuring data integrity.

These practices are crucial in maintaining the accuracy and reliability of data, especially in large and complex datasets.

Integrating Excel with other applications and data sources significantly broadens its capabilities. This might involve importing data from various external sources, linking Excel with databases, or integrating it with other Office applications like Access or Power BI. Understanding these integrations expands the scope of data analysis, enabling more comprehensive and nuanced insights.

For expert users, maintaining security and integrity, particularly in collaborative environments, is paramount. This includes understanding and implementing best practices for sharing workbooks, securing data, and managing user permissions. These practices are essential in protecting sensitive information and ensuring collaborative efficiency.

Continuously adapting to Excel's evolving landscape is a hallmark of an expert. Staying abreast of new features and updates, participating in Excel forums, and engaging in ongoing learning through courses and tutorials are vital for keeping skills sharp and relevant.

In essence, becoming an expert in Excel is a journey that extends beyond basic understanding. It involves a commitment to mastering advanced analysis techniques, creating dynamic data visualizations, automating tasks, optimizing performance, ensuring data integrity, and continually adapting to new features and best practices. This level of proficiency not only enhances your efficiency in Excel but also elevates your capacity for making informed, data-driven decisions, making you an invaluable asset in any data-centric role.

As we conclude this exploration into the depths of Excel, it's clear that this journey is one of continuous discovery and mastery. Excel, far more than a mere spreadsheet tool, is a comprehensive platform for data analysis, visualization, and management. The journey through Excel is characterized by a constant evolution of skills, from understanding the basics to mastering advanced techniques that transform the way data is perceived and utilized.

The mastery of complex calculations, dynamic dashboards, and sophisticated data analysis techniques marks a significant milestone in this journey. These skills not only enhance the ability to navigate through large datasets but also enable the creation of interactive and insightful data presentations. The power of Excel lies in its ability to turn raw data into meaningful stories, providing clarity and direction for decision-making processes.

The exploration of macros and VBA for automation highlights the transformative potential of Excel. By automating repetitive tasks, Excel becomes not just a tool for data analysis but a partner in efficiency, allowing more time for strategic thinking and analysis. The optimization of performance and the emphasis on data integrity further reinforce Excel's role as a reliable and powerful tool in handling and analyzing data.

In essence, the journey through Excel is an ongoing process of learning, adapting, and evolving. It's about harnessing the full potential of this versatile tool to make data-driven decisions with confidence and precision. As the landscape of data and technology continues to evolve, so does the journey in Excel, promising new horizons and possibilities in the world of data analysis.

Book 3: Powerful PowerPoint Presentations

Embarking on the journey to master PowerPoint presentations, you are about to unlock the secrets of creating captivating and effective slideshows. In this comprehensive guide, you will be led through the essential steps and strategies that transform ordinary presentations into powerful tools of communication and engagement.

As we dive into the world of PowerPoint, we begin by establishing a solid foundation. This includes understanding the basic functionalities of the program and the significance of a well-structured narrative in your slides. From the arrangement of content to the choice of design, every decision plays a pivotal role in how your message is received.

The art of PowerPoint is not just about the technicalities of slide creation. It's about harnessing the power of visual storytelling to connect with your audience on a deeper level. You will learn how to craft slides that are not only visually appealing but also strategically designed to hold the attention of your audience and convey your message effectively.

The guide also emphasizes the importance of interactivity and audience engagement. You will explore various techniques to make your presentations more dynamic and engaging, including the use of multimedia, animations, and interactive elements. This not only enhances the visual appeal but also actively involves the audience in the learning process.

Moreover, you will be equipped to handle the common challenges that presenters face, from technical glitches to time management. Tips and strategies will be provided to help you navigate these obstacles with confidence and ease.

This journey will transform your approach to PowerPoint presentations, empowering you to create slides that are not just informative but also inspiring. Get ready to captivate your audience and leave a lasting impact with every presentation you deliver.

30. Beginning with PowerPoint: A Primer

Starting with PowerPoint involves embarking on a journey to create compelling presentations that effectively communicate your message. This powerful tool, integral to the professional world, is designed not just to inform, but to captivate and engage your audience. Mastering PowerPoint starts with a fundamental understanding of its interface and extends to the strategic use of its numerous features.

Initially, getting to know the PowerPoint interface is key. The ribbon, which spans the top of the application, is your control center, housing essential tools across various tabs. Each tab – like 'Home', 'Insert', and 'Design' – provides specific functionalities. Familiarizing yourself with these options is the first step in harnessing the power of PowerPoint.

Creating your first slide marks the beginning of your presentation journey. PowerPoint offers a range of layouts for different purposes, be it a title slide or a content slide. Choosing the right layout is crucial for effectively arranging your information. As you add text to your slides, remember that clarity and brevity are paramount. Overloaded slides with excessive text can overwhelm your audience, diminishing the impact of your message. Use concise bullet points to break down complex information, making it more digestible.

Visual elements play a significant role in enhancing your presentation. Learning to integrate images, shapes, and icons adds a layer of visual interest and helps to underscore your main points. These elements should complement your content, aiding in the storytelling process without overpowering the textual information.

Consistency in design is essential for maintaining a professional and cohesive look throughout your presentation. Utilize PowerPoint's design themes to ensure uniformity in color schemes, fonts, and slide layouts. This consistency not only makes your presentation aesthetically pleasing but also reinforces your message through a unified visual narrative.

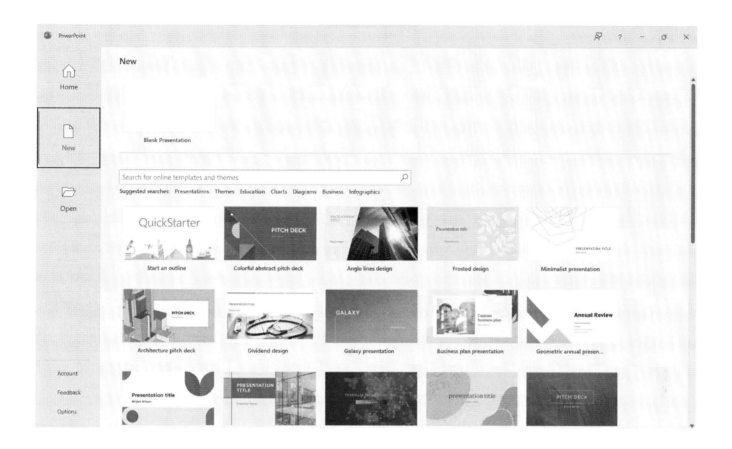

Incorporating multimedia, such as videos and audio clips, can transform your presentation into an engaging experience. PowerPoint allows the embedding of these files directly into your slides. However, it's crucial to integrate multimedia seamlessly, ensuring that it enhances rather than distracts from your overall presentation.

Animations and transitions add a dynamic element to your presentation. Used judiciously, animations can draw attention to key points and aid in information flow. Similarly, slide transitions should complement the pace and style of your presentation. The key lies in subtlety; overusing these effects can lead to a cluttered and distracting presentation.

A crucial part of a successful PowerPoint presentation is your delivery. Familiarizing yourself with the 'Presenter View' can significantly enhance your presentation skills. This feature provides you with a private view of your notes, upcoming slides, and a timer, helping you to deliver your presentation smoothly and confidently.

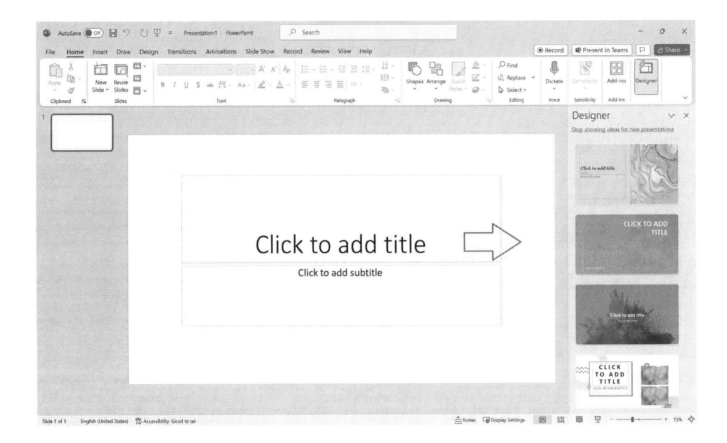

In summary, beginning with PowerPoint is about more than just learning a software tool; it's about developing the skills to create presentations that effectively convey your message and engage your audience. From the initial steps of understanding the interface and creating your first slide to the more advanced aspects of integrating multimedia and mastering animations, each element plays a crucial role in the creation of a powerful presentation. Your journey with PowerPoint is a continuous learning experience, where each presentation offers an opportunity to refine and enhance your skills, making you a more effective and impactful communicator.

31. Designing Engaging Slides

Crafting engaging slides in PowerPoint transcends mere aesthetics; it's an essential part of effective communication in any presentation.

The design of each slide is pivotal, as it not only sets the visual tone but also significantly influences the audience's ability to absorb and retain the information presented.

An effective slide strikes a balance between text and visual elements. Overcrowding slides with text can lead to disinterest or even confusion among the audience. Instead, key phrases or concise bullet points should form the crux of your text content, supplemented by appropriate visuals like images, charts, or graphs. These visuals serve a dual purpose – breaking the monotony of text and illustrating complex ideas more intuitively, thereby enhancing understanding and retention.

Maintaining a consistent theme and layout throughout the presentation is critical. A uniform approach in terms of color schemes, font styles, and background choices imparts a professional look and aids in keeping the audience focused on the content rather than getting distracted by inconsistent design elements. While PowerPoint provides a variety of themes and layouts, customizing them to align with your presentation's message and tone can add a unique touch while upholding consistency.

Color choices in slide design are not just about aesthetics; they play a crucial role in drawing attention and conveying emotions. It's essential to select a palette that is visually harmonious and ensures clear readability of text. The significance of colors can vary across different cultural contexts, so it's important to choose colors that resonate well with the intended audience.

Font selection is equally crucial in slide design. The chosen fonts should embody professionalism and ease of reading. A common mistake is using multiple font styles within a single presentation, leading to a cluttered and disorganized appearance. The font size must be large enough to be legible from a distance, ensuring that your message is clearly communicated to everyone in the audience.

Integrating multimedia elements like images, videos, and audio clips can elevate the engagement level of your slides significantly. However, their use needs to be strategic and purposeful. Each multimedia element should directly support and enhance the key messages of your presentation. Overuse or inappropriate use of these elements can distract from the core message.

Animations and transitions are powerful tools in PowerPoint, adding an element of dynamism to the presentation. They can be effective in highlighting important points and maintaining the audience's interest.

However, they should be used sparingly and thoughtfully to avoid overwhelming the audience and detracting from the main content.

Embracing simplicity is perhaps the most effective strategy in slide design. A clean and uncluttered slide with ample white space not only looks appealing but also facilitates better focus on the key messages. This minimalist approach aids in delivering a clear and impactful presentation.

Before finalizing a presentation, it's crucial to test the slides. This process involves checking the presentation on different devices and screens to ensure consistency in appearance. This step is essential to verify the readability of text, the clarity of images, and the functionality of any embedded multimedia elements.

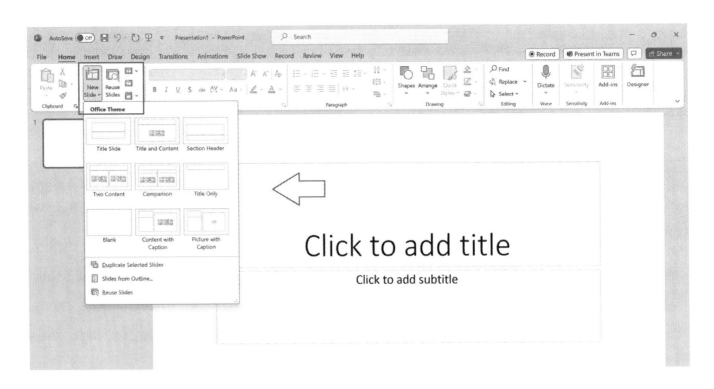

In summary, designing engaging slides is an art that requires thoughtful consideration of various elements – from text and visuals to color and font choices, along with the strategic use of multimedia and animations.

The goal is to create a harmonious, clear, and visually appealing presentation that not only captures the audience's attention but also aids in effectively conveying the intended message. This thoughtful approach to slide design is fundamental in making your PowerPoint presentation not just informative, but also engaging and memorable.

32. Utilizing Themes and Templates

In the art of crafting powerful PowerPoint presentations, the skillful use of themes and templates is pivotal. These tools are not just about aesthetics; they're about creating a visual narrative that complements and enhances the spoken message. Themes are pre-designed color schemes, font styles, and effects that bring a uniform look to the entire presentation, ensuring each slide aligns visually with others. Templates go a step further, offering a structured layout that includes not only design elements but also potential content placement.

The choice of the right theme or template can set the tone of the presentation. A corporate presentation might benefit from a sleek, professional theme, while a more creative topic might call for something vibrant and engaging. The beauty of themes lies in their simplicity and transformative power. With a few clicks, a mundane presentation can adopt a professional and aesthetically pleasing look.

However, the true artistry lies in customizing these themes and templates. Altering a theme's color scheme to match a company's branding, or modifying a template's layout to suit a specific storytelling style can give a unique identity to the presentation. This customization ensures that your presentation stands out, offering a unique flavor while maintaining the professional sheen provided by the theme or template.

It's crucial, however, to ensure that the design complements the content. The primary aim of a presentation is to communicate a message effectively, and the design should aid this process, not distract from it. Themes and templates should serve as a backdrop that elevates the content, making it more engaging and digestible for the audience.

Consistency is another key advantage of using themes and templates. A consistent design theme across slides helps in maintaining the audience's attention and reinforces the narrative. This consistency makes the presentation appear well-planned and cohesive, significantly enhancing its professional appeal.

Moreover, themes and templates are an opportunity to reflect personal or brand identity. Customizing a theme to include specific brand elements like logos and colors can make a presentation an extension of the brand, aiding in brand recognition and recall. This aspect is particularly vital in a corporate setting, where brand identity is paramount.

In essence, utilizing themes and templates in PowerPoint is about creating a harmonious blend of design and content. It's about choosing and tailoring these tools to enhance the message and engage the audience.

A well-chosen theme or template can transform a presentation from ordinary to extraordinary, making it not only a vehicle for information but also an engaging and memorable experience.

By mastering the use of themes and templates, you can elevate your PowerPoint presentations, ensuring they are not only informative but also visually captivating and professionally polished.

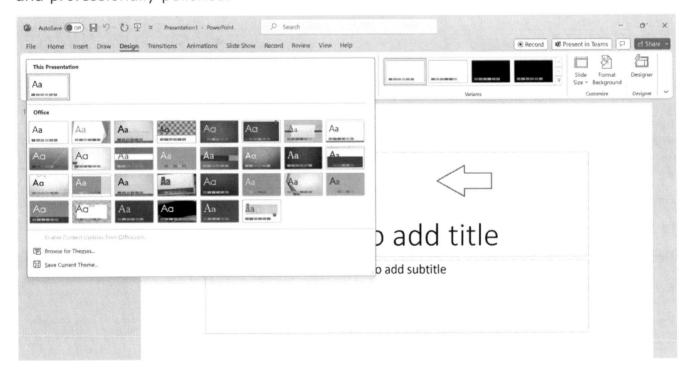

33. Adding and Managing Multimedia

Incorporating multimedia into PowerPoint presentations transforms them from static displays of information into engaging, dynamic narratives. When done effectively, multimedia elements like images, videos, audio, and animations not only capture but also maintain the audience's attention, making the presentation a memorable experience.

Images are a critical component of this multimedia mix. They have the power to convey complex ideas quickly and evoke emotions, thereby enhancing the message. Selecting high-resolution images that are relevant to your presentation's theme is vital. However, their impact lies in strategic usage - the images should complement, not clutter your slides. They should be positioned and sized in a way that they work harmoniously with the text and other slide elements.

Videos add a level of depth and dynamism to presentations that is hard to achieve with still images or text. They can effectively break up the presentation, providing a visual explanation or a change of pace that can re-engage the audience's attention. When embedding videos, it's important to trim them to the essential segments and ensure they play seamlessly within the slide, without the need for manual intervention.

Audio elements, whether they are background music, narrations, or sound effects, can add a unique dimension to your presentation. The key is to use them to support and enhance your message. Any background music should be subtle, complementing the spoken content without overwhelming it. Narrations should be clear, and sound effects should be used sparingly to add emphasis or clarity to your points.

Animations in PowerPoint are more than just decorative elements. When used correctly, they guide the audience's focus, highlight important information, and facilitate smooth transitions between concepts. It's essential to use animations purposefully, ensuring they add to the presentation rather than distract from it. Each animation should be thoughtfully incorporated to enhance the audience's understanding and retention of the content.

Managing these multimedia elements effectively is crucial for a seamless presentation. This includes ensuring compatibility with different devices and software versions, embedding files correctly, and having backups ready for any unforeseen technical issues. Synchronizing these elements with the overall flow of the presentation is also essential. They should align with the narrative and not disrupt the presentation's pacing.

Legal and ethical considerations are paramount when using multimedia in presentations. Always use appropriately licensed or royalty-free images, videos, and music. Respecting copyright laws and giving due credit is not only a legal requirement but also an ethical practice.

Finally, testing all multimedia elements before the actual presentation is crucial. This step is often overlooked but can be the difference between a successful presentation and a technical nightmare. Testing helps identify issues with audio levels, video playback, and animation timings, ensuring that every element contributes positively to the presentation.

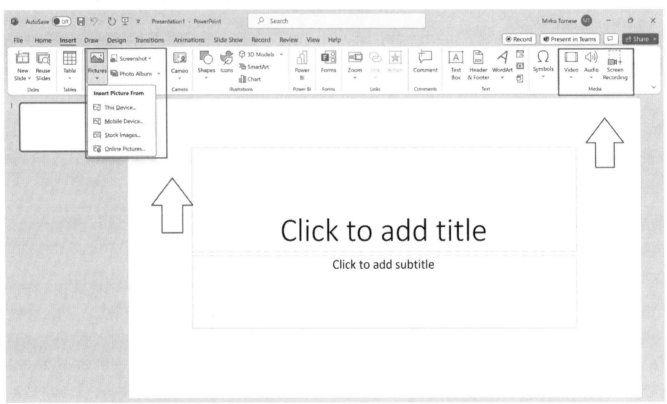

In sum, adding and managing multimedia in PowerPoint presentations is a delicate balancing act. It requires a thoughtful approach to select and incorporate these elements in a way that enhances the presentation. Multimedia should never overshadow the content; instead, it should act as a complement that enriches the overall message. Through careful planning, testing, and ethical usage, multimedia can elevate your PowerPoint presentations from ordinary to extraordinary, leaving a lasting impression on your audience.

34. Animations and Transitions: The Wow Factor

Harnessing the power of animations and transitions in PowerPoint is akin to a skilled artist adding depth and emotion to a painting. Far from being mere embellishments, these elements can significantly elevate a presentation from mundane to mesmerizing. They play a critical role in not just capturing but maintaining the audience's attention, thereby transforming an ordinary presentation into an engaging, memorable experience.

Animations serve as a dynamic tool to guide the audience's focus, illustrate complex concepts, and enhance the storytelling aspect of a presentation. Their effectiveness lies in the purposeful application. Imagine using an animation to highlight a key statistic, visualize a process, or animate a graph. This strategic use can amplify the impact of your message, making key points more noticeable and understandable.

Transitions, often underutilized, are essential in creating a seamless narrative flow. They are the subtle threads that weave individual slides into a coherent story. Each transition has the potential to set the stage for what's next, keeping the audience engaged. The choice of transition should resonate with the mood of your content – a swift transition can energize the audience, while a slow fade might better suit reflective, thought-provoking content.

Customizing animations and transitions is where the real magic happens. PowerPoint offers an array of options to control timing, duration, and direction. Tailoring these elements allows you to synchronize animations with key moments in your speech, creating a powerful audio-visual harmony. This synchronization ensures that visual cues perfectly complement your spoken words, enhancing the clarity and retention of your message.

In data visualization, animations can be particularly transformative. Complex data, when broken down and animated, becomes more digestible and engaging. Through animated graphs and charts, trends and patterns emerge, telling a story that static images or text could not convey as effectively.

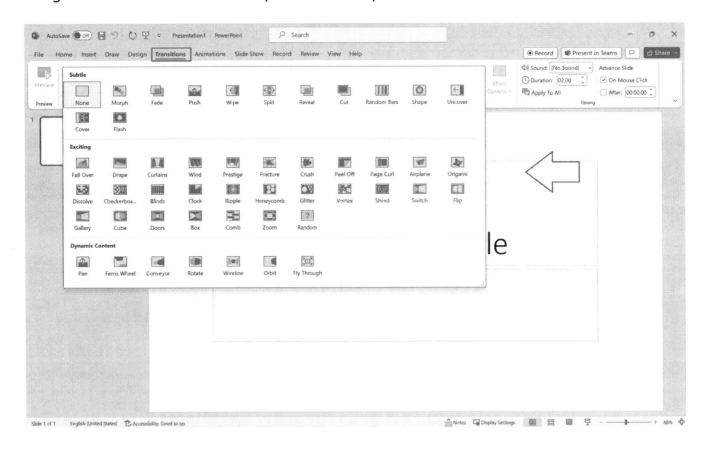

However, the art of using animations and transitions lies in moderation and strategic placement. Overuse or misplaced animations can distract and confuse rather than clarify. They should add to the narrative, not detract from it. Keep animations simple and consistent throughout your presentation to maintain a professional and cohesive feel.

Additionally, it's crucial to test these elements in the environment where you'll present. This ensures that all animations and transitions work flawlessly and align with your delivery. It also prepares you for any technical issues that might arise.

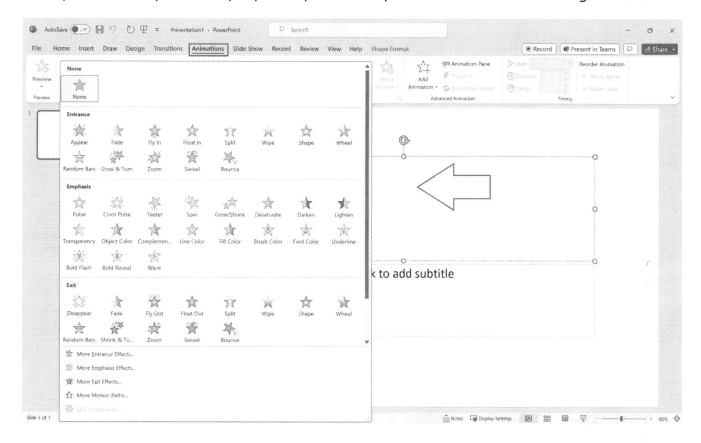

Finally, consider your audience when designing your presentation. What might captivate a young, tech-savvy crowd could overwhelm a more traditional audience. Tailoring your animations and transitions to suit your audience's preferences can make your presentation more relatable and effective.

In essence, animations and transitions in PowerPoint are not just about the 'wow' factor; they are about enhancing communication. They bring your content to life, making it more engaging and memorable. By judiciously using these elements, you can create a presentation that not only delivers information but also tells a compelling story, leaving a lasting impression on your audience. This approach transforms a standard presentation into an experience, ensuring that your message resonates with the audience long after the final slide.

35. Delivering Effective Presentations

Delivering an effective PowerPoint presentation transcends mere content display; it's an art of communication, connection, and persuasion. The essence of a compelling presentation lies in its ability to blend informative content with an engaging delivery, creating a resonating impact on the audience. This requires a deep understanding of your audience, skillful storytelling, clarity in message delivery, and the adept use of multimedia.

When preparing for a presentation, the first step is always understanding your audience. Knowing their interests, background, and expectations helps tailor the content, making it relevant and engaging. Once the audience is understood, the focus shifts to the narrative. A well-crafted story, with a clear beginning, middle, and end, provides a natural flow and structure to the presentation. Each slide should seamlessly transition into the next, like chapters in a book, each contributing meaningfully to the overall narrative.

However, the effectiveness of a presentation is not determined solely by the content; how the content is delivered is equally important. Clarity and conciseness in speech, supported by well-designed slides, ensure the message is both understood and remembered. Avoid cluttering slides with excessive information; each should focus on a single idea, complementing the verbal message, not overshadowing it.

The delivery of the presentation is where personal skills come into play. A confident and clear voice, well-timed gestures, and eye contact are crucial elements that keep the audience engaged. An effective presenter knows how to use the stage, maintaining a dynamic and interactive presence. Moreover, the wise use of multimedia elements – images, videos, animations – can greatly enhance the presentation. These should be used judiciously, adding value to the narrative without becoming distractions.

Engaging with the audience is another vital aspect of effective presentations. Encouraging participation, be it through questions, interactive elements, or discussions, makes the experience more immersive and memorable. Handling the Q&A sessions with openness and readiness to address queries further cements the connection with the audience.

Nerves are natural, especially in public speaking scenarios. Preparation is key to managing these nerves. Familiarity with the content, the venue, and the equipment helps build confidence. Practicing the delivery, perhaps in front of a mock audience, can provide valuable insights into areas of improvement. It's also crucial to remember that a certain level of nervous energy can be beneficial, adding a sense of enthusiasm and earnestness to the delivery.

Feedback post-presentation is invaluable. It provides insights into what worked well and what didn't, paving the way for continuous improvement. Every presentation is a learning opportunity, a chance to hone skills and techniques.

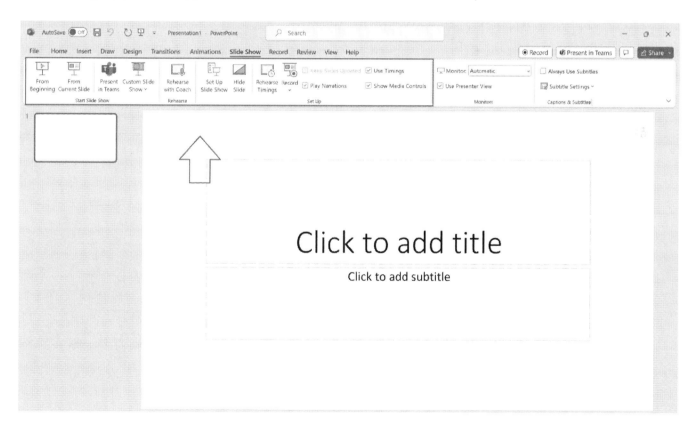

In sum, delivering an effective PowerPoint presentation is a multifaceted skill that goes beyond the slides themselves. It encompasses understanding the audience, crafting and narrating a compelling story, delivering it with clarity and confidence, and engaging with the audience. This synergy of content and delivery, supported by the right use of multimedia and interactive elements, transforms a presentation into an impactful, memorable experience. Continuously seeking feedback and practicing these skills can lead to mastery in the art of PowerPoint presentations, making each one better than the last.

36. Collaborative Presentation Strategies

Collaborative presentations are more than just an amalgamation of individual contributions; they are a symphony of diverse perspectives and skills, harmonized to create a compelling and impactful narrative. In such collaborations, the melding of various backgrounds and expertise enriches the presentation's content, making it multidimensional and robust. This multifaceted approach caters to a broader audience range, addressing various interests and queries more effectively.

Effective team coordination is pivotal in the realm of collaborative presentations. It demands open and clear communication, a well-considered division of tasks, and regular updates on progress. Utilizing a central platform for collaboration, especially cloud-based software, is instrumental. It allows team members to contribute concurrently, keeping everyone on the same page with real-time updates.

The diversity of a team, while a strength, can lead to inconsistencies in style and content. To counter this, establishing a unified presentation style, tone, and structure from the beginning is crucial. This unified approach ensures that the final product, despite having multiple creators, presents a cohesive and seamless narrative.

Capitalizing on individual strengths significantly amplifies the quality of the presentation. Team members might bring various skills to the table, like adept research capabilities, flair for design, data analysis proficiency, or a talent for weaving engaging stories. Assigning tasks based on these strengths not only enhances the presentation's quality but also boosts team efficiency and satisfaction. When the presentation is delivered by multiple speakers, ensuring fluid transitions and a coherent overall narrative is essential. Each speaker should have a thorough understanding of the entire presentation, not just their segment. Practicing these transitions is key to maintaining a smooth flow during the actual presentation.

An essential aspect of collaborative work is the exchange of constructive feedback and the willingness to revise and refine. Regularly scheduled meetings for discussions and feedback foster an environment of continuous improvement. This process ensures alignment with the presentation's objectives and a uniformly high quality across all segments.

Technological tools play a significant role in facilitating collaboration. Features like real-time editing, commenting, and track changes in presentation software make coordination and communication more efficient. For teams not co-located, video conferencing and online collaboration tools are invaluable for remote discussions and rehearsals.

Conflicts, albeit challenging, are an inevitable part of collaboration. Handling disagreements constructively and diplomatically is crucial. Keeping the focus on the shared goal of creating an effective presentation helps navigate through differences and ensures a productive collaborative environment.

In sum, the essence of collaborative presentation strategies lies in the integration of diverse talents and perspectives, coordinated efficiently and harmoniously. A successful collaborative presentation is marked by a unified style, seamless transitions between speakers, constructive feedback, and effective use of technology. It's a process that not only results in a richer, more engaging presentation but also fosters a sense of teamwork and collective achievement. This approach transforms the art of presentation from a solo endeavor to a synergistic activity, culminating in a powerful impact on the audience.

37. Tips for Impactful Slide Design

Creating slides that not only convey your message effectively but also captivate your audience involves a blend of thoughtful design and strategic planning. The key is to marry clarity with visual appeal, ensuring that your presentation resonates with your audience and leaves a lasting impact.

Begin by fully grasping your message and the expectations of your audience. Your slides should be tailored to the content's essence and the preferences of those you are addressing. For instance, a data-centric audience would benefit more from well-designed charts and infographics, while a narrative-heavy presentation might rely more on storytelling through visuals.

The mantra of simplicity cannot be overstated. Each slide should focus on a single idea, using minimal text. This approach helps in preventing the audience from feeling overwhelmed by too much information. Instead, let your spoken words carry the detailed content, using your slides as a visual support to reinforce your message.

Consistency in your slide layout is non-negotiable. Use uniform fonts, colors, and backgrounds to maintain a professional and coherent look throughout your presentation. This consistency in design keeps your audience focused on the content rather than being distracted by inconsistent styling.

When selecting colors and fonts, it's crucial to choose those that reflect the tone of your presentation. A subdued color palette generally works well for professional settings, while more creative discussions may allow for a wider range of bold colors. Contrast is key for readability, so ensure your text stands out against the background. Font choices should prioritize clarity – go for clean, readable fonts like Arial or Helvetica.

Establishing a visual hierarchy helps guide the audience's attention to what's important. The most crucial elements should be the most visually dominant, achieved through variations in size, color, and placement. Titles and key points deserve prominence, while secondary information can be more subtle.

Incorporating high-quality images and graphics is vital. They should be clear and professional, as poor-quality images can detract from your presentation's perceived professionalism. Complex concepts can be made more accessible through well-designed infographics or diagrams, making it easier for your audience to grasp.

Animations and transitions, while potentially effective, should be used judiciously. Excessive use can appear unprofessional, but when used correctly, they can emphasize crucial points or aid in transitioning between topics smoothly.

For data-heavy slides, clarity in data visualization is essential. Keep graphs and charts straightforward and easy to comprehend. Cluttered or overly complex visuals can confuse rather than inform, so always opt for simplicity and clarity.

Accessibility is another critical aspect of slide design. Your presentation should be accessible to everyone in the audience, including those with visual impairments. This means using alt text for images, ensuring good color contrast, and considering font sizes for easy readability.

Lastly, rehearsing with your slides is crucial for a successful presentation. It helps you familiarize yourself with the flow and transition of your content, allowing for any necessary revisions. A well-rehearsed presenter is confident and less reliant on the slides, making for a more engaging and effective delivery.

In sum, impactful slide design is about striking the right balance between aesthetics and functionality. Your slides should not only look good but also serve their purpose – to enhance and clarify your message. Remember, your slides are a tool to aid your presentation, not to overshadow it. With these guidelines, you're well on your way to creating presentations that are not only informative but also memorable.

38. PowerPoint Shortcuts and Secrets

Mastering Microsoft PowerPoint is akin to unlocking a new realm of presentation capabilities. It's not just about how you design your slides, but also about how efficiently and effectively you can navigate and utilize PowerPoint's myriad features. Knowing the right shortcuts and secrets can transform your experience from mundane to magical, saving you time and enhancing your productivity.

Let's delve into some of these lesser-known, yet powerful features and shortcuts that can elevate your PowerPoint game.

Firstly, mastering keyboard shortcuts is a game-changer. For instance, 'Ctrl + D' duplicates objects, 'Ctrl + Z' undoes the last action, and 'F5' starts the slideshow. These shortcuts are just the tip of the iceberg. Learn them, and you'll navigate through the creation process with much more speed and ease.

Next, delve into the magic of 'Quick Access Toolbar'. This customizable toolbar allows you to keep your most-used commands a click away. By adding features like 'Format Painter' or 'Align', you can streamline your workflow significantly. This customization ensures your most-needed tools are always at your fingertips.

Another powerful feature is the 'Slide Master'. This tool is a life-saver for creating consistent formatting across your presentation. Here, you can set a uniform style for fonts, colors, backgrounds, and even add recurring elements like logos or footers. Understanding and using the Slide Master can drastically reduce the time spent on formatting individual slides.

'Presenter View' is a feature often overlooked but incredibly useful. While delivering a presentation, this view provides you with a private interface to view your notes, see upcoming slides, and keep track of time without your audience seeing any of it.

For those who use PowerPoint to present data, 'Data-Driven Charts' are a boon. These charts link directly to your data source, be it an Excel sheet or other databases. When the data updates, so do your charts, automatically. This feature keeps your data presentations accurate and up-to-date with minimal effort.

Then, there's the 'Selection Pane', a lifesaver when working with slides crowded with multiple elements. It allows you to easily select, hide, or reorder objects, making the editing process smoother, especially for complex slides.

'Custom Animations and Transitions' are another area where you can shine. Beyond the standard animations, you can customize motion paths, timing, and triggers. This customization can make your presentation stand out and keep your audience engaged.

Don't forget the power of 'Morph Transition', a relatively new addition to PowerPoint. It lets you create smooth animations and object movements across slides. It's simple: duplicate your slide, move objects where you want them, apply the Morph transition, and watch as elements fluidly move to their new positions.

'Zoom for PowerPoint' is a feature that allows you to create a more interactive and non-linear presentation. Instead of moving slide by slide, you can zoom in on different sections of your presentation in a more dynamic way.

Incorporating 'Hyperlinks' within your presentation can add a new layer of interactivity. Link to external sources, other slides in your presentation, or even email addresses. This technique can turn your presentation into a navigable, interactive experience.

Lastly, don't underestimate the power of 'Templates and Themes'. While creating a presentation from scratch can be rewarding, templates and themes provide a solid foundation to work from. They can inspire and guide your design choices, ensuring a professional look.

By embracing these shortcuts and features, you'll not only save time but also unlock new potentials in your presentations. PowerPoint is more than just a slideshow tool; it's a medium for storytelling, data presentation, and audience engagement. The more you explore its capabilities, the more you can achieve with your presentations. Remember, the key to PowerPoint mastery lies in continual learning and experimentation.

39. Overcoming PowerPoint Challenges

Navigating through the challenges of PowerPoint presentations can be a daunting task, especially when the goal is to create an impactful and engaging presentation. The key lies in understanding common pitfalls and mastering strategies to overcome them. This exploration will equip you with essential tools and insights to tackle these challenges head-on, transforming potential obstacles into opportunities for creative presentation.

The first major challenge many encounter is creating a cohesive narrative. A PowerPoint presentation should not be a random assemblage of slides, but a well-structured story with a clear beginning, middle, and end. To overcome this, start by outlining your main message and supporting points. This roadmap will guide the creation of each slide, ensuring they all contribute to the overarching narrative. Remember, every slide should serve a purpose in advancing your story.

Another common hurdle is managing content overload. It's tempting to cram slides with as much information as possible, but this often leads to cluttered slides that overwhelm the audience. The solution? Embrace simplicity. Use bullet points sparingly, focus on key ideas, and leave room for visual elements and white space. This approach not only makes slides more readable but also more memorable.

Visual design challenges are also frequent. Poorly designed slides can distract or disengage your audience. To combat this, stick to a consistent color scheme and font style throughout your presentation. Use high-quality images and graphics that align with your content. Remember, visual elements should enhance your message, not detract from it.

Engaging the audience is another critical aspect often overlooked. A common mistake is to focus solely on slide content, forgetting about the delivery. Engage your audience by incorporating interactive elements like polls or questions, and by using storytelling techniques to make your content relatable. Also, practice your delivery to ensure you are confident, clear, and engaging.

Technical difficulties can derail even the best presentations. Always have a backup plan for potential issues like software glitches, incompatible file formats, or hardware problems. Check your equipment beforehand, have your presentation saved on multiple devices, and be prepared to present without technology if necessary.

Time management is another crucial challenge. It's easy to get caught up in details and run out of time. To avoid this, rehearse your presentation and time each section. Be prepared to adjust on the fly if you're running long, knowing what content can be trimmed without losing the essence of your message.

Lastly, dealing with questions and interactivity can be tricky. You might face unexpected questions or discussions. Prepare by anticipating potential questions and practicing your responses. During the presentation, listen actively to questions, respond thoughtfully, and use them as opportunities to engage further with your audience.

In conclusion, overcoming PowerPoint challenges requires a combination of careful planning, thoughtful design, audience engagement, technical preparedness, and adaptability. By focusing on these areas, you can create presentations that are not only informative but also compelling and memorable. Remember, each challenge is an opportunity to refine your skills and enhance your presentation's impact. With practice and perseverance, you can master the art of PowerPoint presentations and leave a lasting impression on your audience.

As we conclude this exploration of creating powerful PowerPoint presentations, it's evident that the journey to mastering this skill is both enriching and transformative. Throughout this guide, we've navigated the intricacies of PowerPoint, uncovering the techniques and strategies that make presentations not just informative but impactful and memorable.

We've seen how effective presentations transcend mere data display, becoming a narrative journey that engages and inspires. By understanding the importance of storytelling, design principles, and audience engagement, you've gained the tools to convey messages that resonate and influence. From the basics of slide design to the nuances of animations and transitions, each element has been a building block in creating presentations that captivate.

The journey has also emphasized the importance of adaptability and continuous learning. As technology evolves and audience expectations shift, so too must our approaches to presentation design. You've learned to embrace new features, experiment with different styles, and seek feedback to refine and enhance your skills.

In mastering PowerPoint, you've not only learned to communicate ideas effectively; you've gained the ability to influence, persuade, and inspire. Whether presenting in a boardroom, classroom, or conference, the skills you've developed here will serve you in crafting messages that leave a lasting impact.

As this chapter closes, remember that each presentation is an opportunity to tell a story, to share knowledge, and to connect with your audience. Carry forward these lessons and continue to grow as a compelling communicator and storyteller through the art of PowerPoint.

Book 4: Optimizing Outlook

In an era where digital communication and organization are integral to both personal and professional life, mastering a tool like Outlook becomes more than just a convenience; it's a necessity. The journey to optimizing this powerful software begins with understanding its multifaceted capabilities, extending far beyond mere email management. This guide is crafted to provide a comprehensive look into the depths of what Outlook offers, enabling users to harness its full potential for heightened productivity and efficiency.

The journey starts with familiarizing oneself with the basic functionalities of Outlook, gradually building towards more advanced features. Key aspects like managing emails effectively, mastering the calendar for seamless scheduling, and maintaining an organized contact list are foundational skills that enhance day-to-day operations. As users delve deeper, they encounter more sophisticated elements such as task tracking and advanced email techniques, which streamline workflow and communication.

Customization is a significant aspect of optimizing the Outlook experience. Tailoring the interface and functions to meet individual needs and preferences not only improves usability but also boosts overall productivity. From setting up specific email rules to customizing the calendar and task interfaces, the power of personalization in Outlook is vast and varied.

Security and privacy are paramount in the digital world, and this guide addresses these aspects with the seriousness they deserve. It provides insights into maintaining the security of your data within Outlook and protecting your privacy from potential breaches.

This guide aims to be more than just a manual; it's a journey towards mastering a tool that can transform the way one interacts with the world of digital communication and organization. Whether for professional growth, academic excellence, or personal efficiency, the insights offered pave the way for users to make the most out of their Outlook experience.

40. Getting Started with Outlook

Embarking on the journey of mastering Microsoft Outlook begins with understanding its fundamental purpose: a powerful tool designed to streamline communication, manage schedules, and organize tasks. This segment is dedicated to guiding beginners through the initial steps of navigating and utilizing Outlook to its full potential, setting the stage for more advanced functionalities.

Outlook, more than just an email client, is a comprehensive personal information manager. Its capabilities extend beyond sending and receiving emails, encompassing calendar management, task tracking, and contact organization. The first step in leveraging Outlook's capabilities is setting up your email account. Outlook supports various email services, making it a versatile choice for personal and professional communication.

Once your email is set up, familiarize yourself with the Outlook interface. The layout is intuitively designed, with the primary sections being the inbox, calendar, contacts, and tasks. Each of these sections plays a crucial role in managing your daily activities and communication. The inbox is where you'll spend a significant amount of time, managing emails and ensuring effective communication. Learning how to sort, filter, and search emails efficiently can save time and reduce the overwhelm often associated with email management.

Outlook's calendar function is a powerful tool for scheduling and time management. It allows you to create, edit, and manage appointments and meetings, set reminders, and even share your calendar with others. Understanding how to use the calendar effectively is crucial for keeping track of your commitments and staying organized.

Contact management in Outlook is more than just storing email addresses. It's about creating a database of your professional and personal network. You can store detailed information about your contacts, including phone numbers, addresses, and important dates, which can be synced across devices for easy access.

Task management in Outlook is designed to help you keep track of various tasks and deadlines. You can create, prioritize, and track tasks, set due dates, and even assign tasks to others. This functionality can be a game-changer in managing your workload and ensuring nothing falls through the cracks.

As you become more comfortable with these basic functionalities, you can explore advanced email techniques such as creating rules for incoming emails, using categories and flags for organization, and even setting up automated responses. Customizing your Outlook experience to suit your specific needs can significantly enhance your productivity.

Common issues and troubleshooting are an inevitable part of any software experience. Learning how to address frequent problems like syncing errors, file attachment issues, and managing mailbox size will make your Outlook experience smoother and more efficient.

Security and privacy in Outlook are paramount, especially in a world where digital communication is a primary target for malicious activities. Understanding how to use Outlook's security features, like junk email filtering and sensitivity labels, is crucial for protecting your information.

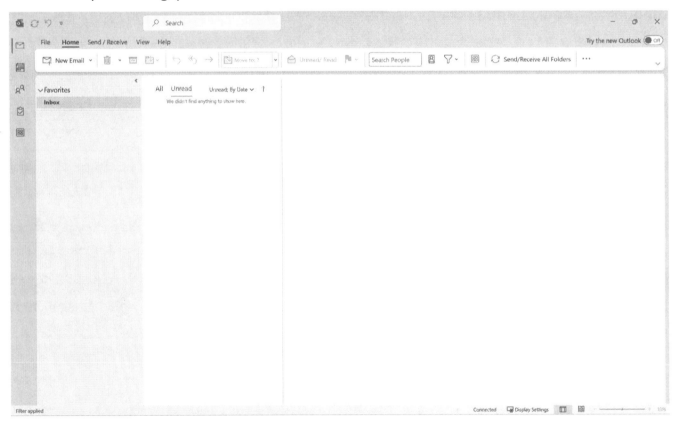

In summary, getting started with Outlook involves familiarizing yourself with its interface, mastering its core functionalities of email, calendar, contacts, and tasks, and then gradually advancing to more complex features. By doing so, you will transform Outlook from a mere email client into a powerful ally in managing your daily professional and personal life. This foundational knowledge sets the stage for diving deeper into the intricacies of Outlook, ensuring you are well-equipped to utilize this versatile tool to its fullest potential.

41. Email Management: Best Practices

In the world of modern communication, managing emails effectively is pivotal for productivity and organization. Email management is not just about keeping your inbox at zero; it's about optimizing the way you interact with this crucial tool to maximize efficiency and minimize stress.

Here, we delve into the best practices for managing emails, specifically tailored for Outlook users, who often juggle a myriad of professional and personal correspondences daily.

First and foremost, understanding the power of organizing your inbox is key. Outlook offers various features like folders, categories, and rules that can be strategically used to keep your inbox streamlined. Create a system of folders for different projects or areas of your life, and use categories to mark emails by priority or type. This system not only declutters your inbox but also makes finding specific emails easier when you need them.

One of the most effective strategies in email management is setting specific times for checking emails. Constantly responding to emails as they arrive can disrupt your workflow and decrease productivity. Instead, allocate certain times of your day for email checking and responding. This approach helps maintain focus on your tasks and reduces the anxiety of an ever-growing inbox.

Utilizing rules in Outlook is another way to automatically manage incoming emails. You can set rules to direct emails from specific senders or with certain keywords into designated folders, mark them as important, or even delete them. This automation saves time and ensures that your inbox contains only what requires your immediate attention.

Effective email management also involves efficient email writing. Keep your emails clear, concise, and to the point. Use subject lines effectively to convey the purpose of the email, making it easier for the recipient to understand the context and respond appropriately. This practice not only benefits you but also respects the time of your recipients.

Another important aspect of email management is dealing with attachments. In Outlook, you can easily manage attachments by saving them directly to your cloud storage, like OneDrive, or your local storage. This way, you keep your inbox light and ensure that important documents are stored securely and accessibly.

Regularly cleaning up your inbox is crucial. Set a routine to go through your email, archive what's important, and delete unnecessary emails. Outlook's clean-up tool can help you remove redundant messages from conversations, making your email threads more manageable and less cluttered.

In addition to these practices, staying on top of your emails involves managing your calendar and tasks in tandem. Outlook integrates these features seamlessly, allowing you to schedule follow-ups and set reminders directly from your emails. This integration ensures that important emails translate into action items or scheduled events, making sure nothing slips through the cracks.

Finally, being aware of security and privacy in email communication is vital. Be cautious of phishing attempts, suspicious attachments, and sharing sensitive information. Outlook provides several security features to protect your email, such as junk mail filters and phishing email protection, which should be utilized to their fullest to safeguard your digital communication.

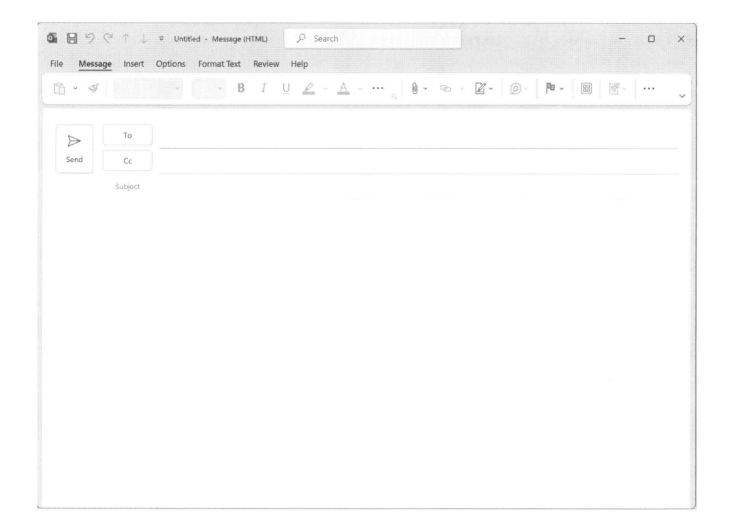

In conclusion, email management in Outlook is an art that combines organization, strategic planning, and the effective use of technological tools. By adopting these best practices, you can transform your email experience from a source of stress to a streamlined, efficient component of your daily routine. It's about creating a system that works for you, one that makes email management a seamless and productive part of your day. Remember, effective email management is not just about dealing with what's in your inbox today, but setting up a sustainable system for the days to come.

42. Mastering Calendar Functions

Mastering the calendar functions in Outlook is an essential skill for anyone looking to optimize their time management and organizational skills. The Outlook Calendar is not just a tool for marking dates; it's a dynamic system for scheduling, planning, and staying ahead in a fast-paced world. This chapter delves into the intricacies of the Outlook Calendar, providing insights and strategies to harness its full potential for personal and professional success.

At the heart of effective calendar management is understanding the interface and functionalities of the Outlook Calendar. The layout is designed to provide a clear and comprehensive view of your schedule, with options to switch between day, week, and month views. Familiarizing yourself with these views allows you to assess your schedule in various granularities, helping you plan both the minute details and the bigger picture of your time.

Creating and managing appointments is a fundamental aspect of the Outlook Calendar. It's about more than just setting a date and time; it involves adding locations, inviting attendees, and setting reminders. Utilize the scheduling assistant feature to find suitable meeting times that work for all participants, thereby avoiding the back-and-forth often associated with meeting coordination. Remember, the key to efficient appointment management is clarity and precision in the details you provide.

Recurring appointments are a powerful feature in Outlook, perfect for regular meetings, weekly calls, or monthly check-ins. Setting up recurring events saves time and ensures consistency in your schedule. It's important, however, to regularly review these recurring appointments to ensure they remain relevant and to avoid cluttering your calendar with outdated or unnecessary meetings.

Reminders in Outlook are a critical tool to keep you on top of your commitments. Customize your reminder settings based on the importance of the event or your personal preference. Whether it's a pop-up notification a few minutes before a meeting or a day-ahead alert for a major event, these reminders are vital for ensuring you never miss an important engagement.

Another significant aspect of the Outlook Calendar is sharing and accessing shared calendars. This feature is invaluable in collaborative environments, allowing you to view colleagues' availability and schedule meetings more efficiently. Respect and privacy are crucial here; be mindful of the information you share and access.

Integrating your calendar with email and task management in Outlook creates a unified system of organization. Convert emails directly into calendar events or tasks, ensuring that actionable items from your emails don't get lost in the shuffle. This integration streamlines your workflow, turning communication into action.

Time zone management is an often-overlooked aspect of calendar mastery, especially crucial for those working across different regions. Outlook's time zone functionality allows you to schedule meetings in different time zones, removing the guesswork and errors associated with time zone conversions.

Customizing calendar views and settings tailors the Outlook Calendar to your personal workflow. Color-code different types of appointments, set the default duration for meetings, or create custom views to filter and display calendar items that are most relevant to you. Personalization makes the calendar an extension of your work style, enhancing efficiency and usability.

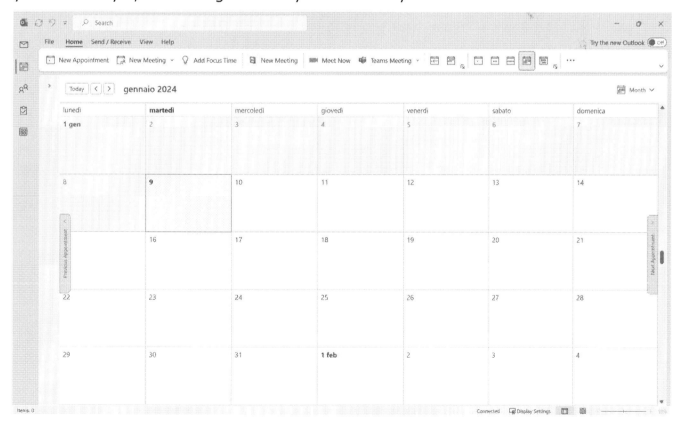

Finally, staying on top of calendar maintenance is crucial. Regularly review and clean up past appointments, delete or update obsolete recurring events, and ensure your calendar reflects your current priorities. A well-maintained calendar is not just a scheduling tool; it's a reflection of your professionalism and attention to detail.

In conclusion, mastering the calendar functions in Outlook is about much more than keeping track of dates and appointments. It's about creating a personalized, efficient system that aligns with your goals, enhances your productivity, and brings structure to the chaos of daily commitments. By fully understanding and utilizing the various features of the Outlook Calendar, you transform it into a strategic ally in managing your most valuable resource: time.

43. Effective Contact Management

Effective contact management in Outlook is not just about storing email addresses and phone numbers; it's about organizing and optimizing your network of professional and personal connections. In today's fast-paced environment, the ability to access and utilize your contact list efficiently can make a significant difference in your productivity and professional relationships.

Central to effective contact management is the initial setup and organization of your contacts. Start by inputting the essential information for each contact, such as name, email, phone number, and company details. This basic data forms the foundation of your contact list, ensuring you have the necessary information at your fingertips when needed. However, effective management goes beyond just the basics. Consider adding additional details such as birthdays, anniversaries, or other personal notes that can help strengthen professional relationships.

Grouping and categorizing contacts is a powerful feature in Outlook that allows you to manage your network more effectively. By creating specific groups, you can organize contacts based on different criteria such as work, family, friends, or even specific projects. This categorization not only helps in sending group emails but also in segmenting your contacts for targeted communication, making your interactions more relevant and efficient.

The search functionality in Outlook is a robust tool to quickly locate contact information. Knowing how to utilize the search efficiently, including using keywords and filters, can significantly cut down the time you spend looking for contact details. Advanced search options, like searching by company name or job title, further refine your search, ensuring you find the right information promptly.

Synchronizing your Outlook contacts with your phone and other devices is a game-changer for accessibility. This synchronization ensures that you have access to your contacts no matter where you are, whether you're in the office or on the move. Regularly updating and syncing your contacts across devices keeps your network current and accessible.

Integrating social media information with your Outlook contacts can provide a broader context to your professional relationships. By linking social media profiles, you have more insights into your contacts' professional updates, interests, and activities. This integration can be particularly useful for networking and building rapport with clients and colleagues.

Effective contact management also involves regular maintenance and updates. Over time, contacts change jobs, phone numbers, and email addresses. Regularly reviewing and updating your contact list ensures that your database is current and reliable. This maintenance includes removing duplicate entries, updating outdated information, and adding new contacts as soon as you receive them.

Sharing contact information can be invaluable, especially in collaborative working environments. Outlook allows you to share contact details with colleagues, enhancing team efficiency. However, it's crucial to handle this sharing responsibly, respecting privacy and data protection laws.

Data protection and privacy are critical aspects of contact management. Ensure that your contact list is backed up regularly to prevent loss of valuable information. Additionally, be mindful of the privacy and data protection laws that apply, especially when storing or sharing sensitive contact information.

Automating contact management using rules and alerts can save time and enhance productivity. For example, you can set rules to categorize contacts automatically or to alert you when you receive emails from specific key contacts. Automation streamlines your contact management process, allowing you to focus on more strategic tasks.

In conclusion, effective contact management in Outlook is about creating a structured and efficient system to store, access, and utilize your network of contacts. By investing time in setting up, organizing, and maintaining your contact list, you enhance your communication efficiency and professional relationships. Remember, your network is one of your most valuable assets; managing it effectively in Outlook helps you leverage this asset to its fullest potential.

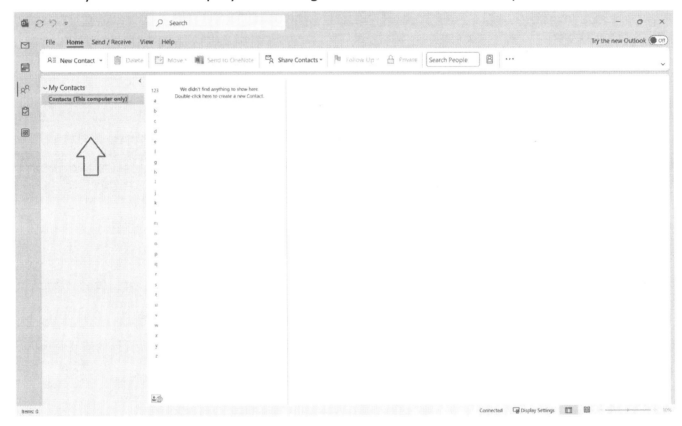

44. Task Tracking and Management

Task tracking and management is a crucial aspect of personal and professional productivity, and Microsoft Outlook offers a comprehensive set of tools to help you stay on top of your tasks effectively. The ability to manage tasks efficiently not only boosts your productivity but also reduces stress, ensures timely completion of projects, and enhances overall work quality.

The foundation of effective task management in Outlook begins with the creation and organization of tasks. Outlook allows you to create detailed tasks, where you can specify the task subject, set start and due dates, and add detailed descriptions. This level of detail helps in clearly defining what needs to be done, making it easier to focus and avoid ambiguity.

Prioritizing tasks is key to effective management. Outlook's task functionality lets you set priority levels, ranging from low to high. This feature is particularly useful in determining which tasks require immediate attention and which can be scheduled for later, helping you to manage your workload more effectively.

Setting reminders for tasks is another vital feature in Outlook. These reminders ensure that you never miss deadlines or forget important tasks. You can customize reminders to alert you at specific times before the task is due, allowing you to plan and allocate time accordingly.

Recurring tasks are a part of most people's work routines. Outlook simplifies managing these tasks by allowing you to set them to recur at regular intervals, be it daily, weekly, monthly, or even yearly. This function is perfect for routine tasks like weekly reports, monthly meetings, or annual reviews.

Delegation of tasks is sometimes necessary, and Outlook handles this efficiently. You can assign tasks to others, and upon acceptance, these tasks appear in their task list. This feature is ideal for team leaders and managers, as it allows for easy delegation and tracking of team tasks.

Tracking the progress of tasks is crucial for staying on top of your workload. Outlook enables you to update the status of tasks, from not started to in progress, completed, or even deferred. This functionality allows you and others involved to have a clear view of the task's progress, fostering better collaboration and accountability.

Integration with calendar and email is one of Outlook's most powerful features. You can link tasks to specific calendar dates and even convert emails into tasks. This integration ensures that all your information is connected and easily accessible, providing a holistic view of your schedule and responsibilities.

Outlook also allows you to categorize tasks, a feature that is particularly useful when dealing with multiple projects or aspects of life. By categorizing tasks, you can group them based on projects, clients, or any other criteria that suit your workflow, making it easier to manage and focus on related tasks.

Sharing tasks with team members is essential for collaborative projects. Outlook's sharing features enable you to share task lists with others, facilitating better teamwork and coordination. This shared approach ensures everyone is on the same page and can track collective progress towards common goals.

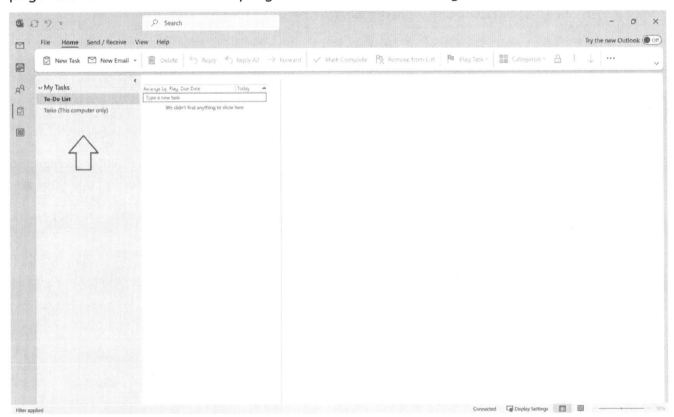

In conclusion, mastering task tracking and management in Outlook is about understanding and utilizing its array of features to suit your workflow. From creating and prioritizing tasks to setting reminders, tracking progress, and integrating with other Outlook tools, these functionalities are designed to optimize your efficiency and productivity. By effectively using Outlook for task management, you can ensure a more organized approach to your work, meet deadlines with ease, and maintain a better work-life balance. Remember, effective task management is not just about completing tasks; it's about doing so in a way that maximizes productivity and minimizes stress.

45. Advanced Email Techniques

Advanced email techniques in Microsoft Outlook go beyond basic sending and receiving. These techniques are designed to enhance productivity, streamline communication, and manage your email more effectively. Here's an in-depth look at these advanced features and how to leverage them to their fullest potential.

1. Email Rules and Automation: Outlook's rules allow you to automate actions for incoming and outgoing emails. You can set rules to automatically sort emails into folders, forward messages to other accounts, or even trigger alerts for specific email types. For instance, you can create a rule to move all emails from a particular client directly into a dedicated folder, ensuring important communications don't get lost in your inbox.

2. Effective Use of Categories and Flags: Categories in Outlook help organize emails by assigning colors or labels, making it easier to spot and manage related emails. Flags, on the other hand, are perfect for marking emails that require follow-up. Combining these features can significantly enhance your ability to track and prioritize your emails.

3. Advanced Search Techniques: Outlook's search functionality is robust, allowing you to find emails quickly. You can search by keywords, sender, date ranges, and even specific attachments. Mastering the search functionality saves time and increases efficiency, especially when dealing with a large volume of emails.

4. Email Templates for Efficiency: If you often send similar emails, creating templates can save time. Templates allow you to pre-write emails and use them as needed, only making necessary adjustments. This feature is ideal for regular status updates, meeting summaries, or frequent inquiries.

5. Scheduling Emails: Outlook allows you to compose an email and schedule it to be sent at a later time or date. This feature is particularly useful for ensuring emails are sent during business hours, or when you want to write an email while the details are fresh but delay sending it until a more appropriate time.

6. Managing Attachments Effectively: Outlook has features to manage attachments efficiently. You can save attachments directly to OneDrive, or even preview attachments without opening them. This feature is especially handy for quickly accessing content without cluttering your device storage.

7. Conversation View for Email Threads: Conversation view organizes your emails by threads, making it easier to follow email chains. This feature is invaluable when tracking discussions over time, as it keeps related emails grouped together.

8. Quick Steps for Common Actions: Quick Steps in Outlook can be used to perform multiple actions on an email with a single click. For example, you can create a Quick Step to move an email to a specific folder and mark it as read. This feature enhances efficiency, especially for repetitive email management tasks.

9. Effective Use of Calendar Invites and Meeting Requests: Integrating your emails with calendar invites and meeting requests is a powerful feature. You can schedule meetings directly from emails, track RSVPs, and even attach necessary documents to the calendar invite.

10. Integrating Email with Other Office Applications: Outlook seamlessly integrates with other Microsoft Office applications. You can send documents directly from Word or Excel, save emails to OneNote, or even link Outlook tasks to Microsoft Planner.

11. Email Encryption for Security: For sensitive information, Outlook's email encryption feature ensures that your emails are securely sent and can only be read by the intended recipients. This feature is crucial for maintaining confidentiality and data security.

12. Custom Views and Folder Management: Custom views allow you to create personalized layouts of your email folders, tailored to how you work. You can also effectively manage your folders, creating subfolders, and even archive old emails to keep your inbox organized.

In summary, these advanced email techniques in Outlook are essential tools for anyone looking to manage their email more efficiently and effectively. By mastering these features, you can reduce the time spent on email management, ensure better organization, improve your communication, and enhance the overall security of your email interactions. Remember, the key to benefiting from these advanced features lies in understanding your unique email management needs and tailoring Outlook's functionalities to meet these requirements.

46. Customizing Your Outlook Experience

Customizing your Outlook experience is a pivotal step in enhancing your productivity and efficiency. By tailoring Outlook to your specific needs, you create a more intuitive and personalized environment that aligns with your work habits and preferences. Let's explore the various ways you can customize your Outlook to make the most out of its capabilities.

Personalizing the Interface: Outlook's interface can be overwhelming with its default settings. Customize it by adjusting the layout, themes, and view settings. You can choose to display emails in a single line or in a more detailed view, adjust the reading pane, or even change the color scheme to something that's more visually appealing to you.

Creating Custom Rules and Alerts: One of Outlook's most powerful features is the ability to create custom rules that automate repetitive tasks. For instance, you can set rules to automatically sort emails into specific folders, flag emails from important clients, or even create alerts for emails with specific words in the subject line.

Utilizing Categories and Folders Effectively: Categories and folders are essential for organizing your emails. You can create custom categories with different colors and assign them to emails based on project, priority, or type. Similarly, creating a structured folder system helps in filing emails appropriately, making them easier to retrieve when needed.

Customizing the Ribbon and Quick Access Toolbar: The Ribbon and Quick Access Toolbar are the core of Outlook's functionality. Customizing these with the commands you use most frequently saves time. You can add or remove buttons, group similar tasks together, and even create custom tabs tailored to your workflow.

Signature and Stationery: Personalize your emails by creating a unique email signature or choosing a stationery that reflects your style. This can include your contact information, a company logo, or even a professional disclaimer.

Customizing Calendar Views and Settings: Tailoring your calendar views helps in better managing your time. You can set your work hours, customize the appearance of your calendar, and create different color codes for various types of appointments or events. This not only helps in visual differentiation but also in better time management.

Task Management Customizations: Outlook's task management can be customized to align with your personal productivity style. You can create custom task folders, set reminders, and even prioritize tasks based on urgency or project.

Setting Up Email Filters: Filters are a great way to ensure that your inbox contains only what's relevant to you. Set up filters to manage junk email effectively, block unwanted senders, or to ensure important emails stand out.

Integrating Add-Ins and Plugins: Enhance Outlook's functionality by integrating add-ins and plugins that suit your specific needs. Whether it's a CRM tool, project management plugin, or a simple utility tool, these add-ons can significantly boost your productivity.

Managing Notifications: In a world of constant digital interruptions, managing notifications is crucial. Customize your Outlook notifications to receive alerts only for critical emails or turn them off during focused work hours. This helps in reducing distractions and improving concentration.

Archiving and Backup Settings: Customize your archiving and backup settings to ensure your data is safe and retrievable. Determine how often you want to archive your emails and set up a backup routine to protect against data loss.

Accessibility Settings: Outlook also offers various accessibility features. Customize these settings to suit your needs, whether it's changing the font size, adjusting the contrast, or using the built-in screen reader.

In conclusion, customizing Outlook goes beyond mere aesthetic changes; it's about creating an environment that caters to your unique working style, enhances your productivity, and streamlines your daily tasks. By meticulously setting up Outlook, you can transform it from a standard email client into a powerful personal productivity hub. Remember, the goal of customization is to make your daily work more efficient and less cluttered, allowing you to focus on what truly matters.

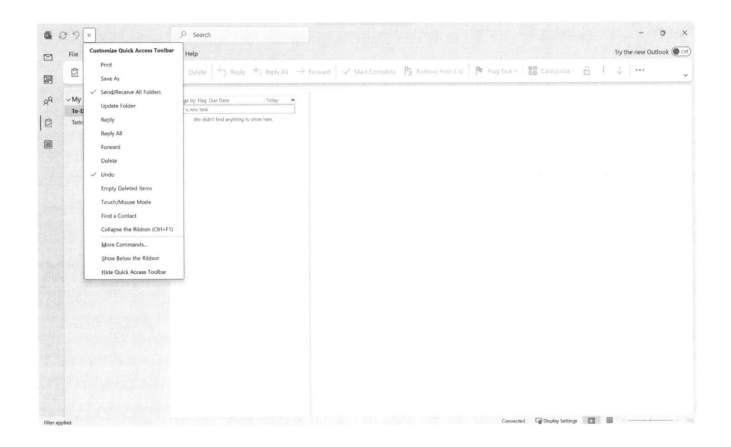

47. Dealing with Common Outlook Issues

Dealing with common Outlook issues is a crucial skill for managing a smooth and productive workflow. Like any sophisticated software, Outlook comes with its challenges, ranging from basic operational glitches to more complex technical hiccups. Understanding how to effectively troubleshoot these issues not only saves time but also ensures a seamless experience.

Troubleshooting Email Delivery Problems: One of the most common issues in Outlook is email delivery problems. This could manifest as emails not being sent or received. Start by checking the internet connection and ensuring Outlook is online. Review the Outbox for unsent emails and Sent Items to confirm if emails are being sent. Check for error messages that can indicate whether the problem is with the recipient's email server or something on your end.

Resolving Syncing Issues: Syncing issues are prevalent, especially when using Outlook on multiple devices. Ensure that all devices are updated to the latest version of Outlook. Sometimes, simple steps like restarting the application or switching the sync settings off and on can resolve the issue. If the problem persists, consider removing and re-adding your account to the device.

Handling Performance Lag: Outlook can sometimes run slow or become unresponsive. This could be due to a large mailbox size, numerous add-ins, or outdated software. Regularly archiving older emails and attachments can help. Also, disable any unnecessary add-ins and keep your Outlook updated to the latest version.

Dealing with Search Function Issues: If Outlook's search function isn't working properly, rebuilding the search index is a common fix. You can find this option in the advanced settings of Outlook. Remember, rebuilding the index might take time, especially if you have a large number of emails.

Addressing Calendar Synchronization Errors: Calendar synchronization issues can be a headache, especially when it comes to meetings and appointments. Check your time zone settings and ensure they are correctly configured. If you are using a shared or public calendar, verify the permission settings to make sure you have the right access.

Fixing Attachment Problems: Difficulty with opening or sending attachments in Outlook is another frequent issue. Ensure the file size does not exceed the limit set by your email server. If you're unable to open an attachment, it might be because of your security settings or the file type. Adjusting the Trust Center settings can sometimes resolve this.

Resolving Error Messages: Outlook may display various error messages, often indicating issues with server settings, password errors, or corrupted files. Take note of the error message and use it to guide your troubleshooting steps. Microsoft's support website and community forums are valuable resources for understanding specific error codes.

Dealing with Account Setup Challenges: Setting up a new account in Outlook can sometimes be problematic. Ensure you have the correct server settings, username, and password. For corporate accounts, consult your IT department as there may be specific configurations or VPN requirements.

Recovering Deleted Items: Accidentally deleted emails, contacts, or calendar items can usually be recovered from the Deleted Items or Trash folder. If items have been permanently deleted, you can use the Recover Deleted Items feature, but this is often subject to your organization's email retention policies.

Managing Add-ins and Plug-ins: Add-ins enhance Outlook's functionality but can sometimes cause conflicts or errors. If you suspect an add-in is causing a problem, start Outlook in Safe Mode and disable the add-ins to identify the culprit.

Addressing Outlook Startup Issues: If Outlook fails to start, use the Inbox Repair Tool (ScanPST.exe) to fix any issues with your Outlook data files. Sometimes, running Outlook as an administrator can help resolve startup issues.

Navigating Compatibility Issues with Other Software: Compatibility issues with other software on your computer can cause problems with Outlook. Ensure that any other office suites or email programs do not conflict with Outlook.

In summary, becoming adept at solving common Outlook problems enhances your ability to maintain productivity and reduces downtime. Most issues have straightforward solutions, and with a bit of patience and troubleshooting, they can be resolved efficiently. Remember, a well-maintained Outlook system is less prone to problems, so regular updates, backups, and maintenance are key to a smooth experience.

48. Security and Privacy in Outlook

In today's interconnected world, ensuring the security and privacy of your Outlook account is crucial. As a comprehensive platform for emails, contacts, and calendar management, Outlook is a repository of sensitive information that requires stringent protection. This comprehensive guide is designed to equip you with strategies and best practices to safeguard your Outlook experience.

Start with a solid foundation by understanding the security features Outlook offers. These include Junk Email filters to sort potential spam, attachment handling protocols, and phishing protection mechanisms. Employing these tools effectively can significantly bolster your account's defense against common email threats.

The cornerstone of any secure account is a robust password. It's advisable to craft a password that's not only strong but also unique. Steer clear of easily guessable passwords and include a mix of characters, numbers, and symbols. Regularly updating your password and ensuring it's not replicated across multiple accounts is essential.

Two-Factor Authentication (2FA) offers an added security layer. With 2FA, access to your account requires your password plus a second verification form, like a code sent to your mobile device. This method dramatically reduces unauthorized access risks.

Be vigilant about email attachments and links, as they are common avenues for security breaches. Exercise caution, particularly with emails from unknown or dubious sources. If uncertain, verify the sender's authenticity before engaging with the content.

Keeping Outlook updated is vital. Regular updates often include security patches and new features that fortify your account against known vulnerabilities.

For confidential information, consider using email encryption. Encrypting emails ensures that your message content remains unreadable to anyone but the intended recipient, adding an extra layer of security for sensitive communications.

Reviewing and adjusting your privacy settings is also important. This includes scrutinizing permissions granted to third-party apps and add-ins connected to Outlook. Being mindful of the data you share and with whom is crucial for maintaining your privacy.

Phishing scams are increasingly sophisticated, making awareness critical. Stay alert for tell-tale signs like grammatical errors, urgent requests for personal information, or unfamiliar sender addresses.

Public Wi-Fi networks are less secure, so it's advisable to avoid accessing sensitive Outlook data when connected to them. For sensitive transactions, use a secure, private network.

Securing the devices you use to access Outlook is equally important. This includes installing robust antivirus software, using firewalls, and keeping your operating system updated. Additionally, employ physical security measures like lock screens and consider remote wiping capabilities for your devices in case they are lost or stolen.

Backing up your Outlook data regularly can be a lifesaver. In case of a security breach or technical failure, having a backup ensures that your essential emails, contacts, and calendar entries are not permanently lost.

Staying informed about the latest cybersecurity threats and best practices is crucial. Share this knowledge with your network, as collective awareness and vigilance are key to maintaining a secure digital environment.

Finally, proactive reporting of any unusual activities in your Outlook account is essential. This could be unrecognized emails in your Sent folder or alerts of login attempts from unfamiliar locations. Prompt reporting can prevent potential security breaches.

In sum, safeguarding your Outlook account involves a combination of using the right tools, adopting strong security practices, and staying informed. Always remember, the best defense in the digital world is a proactive and informed approach to security and privacy. By taking these steps, you can ensure that your Outlook experience remains secure, allowing you to focus on your productivity and communication needs without undue concern for your digital safety.

As we conclude this comprehensive exploration into the multifaceted world of Outlook, it's essential to reflect on the journey undertaken. From the initial steps of understanding the interface to mastering advanced functionalities, this guide has endeavored to provide a thorough grounding in all aspects of this indispensable tool. The aim has been to transform users from novices to confident, proficient Outlook users, equipped to handle the demands of modern digital communication and organization.

Throughout this guide, emphasis has been placed on not just the technical know-how but also on adopting best practices that enhance efficiency and productivity. The exploration of email management, calendar functions, and contact organization has laid a solid foundation for effective communication. The foray into advanced techniques and customization options has further empowered users to tailor their Outlook experience to their specific needs, ensuring a more personal and efficient workflow.

The critical aspect of security and privacy in the digital realm has been addressed, providing users with the knowledge to safeguard their information in an increasingly interconnected world. This insight is invaluable, as it ensures that users can navigate the digital landscape with confidence and security.

In essence, this guide has aimed to be a transformative experience, equipping users with the skills and knowledge to optimize their use of Outlook. Whether for professional development, academic endeavors, or personal organization, the mastery of Outlook is a valuable asset in today's fast-paced, technology-driven world. With the insights and strategies provided, users are well-equipped to harness the full potential of Outlook, making it a powerful ally in their digital journey.

Book 5: OneNote for Organization

In an era where information is abundant and organization is key, a tool that streamlines the process of gathering, managing, and sharing ideas is indispensable. The digital realm offers myriad solutions, but one stands out for its versatility and integration capabilities. This platform is more than just a digital notebook; it's a comprehensive tool designed to enhance productivity and organization in both personal and professional settings.

The journey through this platform begins with understanding its basic functionalities - how to create and manage digital notebooks, which serve as the cornerstone of organization. These notebooks are not mere repositories of information; they are dynamic spaces where ideas can be captured, cultivated, and connected. As users delve deeper, they discover strategies for effective note-taking, ensuring that every piece of information is captured meaningfully and efficiently.

But the capabilities of this tool extend far beyond note-taking. It offers robust features for organizing information, including the use of sections and pages that provide structure to the myriad of thoughts and ideas. The use of tags furthers this organization, allowing for quick retrieval of information in an intuitive manner.

The integration of multimedia elevates the note-taking experience, allowing for the incorporation of diverse content types, from images to videos, making information not only more accessible but also more engaging. The sharing and collaboration features bring a communal aspect to note-taking, making it an inclusive tool for teams and groups, fostering a collaborative environment that is essential in today's interconnected world.

In essence, this platform is a testament to the evolution of note-taking and organization. It embraces the digital age's demands, providing a versatile, integrated, and comprehensive solution for managing the ever-growing influx of information in our daily lives.

49. Introduction to OneNote

Embarking on the journey of mastering OneNote is akin to discovering a digital canvas for your thoughts, ideas, and information. As a versatile and powerful tool within the Office 365 suite, OneNote stands out as a dynamic application that redefines the way we capture, organize, and share information. This introduction is designed to guide you through the fundamental concepts of OneNote, laying the foundation for a more organized and productive approach to note-taking and information management.

OneNote's interface is both intuitive and flexible, making it an ideal platform for users of all proficiency levels. Unlike traditional note-taking methods, OneNote offers a non-linear approach. You can think of it as an endless digital notebook, where your ideas aren't confined to the rigid structure of pages and lines. Here, your creativity can flow unimpeded, as you jot down notes, make lists, or sketch ideas.

The heart of OneNote lies in its organizational prowess. Notebooks, the primary structural element, serve as the overarching categories under which your information is stored. Within each notebook, you have the liberty to create various sections and pages, allowing for a layered organization that mirrors the complexity and depth of your projects. This hierarchical structure is essential for keeping your thoughts and data well-arranged and easily accessible.

One of OneNote's strengths is its ability to cater to diverse note-taking styles. Whether you prefer typing out detailed notes, bullet point lists, or visually mapping concepts, OneNote's flexible interface adapts to your preferences. Its ability to accommodate various media types, from text and images to audio recordings and video clips, ensures that all forms of information can be seamlessly integrated into your notes.

Tags in OneNote are powerful tools for categorization and prioritization. With tags, you can mark important items, track tasks, or highlight questions. This feature enhances the efficiency of reviewing notes, ensuring that key information is always at your fingertips.

OneNote's power is amplified when used in collaboration. The shared notebooks feature enables teams to work together in real time, making it an invaluable tool for collaborative projects, meeting minutes, or shared resource pools. The ability to sync across devices further enhances its utility, ensuring your notes are always accessible, whether you're on a laptop at work, a tablet at a coffee shop, or your smartphone on the go.

For the modern professional, student, or anyone looking to streamline their organizational process, OneNote stands as a beacon of efficiency. Its capacity to integrate multimedia, collaborate in real-time, and sync across devices makes it a cornerstone tool in the realm of digital productivity.

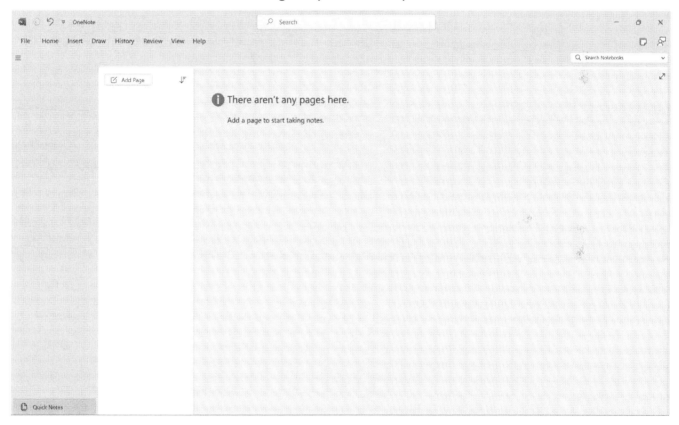

In summary, OneNote offers a unique and powerful approach to note-taking and information management. Its flexible structure, combined with robust organizational features, makes it an essential tool for anyone looking to optimize their workflow.

As we delve deeper into the nuances of OneNote in the subsequent sections, you will discover ways to tailor this tool to your specific needs, elevating your ability to organize, retrieve, and share information like never before. Welcome to the world of OneNote, where organization meets innovation.

50. Creating and Managing Notebooks

Diving into OneNote begins with an exploration of its core feature: the digital notebook. These versatile, electronic versions of traditional notebooks are where your ideas, information, and collaborative content live. Excelling in creating and managing these notebooks is central to leveraging OneNote's capabilities, making it an indispensable tool for organization and productivity.

Imagine each notebook as a specialized container for different facets of your life or work. You could have one for managing projects, another for personal reflections, and yet another for academic research. This segmentation is essential for keeping thoughts organized and clear. When creating a new notebook, consider its purpose—personal, professional, or collaborative. This decision influences its structure, section titles, and the granularity of its pages.

The next stage is structuring your notebook. Like a binder filled with dividers, OneNote notebooks are organized into sections and pages. Sections could be themed—'Meetings', 'Ideas', 'Research'—offering an organized way to categorize your notes. Pages within these sections are where the details live. The flexibility of OneNote is in its ability to accommodate as many sections and pages as you need, all modifiable at any moment.

Customization plays a significant role in making OneNote work for you. From color-coding sections for easy identification to using custom tags for quick referencing, the application offers various ways to make each notebook uniquely yours. These options not only enhance the visual appeal but also boost efficiency, reflecting your style and workflow.

As your collection of notebooks grows, managing them effectively becomes crucial. Regular reviews keep them relevant and up-to-date. It's important to archive or delete notebooks that are no longer in use, maintaining a tidy digital workspace. Thanks to OneNote's cloud-based system, your notebooks are synchronized across all devices, ensuring you have access to your latest data, whether on your computer, tablet, or smartphone.

Collaboration is another area where OneNote excels. You can share notebooks with others for joint projects or planning activities. This feature transforms OneNote into a dynamic space where team members or family can contribute and stay updated. Managing who can view or edit these shared notebooks is essential for maintaining control over your content.

To maintain optimal performance, regular upkeep of your notebooks is recommended. This involves organizing sections and pages, updating content, and checking shared access permissions. Such maintenance ensures a streamlined environment conducive to productivity.

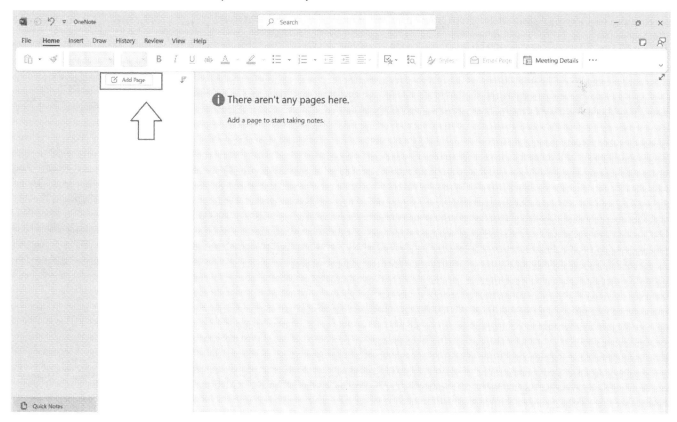

In sum, understanding and mastering notebooks in OneNote can transform it from a simple note-taking app to a powerful tool for managing various aspects of your life. Thoughtful creation, organization, customization, and maintenance of your notebooks elevate OneNote to a critical component of your organizational toolbox. Whether for personal, professional, or collaborative use, well-managed notebooks in OneNote can greatly enhance your efficiency and organization.

51. Effective Note-Taking Strategies

Effective note-taking is an art that transforms the way we capture, retain, and retrieve information. In OneNote, this art is elevated through its digital platform, providing a canvas for ideas, information, and collaboration. To harness the full potential of OneNote, it's crucial to understand and apply effective note-taking strategies that cater to diverse needs and styles.

The first step in effective note-taking is understanding the purpose of your notes. Are they for capturing fleeting ideas, detailed project plans, or research summaries? Identifying the purpose sets the tone for how you structure and approach your note-taking. In OneNote, this translates to deciding whether your notes need to be brief and to-the-point, detailed and comprehensive, or visually rich.

Once the purpose is clear, the next step is to create a system for organizing notes. OneNote's structure of notebooks, sections, and pages is incredibly versatile, allowing for a range of organizational methods. You might create a notebook for each major project or subject, with sections for different themes or topics and pages for individual meetings, ideas, or tasks. This structure helps in keeping notes orderly and makes retrieval quick and intuitive.

OneNote also excels in its ability to accommodate various note-taking methodologies. Whether you prefer linear, Cornell, mind mapping, or the box method, OneNote can be tailored to fit these styles. Its flexible canvas allows you to take notes in the way that best suits your learning style or the demands of the task at hand. This flexibility is key to making note-taking an effective tool for understanding and processing information.

Another crucial aspect of note-taking in OneNote is the use of tags. Tags act as visual cues, highlighting important information, tasks, or questions. They make it easy to categorize and prioritize information, which is particularly helpful when reviewing notes. OneNote's search functionality, combined with tags, turns finding specific pieces of information in a sea of notes into a simple task.

Incorporating multimedia into notes is another powerful feature of OneNote. The ability to embed images, videos, links, and even audio recordings can make notes more comprehensive and engaging. This is particularly useful for visual learners or when capturing complex information that benefits from visual aids.

Review and revision are integral parts of effective note-taking. Regularly revisiting notes to summarize, clarify, or reorganize information helps reinforce understanding and retention. OneNote's digital format makes editing and updating notes a seamless process, encouraging ongoing interaction with the material.

Collaboration in note-taking can also enhance its effectiveness. Sharing OneNote pages or notebooks with peers or colleagues allows for collective note-taking and brainstorming. This collaborative approach can lead to more comprehensive and diverse perspectives on the subject matter.

Lastly, syncing OneNote across devices ensures your notes are always accessible, whether you're on a computer, tablet, or smartphone. This ubiquity means you can capture thoughts and ideas as they occur, regardless of your location, making OneNote an ever-present companion in your note-taking journey.

In conclusion, effective note-taking in OneNote is about more than just recording information. It's about creating a personalized system that makes information easy to organize, retrieve, and understand. By combining purposeful structure, flexible methodologies, multimedia integration, regular review, and collaboration, OneNote becomes an indispensable tool for managing the wealth of information we encounter daily. Whether for professional development, academic success, or personal organization, mastering note-taking in OneNote can significantly enhance productivity and understanding.

52. Organizing with Sections and Pages

Organizing information effectively is crucial in our fast-paced, information-rich world. OneNote, with its dynamic and flexible platform, provides a multitude of ways to organize your data through sections and pages, transforming the way we categorize, access, and interact with our notes.

The beauty of OneNote lies in its ability to mimic the structure of a physical notebook but with far greater capabilities. Imagine walking into a library where books represent your notebooks in OneNote. Each book has chapters (sections) and pages, but unlike a physical book, you can effortlessly add, remove, or rearrange these as your project evolves or your needs change.

Let's delve into the art of using sections in OneNote. Sections are akin to chapters in a book, serving as a broad categorization of your notes. For instance, if you have a notebook for a project, you can create separate sections for 'Meeting Notes', 'Research', 'Ideas', and 'Tasks'. Each section acts as a container for related content, making it easier to find and manage information.

The flexibility of sections is one of OneNote's strengths. You can color-code sections for quick identification, or even group related sections together for a more structured organization. This flexibility allows you to customize the notebook to mirror the way you think and work, making it a more natural extension of your cognitive process.

Pages in OneNote are where the details live. Under each section, you can create as many pages as needed. This is where you jot down your meeting notes, brainstorm ideas, track tasks, or store research. The ability to create subpages adds another layer of organization, allowing you to break down complex topics into manageable chunks. For instance, under the 'Meeting Notes' section, you could have a main page for 'Weekly Team Meetings' and subpages for each date.

OneNote's search functionality works hand-in-hand with its organizational structure. You can quickly search across all your notebooks, sections, and pages, making it easy to find specific information, no matter how deeply it's buried. This powerful search capability is particularly useful in extensive notebooks with a large number of sections and pages.

Linking between pages and sections in OneNote is another powerful feature. You can create hyperlinks to connect related notes, providing quick navigation and context. This interconnectedness turns your notebook into an interactive web of information, mirroring the complex networks of ideas and data in our minds.

Organizing with sections and pages in OneNote isn't just about keeping your notes tidy; it's about reflecting your unique way of thinking and working. It's about creating a personalized information architecture that aligns with your workflow. Whether you're a student organizing study notes, a professional managing project details, or someone capturing personal memories and ideas, the way you structure your OneNote notebook can significantly impact your efficiency and productivity.

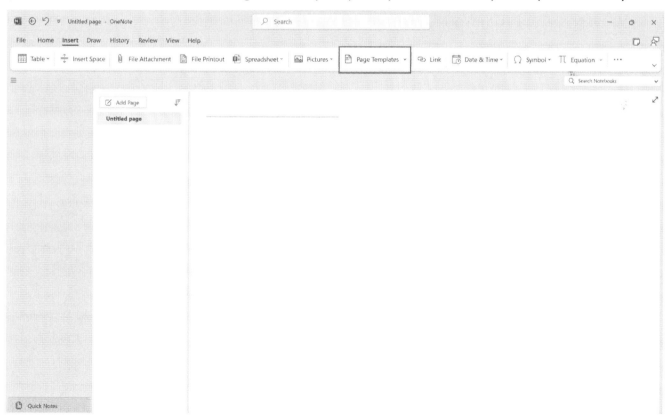

In conclusion, mastering the organization of sections and pages in OneNote is like having a superpower for your notes. It allows you to capture the chaos of information in your head and lay it out in a structured, accessible, and manageable way. This organization leads to better recall, clearer thinking, and more efficient working. With practice, your OneNote notebooks can become a mirror of your mind, helping you capture and organize your thoughts in a way that makes sense to you, thereby enhancing your ability to think, plan, and create.

53. Utilizing Tags for Efficiency

In the realm of digital note-taking, efficiency is key. OneNote, a versatile and dynamic tool, offers a feature that is often underutilized but highly effective in boosting productivity: Tags. This feature is not just about labeling; it's about transforming your note-taking into an efficient, organized, and interactive experience.

Tags in OneNote are more than mere labels. They are powerful markers that help you categorize, prioritize, and locate information quickly. Imagine being able to sift through pages of notes and instantly find critical items, action points, or key questions. This is the power that tags bring to your fingertips.

The diversity of tags in OneNote caters to various needs and preferences. You can use them to mark important information, identify questions, list to-dos, flag items for follow-up, and much more. The beauty of these tags is their flexibility; you can customize them to suit your personal or professional requirements. For instance, a student might use tags to highlight key concepts, while a project manager might use them to track tasks and deadlines.

One of the standout features of tags is their searchability. With OneNote's search function, you can quickly find all instances of a specific tag across your notebooks. This is incredibly useful for reviewing action items before a meeting or compiling study materials for an exam. The search feature turns your notebook into a dynamic database, where information retrieval is just a tag away.

But tags are not just about organization; they also enhance interactivity within your notes. You can create a checklist with clickable to-do tags, turning your notes into an interactive task manager. This interactivity extends to team collaboration as well, where team members can assign and track tasks within shared notebooks.

The use of tags also fosters a consistent note-taking habit. By standardizing the way you mark and categorize information, you create a uniform structure within your notes. This consistency is crucial for long-term note management, especially when dealing with extensive data over time.

Consistency in tagging ensures that your notes remain navigable and comprehensible, even as they grow in volume and complexity.

Another aspect of tags is their role in bridging the gap between digital and mental organization. By tagging items, you are effectively mapping your thought process onto your digital notes. This mapping aids in better recall and understanding, as the tags serve as cognitive cues, guiding you through the intricacies of your information.

Moreover, tags are an invaluable tool in project management and research. They allow you to track progress, categorize research sources, and create an easily navigable repository of information. Whether you are managing a complex project or compiling research for a paper, tags can simplify the process, making it more efficient and manageable.

In conclusion, the use of tags in OneNote is not just a feature – it's a strategy for efficient note management. It transforms the way you interact with your notes, turning them into a structured, searchable, and interactive extension of your mind. Tags enable you to sift through the noise, focus on what matters, and access the right information when you need it. Whether you are a student, a professional, or someone who loves to keep their life organized, mastering the use of tags in OneNote can significantly elevate your productivity and efficiency. With tags, your notes become more than just a collection of information; they become a powerful tool for organization, recall, and action.

54. Integrating Multimedia in Notes

In today's digital age, the art of note-taking transcends beyond mere text. OneNote, a versatile platform for note organization, has embraced this evolution, allowing the integration of multimedia into notes. This capability transforms how information is recorded, accessed, and understood, making note-taking a more dynamic, interactive, and comprehensive process.

Multimedia in OneNote includes a range of elements such as images, audio recordings, videos, links, and files. Each of these elements plays a unique role in enriching the note-taking experience. Images, for instance, can serve as visual aids, breaking the monotony of text and providing a quick reference point. Whether it's a snapshot of a whiteboard, a graph, a photograph, or a scanned document, images add context and depth to notes.

Audio recordings are another powerful feature. For students attending lectures or professionals in meetings, the ability to record audio directly into OneNote is invaluable. It ensures no detail is missed, allowing for playback at a later time for revision or clarification. This feature is particularly beneficial for auditory learners who absorb information better through listening.

Videos, whether embedded or linked, can transform notes from static pages into interactive learning platforms. Embedding instructional videos, for instance, directly into notes can provide immediate access to tutorials or demonstrations relevant to the topic at hand. This integration of video content makes learning more engaging and accessible.

Hyperlinks in OneNote are more than just web addresses; they are gateways to additional information. Linking to external resources, research papers, articles, or even other sections within OneNote itself creates a network of information that is easily navigable and interconnected. This interconnectedness ensures that notes are not isolated islands of information but part of a broader, interconnected knowledge base.

OneNote also allows for the attachment of files, making it a central hub for all related documents. This feature simplifies organization, as all relevant materials, be it spreadsheets, presentations, or word documents, can be stored and accessed in one place. This integration is particularly useful for project management, research, or any activity that involves a variety of documents.

Integrating multimedia into notes isn't just about adding content; it's about enhancing the way information is processed and remembered. Visual aids like images and videos can help in better retention of information, while audio recordings offer an alternative way to review and absorb details.

These multimedia elements cater to different learning styles, whether visual, auditory, or kinesthetic, making learning more inclusive and effective.

Moreover, multimedia integration in OneNote is instrumental in catering to the diverse needs of its users. For professionals, it means having a comprehensive repository of meeting notes, project details, and presentations. For students, it signifies a dynamic learning environment where lectures, study materials, and research coexist seamlessly. For individuals, it provides a versatile platform for personal organization, planning, and creativity.

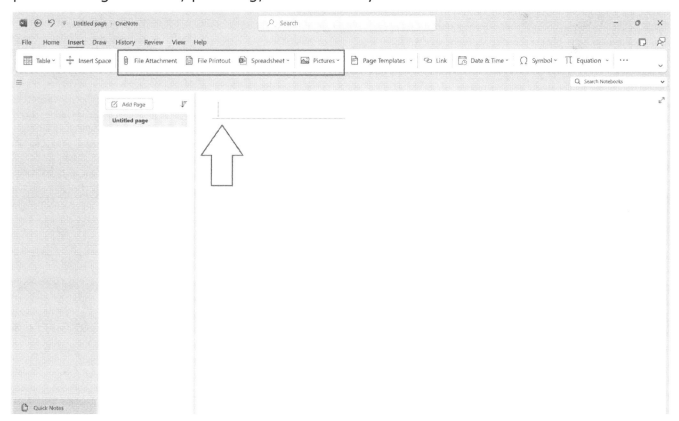

In addition to enhancing individual note-taking, multimedia integration plays a significant role in collaborative efforts. Shared notebooks in OneNote, enriched with multimedia elements, facilitate better communication and understanding among team members. A shared notebook with text, images, audio, and video becomes a rich resource for collaborative learning, planning, and execution.

The process of integrating multimedia in OneNote is also remarkably user-friendly. Whether it's dragging and dropping images, recording audio, embedding videos, or attaching files, the platform is designed for ease of use. This ease ensures that the focus remains on the content and its organization, rather than on the technical aspects of integration.

In conclusion, the integration of multimedia in OneNote is not just a feature; it's a paradigm shift in how we approach note-taking. It transforms notes from static text into vibrant, multifaceted, and interactive resources. This integration aligns with the way we experience the world – a blend of text, visuals, sound, and interconnectivity. By embracing multimedia in OneNote, we open ourselves to a richer, more engaging, and more effective note-taking experience, one that resonates with the digital age we live in.

55. Sharing and Collaborating in OneNote

The advent of OneNote has revolutionized how we manage and organize our digital lives, and its capability for sharing and collaboration is a cornerstone of this transformation. In an age where teamwork and remote working are more prevalent than ever, OneNote's collaborative features stand out as a beacon of efficiency and connectivity.

This chapter delves into the heart of sharing and collaborating in OneNote, exploring its functionalities, benefits, and the impact it has on group dynamics and individual productivity.

OneNote's sharing feature is not just about allowing multiple users to view a notebook; it's about creating a dynamic, interactive, and real-time workspace.

Whether it's a team project, a family plan, or a shared resource among students, OneNote's sharing options cater to a variety of needs. Users can share entire notebooks or specific sections, depending on the level of access and collaboration required. The flexibility of these sharing options ensures that users can maintain control over their content while also promoting teamwork and idea exchange.

Collaboration in OneNote is more than just simultaneous access to documents. It's an interactive experience where team members can contribute, edit, and communicate in real-time. With features like live typing, where users can see each other's edits as they happen, collaboration becomes a dynamic and engaging process. This immediacy not only enhances productivity but also ensures that ideas and feedback are exchanged promptly, keeping everyone on the same page.

The integration of OneNote with cloud services like OneDrive and SharePoint further amplifies its collaborative prowess. These integrations allow notebooks to be stored in a shared space accessible to all team members, regardless of their physical location. This means that a team spread across different time zones can still collaborate effectively, making OneNote a powerful tool for global teams.

OneNote also shines in its ability to track changes and revisions. This tracking is crucial in a collaborative environment as it provides transparency and accountability.

Users can easily see who made specific changes and when, which is invaluable for project management and review processes. This level of tracking fosters a sense of responsibility and ensures that all contributions are acknowledged and valued.

The ability to comment within notebooks is another feature that elevates OneNote's collaborative utility. Comments can be added to specific parts of a note, allowing for focused and contextual discussions.

This feature is particularly useful for feedback, brainstorming sessions, or clarifying information without altering the original content of the note.

OneNote's collaboration tools are also inclusive, catering to diverse needs and preferences. Features like audio recording and search functionalities ensure that all types of users, including those with different learning styles or disabilities, can contribute and access information effectively.

This inclusivity not only enhances the collaborative experience but also ensures that everyone's voice is heard and valued.

In educational settings, OneNote's collaborative features have transformed how students and teachers interact. Teachers can create shared notebooks for their classes, where students can find course materials, submit assignments, and collaborate on projects. This interactive learning environment fosters a sense of community and encourages active participation from students.

In a corporate environment, OneNote facilitates effective meeting management and project collaboration. Teams can create shared notebooks for meeting notes, project plans, and resource pooling, streamlining communication and ensuring that all team members are aligned with their goals and responsibilities.

Moreover, the ease of use and intuitive design of OneNote's collaborative features mean that teams can focus on their work without being bogged down by complex processes or technical difficulties. This ease of use, combined with its powerful features, makes OneNote an essential tool in the arsenal of any team or individual looking to enhance their productivity and collaborative efforts.

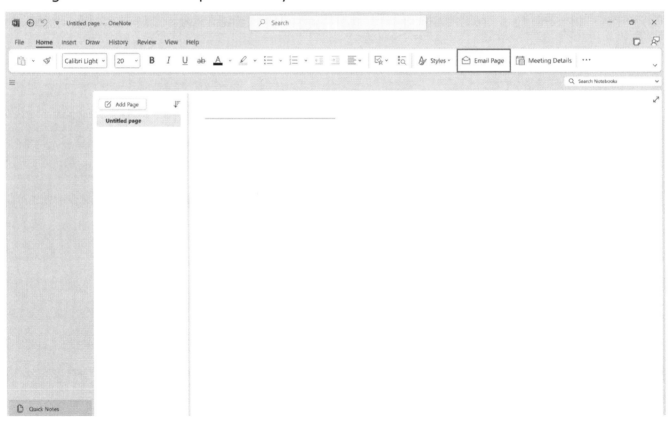

In conclusion, the sharing and collaborative capabilities of OneNote are pivotal in today's interconnected and fast-paced world.

They transform the way individuals and teams interact, collaborate, and achieve their goals.

By harnessing the power of these features, users can create a more organized, efficient, and inclusive workspace, whether it be in a classroom, a corporate office, or a personal project. In embracing these features, OneNote users are not just optimizing their organizational skills; they are opening doors to new possibilities of teamwork and productivity.

56. OneNote on Different Devices

In today's world, where flexibility and mobility are paramount, OneNote stands out as a versatile tool that seamlessly adapts to various devices, enhancing productivity and organization regardless of location or hardware. The ability to use OneNote across different devices – from desktops and laptops to tablets and smartphones – reflects the evolving nature of work and lifestyle in the digital era. This chapter delves into how OneNote on different devices revolutionizes note-taking and information management, offering a comprehensive guide to harnessing its full potential.

OneNote's cross-platform capability ensures that users have access to their notes anytime, anywhere. Whether it's a quick note on a smartphone, a detailed report on a laptop, or a sketch on a tablet, OneNote synchronizes content across all devices. This synchronization is not just a convenience; it's a game changer for professionals, students, and anyone who values the ability to capture and access information on the go.

The desktop version of OneNote, typically used on PCs and Macs, offers a robust set of features for comprehensive note-taking and organization. It allows for intricate notebook structuring with sections and pages, detailed formatting options, and the ability to integrate a wide range of multimedia elements.

This version is ideal for intensive tasks, such as project planning, research compilation, or course preparation, where detailed note organization and formatting are paramount.

On tablets, OneNote capitalizes on the touch interface, offering a natural and intuitive note-taking experience. Users can handwrite notes, draw diagrams, or annotate images with ease, making it an ideal platform for brainstorming sessions, illustrative note-taking, or when working on the move. The seamless integration of stylus and touch inputs on devices like iPads and Microsoft Surface tablets further enhances this experience, blurring the line between traditional paper-based note-taking and digital organization.

The smartphone version of OneNote is designed for speed and efficiency. It provides a quick and easy way to capture ideas, to-do lists, or reminders when on the move. The simplified interface focuses on essential features, such as quick note capture, voice notes, and camera integration, making it an indispensable tool for those moments when ideas strike unexpectedly.

OneNote's cloud-based architecture is the cornerstone of its multi-device capabilities. By storing notebooks in the cloud, for instance, on OneDrive or SharePoint, OneNote ensures that all updates made on one device are immediately available on all others. This seamless synchronization not only safeguards against data loss but also ensures that the latest version of a note is always at hand, regardless of the device used.

The integration of OneNote with other Microsoft Office applications adds another layer of productivity, especially on desktops and laptops. Users can easily link their notes to Outlook for meeting details or tasks, embed Excel spreadsheets, or reference PowerPoint slides, creating a cohesive and interconnected digital workspace.

In the realm of education, OneNote's versatility across devices has a profound impact. Students can take notes on a laptop during a lecture, review and annotate them on a tablet at home, and quickly revise key points on their smartphone before an exam.

Similarly, teachers can prepare lessons on their primary device and have access to their material in the classroom on a different device, adapting to different teaching environments with ease.

For professionals, this cross-device functionality means that the transition between office, home, and fieldwork is smoother. They can start a meeting agenda on their office desktop, make real-time edits on a tablet during the meeting, and complete follow-up actions on their smartphone.

Despite its diverse functionalities across devices, OneNote maintains a consistent and user-friendly interface, ensuring that users don't need to relearn the tool on each device. This consistency is key to OneNote's effectiveness as a multi-platform tool, as it minimizes the learning curve and maximizes user adaptability.

In summary, OneNote's adaptability across different devices is not just a feature; it's a reflection of the modern digital lifestyle. It caters to the diverse needs of users who juggle multiple roles and responsibilities across various environments. By mastering OneNote on different devices, users can ensure that their productivity and organizational skills are not confined to a single location or device but are as mobile and flexible as their lives demand.

57. Advanced OneNote Features

Delving into OneNote's advanced features unveils a world of possibilities that extend far beyond basic note-taking. This platform caters to diverse needs, from academic research to business project management and personal organization. The advanced functionalities of OneNote provide an unparalleled experience in managing information efficiently and effectively.

Custom tags and searches in OneNote allow for a personalized organization. Users can create unique tags fitting their specific needs, like tags for research themes or project stages. This personalized approach, coupled with powerful search capabilities, streamlines information retrieval, making it a swift and hassle-free process.

Linking notes and ideas within OneNote enhances the coherence of information. Users can interconnect related ideas across different sections or notebooks, a feature invaluable for complex projects where information is dispersed.

This interconnected approach aids in maintaining a structured and intuitive flow of information.

OneNote's integration with the Microsoft Office Suite enhances its utility. Users can import data from Word or Excel directly into their notebooks. Furthermore, OneNote's synchronization with Outlook calendar events enables users to efficiently take and link notes to specific meetings, ensuring organized and accessible meeting documentation.

Audio and video recording capabilities take note-taking to a new dimension. This feature allows capturing lectures or meetings in multimedia formats, accommodating various learning and working styles. The ability to search spoken words within audio recordings is especially beneficial for reviewing and navigating through lengthy recordings.

Handwriting recognition and drawing tools cater to those who prefer writing by hand. OneNote transforms handwritten notes into text, making them searchable and editable. Additionally, the drawing tools enable users to sketch diagrams, annotate images, or write notes, supporting a wide range of creative and organizational tasks.

Collaboration in OneNote is robust and dynamic. Multiple users can edit a shared notebook simultaneously, making it ideal for collaborative projects and group work. Real-time synchronization of changes ensures that every team member is up-to-date, fostering a cohesive and efficient collaborative environment.

OneNote's page history feature tracks the evolution of content, allowing users to view and recover past versions of a page. This capability is crucial for retrieving information and understanding the development of ideas over time.

The integration of OneNote with cloud services like OneDrive offers flexibility and accessibility. Users can access their notes from any device, anywhere, ensuring that their data is always within reach. This feature is complemented by offline access, allowing users to continue their work even without internet connectivity, with all changes being synchronized once they're back online.

OneNote also provides options for local backups, adding an extra layer of data security. This ensures that users have a reliable backup of their important notes, safeguarding against data loss.

Security features in OneNote include password protection for sections and encryption of sensitive information. These features provide users with the assurance that their confidential data is secure, which is crucial when handling sensitive personal or business information.

The customizable user interface in OneNote allows users to tailor the platform to their preferences. Adjusting the layout, choosing color schemes, and modifying toolbars can significantly enhance productivity and user experience.

In essence, the advanced features of OneNote transform it from a simple digital notebook into a multifaceted tool for comprehensive information management. Whether it's for enhanced organization through tags and links, multimedia integration, efficient collaboration, or data security, OneNote's advanced functionalities provide users with the tools they need to manage information more effectively. By mastering these features, users can unlock the full potential of OneNote, turning it into an indispensable component of their digital toolkit. This platform is not just about taking notes; it's about revolutionizing the way information is managed, accessed, and shared.

As we conclude this exploration of a versatile digital tool, it's clear that the journey through its features and capabilities has been one of discovery and empowerment. Each aspect, from the creation and management of notebooks to the advanced features, has highlighted the tool's ability to adapt to various needs, providing a flexible and dynamic solution for organization and productivity.

Through effective note-taking strategies and the organization of information into sections and pages, users have learned how to create a structured yet flexible framework. The integration of multimedia has transformed the way information is captured, making it more engaging and multi-dimensional. The ability to tag and search content efficiently has further enhanced the utility of this tool, making it an invaluable resource in both personal and professional contexts.

Collaboration features have opened up new avenues for teamwork and idea-sharing, emphasizing the importance of collective knowledge and cooperative work. The adaptability of this tool across different devices has ensured that users have access to their information anytime, anywhere, seamlessly integrating into their daily workflow.

In essence, this tool represents more than just a digital platform for note-taking and organization. It embodies a comprehensive approach to managing information in the digital age, catering to the diverse needs of its users with ease and efficiency. It stands as a testament to the power of digital tools in enhancing productivity, creativity, and collaboration in an ever-evolving world.

Book 6: Teams for Collaboration

In today's fast-paced digital world, the ability to collaborate effectively is more crucial than ever. The shift towards remote work and the increasing need for efficient team communication have made mastering collaboration tools a necessity. This text aims to guide users through the multifaceted functionalities of one such indispensable tool: Microsoft Teams. Designed as a comprehensive platform for communication and collaboration, Teams integrates chat, video meetings, file storage, and application integration, offering a one-stop solution for modern workplace needs.

As we delve into the chapters, we explore various aspects of Teams, starting from its fundamental setup to advanced features. We address the initial steps of getting acquainted with the interface, setting up teams and channels, and customizing settings to suit your unique needs. The journey then advances to effective communication techniques, emphasizing the importance of clear and concise exchanges and how to achieve them using Teams.

Collaboration extends beyond mere communication. It encompasses file sharing, project management, and seamless integration with numerous applications. Our discussion includes strategies to enhance productivity through task management and app integration, ensuring that Teams becomes an integral part of your workflow.

The essence of this guide lies in not just understanding the functionalities of Teams but also in mastering them for remote collaboration. We focus on how to conduct productive meetings, manage remote teams, and establish best practices for remote work. Finally, we tackle common challenges and provide troubleshooting tips to ensure a smooth, uninterrupted experience.

As we embark on this journey, the goal is to transform your Teams experience from just another tool to a vital component of your collaborative endeavors, enhancing efficiency and productivity in the modern digital workspace.

58. Introduction to Microsoft Teams

In the realm of modern workplace collaboration, Microsoft Teams emerges as a pivotal tool, revolutionizing how teams communicate, collaborate, and streamline their workflows. This platform is not just an application; it's a comprehensive ecosystem that transforms traditional work paradigms into dynamic, interconnected experiences.

At its core, Microsoft Teams is a hub for teamwork, seamlessly integrating chat, video meetings, file sharing, and more. Its strength lies in its ability to bring together people, conversations, and content, enabling teams to work more effectively and stay connected, whether they are in the same building or spread across the globe.

The foundation of Teams is its chat-based workspace, offering a real-time communication channel that is both informal and efficient. This immediacy fosters a quick exchange of ideas, hastening decision-making processes, and keeping team members aligned on their projects. Beyond text, the platform supports rich media sharing, such as images, videos, and documents, enhancing the depth and clarity of communication.

One of the most transformative features of Teams is its deep integration with the broader suite of Office 365 applications. Whether it's Word, Excel, PowerPoint, or SharePoint, these tools are woven into the fabric of Teams, making it a centralized location for all your collaborative needs. This integration not only simplifies access to documents and data but also ensures that the most current versions are always at hand, reducing the confusion of multiple document versions.

Video conferencing in Teams brings a new dimension to remote communication. With features like background blur and custom backgrounds, it helps maintain professionalism and minimizes distractions during meetings. The ability to record meetings and access transcripts later adds to its versatility, ensuring that no critical information is lost.

The customizable nature of Teams is one of its key strengths. Each team can tailor its workspace to suit its unique needs, using channels to segment conversations by topic, project, or department. These channels become a focal point for collaboration, offering a structured way to organize discussions and files.

Another powerful feature is the ability to integrate third-party apps and services, expanding Teams' capabilities. From project management tools like Asana or Trello to customer relationship management services like Salesforce, these integrations enable a seamless workflow within a single interface.

Microsoft Teams also excels in the realm of security and compliance, with advanced features that protect sensitive information while ensuring regulatory compliance. This aspect is crucial for organizations that handle confidential data, offering peace of mind that their communications and documents are secure.

For teams that are spread across different time zones, the asynchronous communication capabilities of Teams are invaluable. Team members can catch up on conversations at their own pace, contribute when it suits them, and stay informed without the pressure of real-time responses.

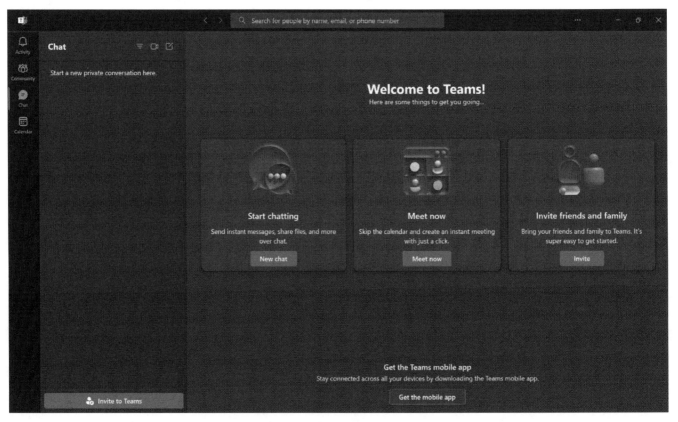

In summary, Microsoft Teams is more than just a tool; it's a game-changer in the way teams work together. It offers a versatile, secure, and integrated platform that adapts to the ever-evolving needs of modern teams. Whether it's for small projects or large-scale collaborations, Teams empowers organizations to achieve more together, breaking down barriers and fostering a culture of open communication and collaboration.

59. Setting Up and Managing Teams

Embarking on the journey of setting up and managing Microsoft Teams, one must understand it's more than just about the technical aspects; it's about creating a digital environment that fosters collaboration, efficiency, and a connected team.

Beginning with the creation of your team, you're setting the foundation for your digital workspace. This is where you define the purpose, outline objectives, and add members. Carefully consider the composition of your team.

Different teams can be formed to mirror your organizational structure – be it by department, project, or any other division that aligns with your objectives.

Assigning roles is a critical step. You'll have owners, who possess overarching control and can configure team settings, and members, who generally have more limited permissions. This distinction in roles is essential for maintaining order and clarity within the team.

The use of channels within a team is a method to compartmentalize conversations and content by specific topics or projects. This keeps discussions relevant and focused. Further structure is provided through the integration of tabs within these channels. These tabs act as direct links to important files, apps, or services, ensuring that everything necessary for collaboration is at your team's fingertips.

The integration of SharePoint for file storage in Teams simplifies file sharing and collaboration. The key to making the most of this feature is an organized approach to file storage. Establishing a logical file structure within the Files tab of each channel will streamline the process of finding and working on documents.

Customization plays a significant role in optimizing your Teams experience. The platform offers a variety of apps, bots, and connectors to augment its functionality. The integration of these tools should be based on the specific needs and workflows of your team. For example, adding task management apps or analytics tools can significantly enhance productivity and decision-making.

Teams excels in facilitating communication, especially with its robust meeting features. The ability to schedule and conduct meetings directly within the platform, coupled with features like screen sharing, digital whiteboarding, and session recording, makes it a powerful tool for keeping everyone connected and informed.

Managing the flow of information via notifications is crucial. Both team members and owners should understand how to tailor notification settings to strike a balance between staying informed and avoiding information overload. Additionally, familiarizing yourself with other team settings, such as guest access and permissions, ensures a secure and well-managed collaborative environment.

Effective management of a team in Microsoft Teams is an ongoing endeavor. It requires regular engagement with your team members, openness to feedback, and a willingness to adapt and evolve practices as needed. The landscape of digital collaboration is continuously changing, and your approach should be flexible enough to accommodate these changes.

In summary, setting up and managing a team in Microsoft Teams is a multifaceted process that extends beyond mere technical setup. It involves understanding your team's dynamics, continuously adapting to new challenges, and utilizing the comprehensive features of Teams to build a highly collaborative and effective workspace. With thoughtful planning and proactive management, Microsoft Teams can significantly transform your team's communication and collaboration, driving towards achieving your collective goals.

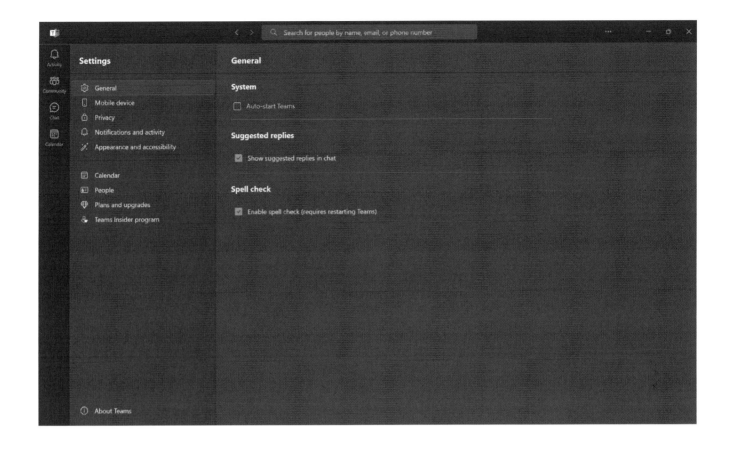

60. Effective Communication in Teams

In the digital workplace, where virtual interactions are a norm, mastering effective communication is crucial. Microsoft Teams has revolutionized the way teams interact, collaborate, and share ideas. It's not just about the tool's capabilities; it's also about how teams use these features to foster a culture of open, transparent, and effective communication.

The cornerstone of any team's success is open communication. Encourage your members to share their ideas, thoughts, and feedback freely. This can be facilitated through regular team meetings and discussions on Teams, promoting an environment where every voice is heard. Casual chats and video calls on Teams also play a significant role in maintaining this culture, especially for remote teams. They help in simulating the informal, spontaneous conversations that occur in physical offices, thus maintaining a personal connection among team members.

Clarity is pivotal in digital communication. Without the non-verbal cues present in face-to-face interactions, messages can often be misconstrued. Team members should aim for clear, concise messaging.

For significant announcements or instructions, using the 'mark as important' feature or breaking down information into bullet points can aid in ensuring the message is understood. When complexity arises, opt for a video call to discuss the matter thoroughly.

Teams is designed to keep conversations organized through the use of channels. These can be leveraged to segregate discussions based on topics, projects, or departments. Using channels effectively ensures that conversations are on-point and information is easy to retrieve. It also helps in reducing the clutter of irrelevant messages, which can be overwhelming and counterproductive.

Balancing between synchronous (instant messaging, video calls) and asynchronous communication (posted messages, shared files) is vital. This balance allows team members to contribute at their own pace and convenience, which is especially important for teams spread across different time zones. It also reduces the pressure of immediate responses, allowing for thoughtful, well-considered communication.

Meetings are integral to team communication. Teams' seamless integration with Outlook for scheduling and its features like screen sharing and meeting recording make it an excellent tool for productive meetings. However, it's important to be mindful of meeting overload. Ensure each meeting has a specific agenda and objective, and share the minutes or recordings post-meeting for those who couldn't attend.

Regular feedback is a powerful tool for team growth. Schedule check-ins to gather insights on project progress or the team's use of Teams itself. These could range from personal one-on-one calls to broader team surveys. Feedback sessions are crucial for identifying areas of improvement and celebrating successes.

Recognition plays a critical role in fostering a positive work environment. Celebrating achievements, whether through the Teams' Praise feature or acknowledgments in team channels, boosts morale and encourages a culture of appreciation.

Continuous learning and training are key to effective communication. Regular training sessions on Teams' functionalities and digital communication best practices can be immensely beneficial.

Tailoring these sessions to the needs of your team ensures everyone is up-to-date with the tool's capabilities and best practices.

The integration of bots and apps can significantly enhance communication efficiency. From scheduling meetings to conducting quick polls, these tools can streamline processes and enrich the Teams experience. Explore and experiment with different tools to find the ones that align with your team's communication style.

Finally, staying adaptable to change is crucial. As Teams continues to evolve, so should your communication strategies. Keeping up with new features and updates, and being willing to adjust your practices accordingly, can open up new avenues for improving team communication.

In essence, effective communication in Teams transcends just the technical aspects of the platform. It's about nurturing an environment where every team member can communicate openly, clearly, and effectively, leveraging the full potential of Teams to drive productivity and foster a cohesive, collaborative team culture.

61. Collaborating with Channels and Tabs

In the dynamic realm of Microsoft Teams, channels and tabs are more than just features; they're the backbone of collaboration. These tools have revolutionized how we work together, breaking down barriers and fostering an environment of shared goals and seamless cooperation.

Channels are the heartbeat of Teams, offering organized spaces for specific topics, projects, or departments. They enable focused discussions, keeping all relevant communication and documents in one easily accessible location. Think of channels as dedicated workspaces where team members can discuss, share, and collaborate without the clutter of unrelated conversations. By creating channels for different needs, you ensure that every discussion has a purpose and a place.

When setting up channels, it's essential to be strategic. Public channels are ideal for broad topics relevant to the entire team, while private channels cater to more sensitive discussions, needing a select audience.

This setup promotes transparency where it's needed and privacy when required.

Tabs, the unsung heroes of Teams, provide quick access to frequently used documents, tools, and applications. They're customizable per channel, ensuring that every team has the tools they need at their fingertips. By integrating apps like Planner or OneNote, you create a multi-functional workspace that can handle tasks, notes, and planning, all within Teams. This integration streamlines workflows, reducing the need to switch between multiple applications.

Collaborating in real-time is a breeze with the file-sharing capabilities within channels. No more lengthy email threads or lost documents. Files shared in a channel are stored in the SharePoint folder associated with the team, ensuring easy access and version control. This centralized storage encourages collaborative editing and feedback, fostering a culture of collective effort and continuous improvement.

The use of mentions (@name) within channels is a powerful way to grab attention. Whether it's highlighting a task for a colleague or bringing a discussion point to someone's notice, mentions ensure that messages don't get lost in the shuffle. This feature is particularly useful in large teams where information overload can easily occur.

Regularly pinning important messages or documents as tabs keeps critical information at the forefront. This practice helps new members quickly catch up and serves as a constant reminder for the team of crucial deadlines, guidelines, or resources.

Channels also support video and voice meetings, making them ideal for team check-ins or quick huddles. These impromptu or scheduled gatherings within the channel context keep the conversation and decisions aligned with the channel's purpose.

But it's not all about work; channels can also foster a sense of community. Creating a 'Water Cooler' or 'Fun Zone' channel for non-work-related conversations can enhance team bonding.

These social channels allow team members to share personal wins, interesting finds, or just have a casual chat, which is crucial in building a cohesive remote or hybrid team.

Regularly reviewing and organizing your channels and tabs is crucial for maintaining an efficient workspace. As projects conclude or priorities shift, archiving or reorganizing channels ensures that the Teams environment remains relevant and clutter-free.

Lastly, don't forget to take feedback from the team on the effectiveness of channels and tabs. Continuous improvement should be the goal, with adaptations and changes made as needed. This adaptability ensures that the collaborative environment within Teams evolves with the team's needs.

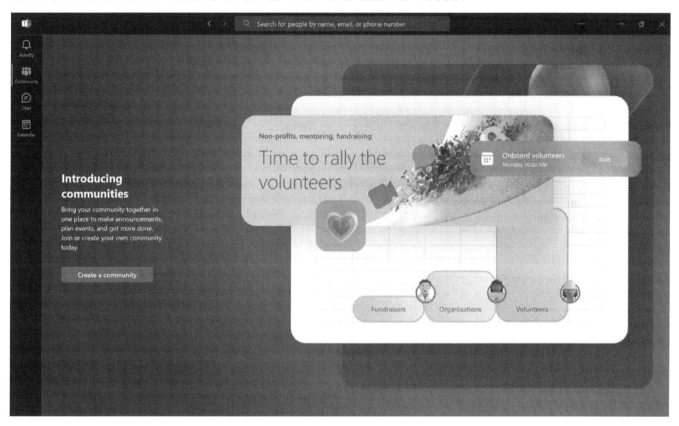

In conclusion, channels and tabs in Microsoft Teams are more than just features; they're a framework for building a highly efficient, collaborative, and engaged team. By leveraging these tools effectively, you can transform how your team communicates, collaborates, and connects, no matter where they are.

With the right approach, channels and tabs can be the key to unlocking the full potential of your team in the digital workspace.

62. Integrating Apps and Tools

In the dynamic ecosystem of Microsoft Teams, the integration of apps and tools stands as a testament to its versatility and user-centric design. This functionality is not just an added feature; it's a pivotal aspect that transforms Teams from a mere communication platform into a comprehensive workspace, addressing diverse professional needs and enhancing overall productivity.

The beauty of Teams lies in its ability to adapt to different workflows and integrate a myriad of tools, from project management to customer relationship management (CRM) systems, all within its interface. This seamless integration means that users can access a variety of tools without the need to switch between different apps or windows, thereby streamlining workflows and saving valuable time.

Project management tools like Planner or Trello can be integrated into Teams, allowing for real-time task tracking and collaboration. Teams can set up their boards, assign tasks, set deadlines, and monitor progress, all within the Teams environment.

This integration ensures that project updates are transparent and accessible, keeping everyone on the same page.

For those who handle customer interactions, integrating CRM tools like Salesforce or Dynamics 365 into Teams can be a game-changer. Sales teams can access customer data, manage leads, and track sales opportunities directly through Teams. This integration not only saves time but also provides valuable context to customer conversations and collaborations.

Another significant integration is with file storage services like SharePoint and OneDrive. These services enable users to store, share, and collaborate on documents seamlessly. The integration ensures that the most recent version of a document is always available, reducing the risk of version conflicts and data loss.

Teams also supports integration with a host of Microsoft 365 apps like Excel, Word, and PowerPoint. This integration allows users to create, edit, and collaborate on documents without leaving Teams. It's particularly useful for co-authoring documents, where team members can work simultaneously on the same file, regardless of their physical location.

For software development teams, integrating development tools like GitHub or Azure DevOps can significantly boost efficiency. Developers can manage their repositories, track issues, and collaborate on code directly within Teams. This integration fosters a collaborative development environment where code reviews and discussions can happen in real-time.

In the realm of data analysis and reporting, integrating tools like Power BI into Teams provides teams with easy access to data insights. Users can view and interact with dashboards and reports directly within their Teams channels, making data-driven decision-making more accessible and timely.

Teams also supports integration with third-party apps and bots, offering a wide range of functionalities from polling and surveys to wellness and productivity tools. These integrations can enhance team engagement, gather feedback, and even support the mental and physical well-being of the team members.

One of the most critical aspects of integrating apps into Teams is the ability to customize the experience based on the team's unique needs. Each team can tailor its workspace by adding the apps that are most relevant to its work, ensuring that the tools they need are always just a click away.

However, with great power comes great responsibility. It's crucial to manage these integrations effectively to avoid clutter and maintain a streamlined workspace. Regular audits of the integrated apps and user training on how to utilize these tools effectively can go a long way in maximizing the benefits of these integrations.

In conclusion, the integration of apps and tools in Microsoft Teams is a powerful feature that, when leveraged correctly, can transform the platform into a comprehensive workspace tailored to a team's specific needs. This integration not only enhances productivity and collaboration but also ensures that Teams remains a central hub for all professional activities, adapting and evolving with the ever-changing business landscape.

63. Conducting Productive Meetings

The modern workplace, increasingly reliant on virtual collaboration, has elevated the importance of mastering the art of conducting productive meetings. Microsoft Teams, integral to Office 365, emerges as a pivotal tool in this realm, offering features that enable meetings to be as interactive and effective as possible. The successful orchestration of these meetings hinges not just on utilizing technological features but also on implementing strategies that foster engagement, clarity, and operational efficiency.

At the forefront of effective meeting management is a comprehensive understanding of Microsoft Teams' functionalities. This encompasses mastering the scheduling process, utilizing video and audio features, screen sharing, and engaging through collaborative tools like whiteboards and integrated apps. This foundational knowledge sets the stage for smooth and efficient meetings.

Preparation, a cornerstone of any successful meeting, involves setting clear agendas, defining objectives, and ensuring all participants have necessary resources beforehand. Teams' calendar integration facilitates this process by allowing meeting invites to include all relevant information and materials, ensuring participants are well-prepared and meetings remain focused.

Active participation is crucial in virtual meetings. Microsoft Teams aids this through interactive tools like live polls, Q&A sessions, and chat functionalities, which can be leveraged to foster interaction, solicit feedback, and ensure inclusivity. Such engagement not only enriches the meeting experience but also ensures diverse perspectives are considered.

Effective time management is another key aspect. Starting and ending meetings punctually, adhering to the agenda, and allocating time effectively for each discussion point are vital. Teams' features such as timers and scheduling aids help the host maintain the meeting's pace and focus.

Clear communication underpins productive meetings. In a virtual setting, where non-verbal cues are limited, this becomes paramount. Ensuring speech clarity, employing visual aids, and managing participant contributions without interruptions are essential practices. Teams' video functionality can further enhance personal interaction and communication effectiveness.

The productivity of a meeting is also gauged by post-meeting activities. Using Teams for sharing meeting minutes, outlining action items, and assigning tasks ensures continuity and accountability. Integration with other Office 365 tools like Planner or To-Do is instrumental in tracking and managing these tasks.

Technical challenges are inevitable in virtual meetings. A proactive approach, including familiarity with Teams' troubleshooting guides and providing participants with basic tips, can mitigate disruptions caused by technical issues.

Feedback and continual improvement are vital for enhancing meeting quality. Tools like Microsoft Forms or Teams' polling features offer a means to gather participant feedback, providing insights into the meeting's effectiveness and areas for improvement.

In summary, productive meetings in Microsoft Teams are the result of a blend of technological proficiency and effective meeting strategies. By preparing adequately, engaging participants actively, managing time efficiently, communicating clearly, ensuring follow-through, addressing technical issues competently, and seeking continuous feedback, Teams can be leveraged to its fullest potential. This approach maximizes the benefits of virtual collaboration and significantly contributes to achieving organizational objectives. Effective meetings in Teams are not just about efficiency; they're about creating a collaborative and enriching environment that drives collective progress.

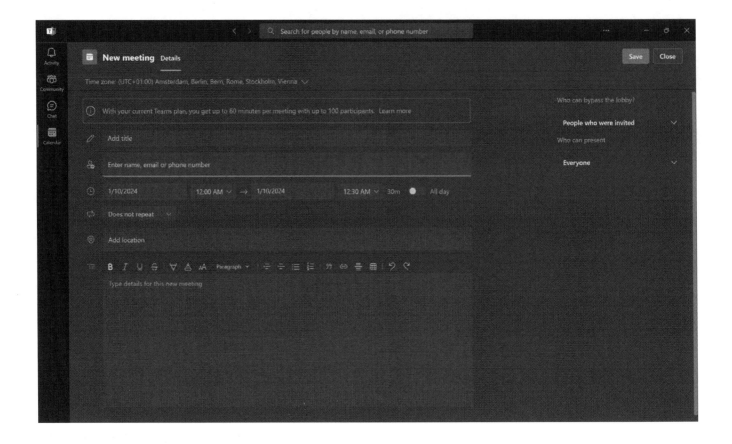

64. Advanced Teams Features

Delving into the advanced features of Microsoft Teams reveals a multitude of functionalities that propel collaboration and efficiency to new heights. These features, often underutilized, can transform the way teams communicate, collaborate, and manage their work in a digital environment. By leveraging these advanced capabilities, users can harness the full potential of Teams, turning it into not just a communication tool, but a comprehensive collaboration hub.

One of the standout advanced features is the integration of third-party apps and services. Teams allows users to connect a wide range of external applications directly into their workspace. This integration means that tools for project management, customer relationship management, and many others can be accessed without leaving Teams. The resulting seamless workflow minimizes the need to switch between different apps, thereby saving time and reducing the risk of data silos.

Another notable feature is the advanced meeting capabilities. Beyond the basic video conferencing, Teams offers features like live events, webinar hosting, and large-scale virtual conferences. These tools are invaluable for organizations conducting large meetings or engaging with a broader audience. Additionally, features like background blur and custom backgrounds enhance the professionalism and privacy of video calls.

Teams also offers sophisticated file collaboration features. Users can co-author documents in real-time, with changes saved automatically to the cloud. This real-time collaboration extends to all Office 365 applications like Word, Excel, and PowerPoint, ensuring that team members can work together on documents without the hassle of version control or email attachments.

The automation of routine tasks is another advanced feature that Teams supports. Using the Microsoft Power Automate integration, users can create custom workflows that automate repetitive tasks, such as scheduling meetings, managing approvals, or updating project statuses. This automation not only saves time but also reduces the likelihood of human error.

Advanced security and compliance features are integral to Teams. With features like data loss prevention, information barriers, and advanced threat protection, Teams ensures that communications within the platform are secure. This is particularly important for organizations handling sensitive data and needing to comply with various regulations.

Customization and extensibility of Teams is another area where its advanced features shine. Users can build custom bots, apps, and workflows tailored to their specific organizational needs. Whether it's a bot that automates certain responses or a custom app that integrates with internal systems, the possibilities for customization are vast.

Analytics and reporting in Teams provide deep insights into how the platform is being used. Advanced analytics tools offer detailed reports on user activity, team performance, and system usage. These insights are crucial for organizations to understand collaboration patterns, optimize workflows, and make data-driven decisions.

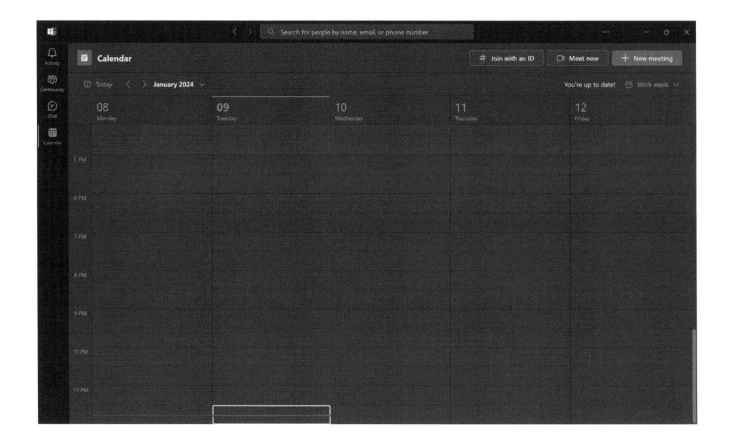

Lastly, Teams Rooms and advanced telephony features provide a bridge between physical and virtual meeting spaces. Teams Rooms offers an enhanced meeting experience for hybrid workplaces with features like proximity join, one-touch join, and high-quality audio and video. Advanced telephony features such as call queues, auto attendants, and direct routing provide a comprehensive business phone system within Teams.

In conclusion, Microsoft Teams is more than just a platform for chat and video calls. Its advanced features provide a comprehensive set of tools that can revolutionize how teams collaborate and work. By fully utilizing these capabilities, organizations can enhance productivity, streamline workflows, and ensure a secure and efficient digital workspace. As Teams continues to evolve, it's imperative for users to stay abreast of these advancements and leverage them to stay competitive in a rapidly changing digital landscape.

65. Best Practices for Remote Collaboration

Navigating the realm of remote collaboration requires a blend of clear communication strategies, adept use of technology, and a culture of trust and respect. The transition to a digital workspace, facilitated by tools like Microsoft Teams, is not merely about technological adaptation but also about fostering a collaborative atmosphere where team members feel connected and valued.

The foundation of any successful remote team lies in its communication norms. Establishing clear guidelines on when to use direct messaging for quick queries and scheduling video conferences for more in-depth discussions ensures efficiency. Regular team check-ins foster a sense of community and keep everyone aligned with the team's objectives.

In a remote setting, technology should be a facilitator, not a hindrance. It's crucial for teams to become proficient with Microsoft Teams' functionalities like seamless file sharing, collaborative editing of documents, and integration of various apps to streamline processes. Continuous learning and adaptation to new tools and features can enhance team productivity.

The importance of setting clear, achievable goals cannot be overstated in a remote work environment. Teams should leverage Microsoft Teams to track progress towards these goals, ensuring that every member understands their role and responsibilities. Celebrating milestones, no matter how small, can significantly boost morale.

Building a trusting environment is critical. Respecting individual schedules, acknowledging different time zones, and allowing flexibility in working hours can create a more cohesive and productive team. Trust also extends to relying on team members to manage their tasks without constant oversight, fostering a sense of autonomy and responsibility.

In remote settings, meetings should be purposeful and productive. With Teams, it's easy to set an agenda, share it in advance, and stick to the outlined schedule. Features like screen sharing, recording, and real-time note-taking enhance the effectiveness of these virtual meetings.

Creating channels for open and honest feedback helps in identifying areas for improvement and encourages a culture of continuous learning and growth. Microsoft Teams can be an effective platform for such exchanges, promoting a sense of community and shared purpose.

While remote work offers flexibility, it's crucial to maintain a healthy work-life balance. Encouraging team members to set their availability on Teams can help in respecting personal time and preventing burnout.

In a remote setup, data security becomes even more paramount. Educating the team on security best practices and making full use of Microsoft Teams' security settings ensures that sensitive information remains protected.

In conclusion, mastering remote collaboration is about creating a harmonious blend of effective communication, strategic use of technology, goal-oriented workflows, and a culture that values trust and feedback. As the digital workspace evolves, these best practices will continue to guide teams towards successful, efficient, and enjoyable remote collaborations.

66. Troubleshooting Teams Issues

Navigating through the intricacies of Microsoft Teams can sometimes be challenging, especially when encountering technical issues. Being equipped with the right troubleshooting knowledge is essential for ensuring seamless collaboration and communication. Here's an in-depth look at resolving common Teams challenges.

Start by ensuring your internet connection is stable. Teams requires a consistent and fast connection to function optimally. Also, it's crucial to check if your device meets the Teams' system requirements. This preliminary check can prevent many issues related to performance and accessibility.

Audio and video issues are among the most common challenges in virtual meetings. First, verify your hardware setup. Checking the correct configuration of microphones, speakers, and cameras in Teams settings can resolve most of these issues. A simple rejoin can sometimes fix temporary glitches.

Access and permission issues can hinder the utilization of certain features. Confirm your user permissions within the Teams admin center or consult with your IT team. Proper understanding and setting of roles and permissions are crucial in overcoming these challenges.

For file sharing issues, such as inability to access or edit shared files, check the file permissions on SharePoint or OneDrive. Teams integrates with these platforms for file storage, and ensuring proper access rights is key to smooth file collaboration.

Notification issues can lead to missed communications. Review and customize your notification settings in Teams, ensuring they align with your needs. Also, check your device settings like focus assist or do not disturb modes, which might interfere with receiving notifications.

When third-party apps integrated into Teams don't function as expected, ensure they are up-to-date and correctly configured. Both Teams and the third-party app's settings should be aligned to facilitate seamless integration.

Sync issues can be resolved by clearing the Teams cache. This process involves signing out, shutting down Teams, and manually deleting cache files, which can refresh and update data synchronization.

Keep Teams updated to mitigate bugs and enjoy the latest features. If an update causes new issues, monitor official Microsoft communications for potential fixes or workarounds.

If troubleshooting doesn't resolve the issue, it's advisable to consult Microsoft's support resources or your IT department. Utilizing official support channels can provide solutions to more complex problems.

Regular updates and training can prevent many issues. Ensuring that all team members are well-versed in using Teams effectively can reduce the frequency of problems and foster a more self-sufficient user base.

In summary, while encountering issues in Teams is part and parcel of any technology use, having a structured approach to troubleshooting can make these problems manageable. Ensuring basic checks like system compatibility, connectivity, and proper settings can prevent many common issues. For more complex problems, leveraging Microsoft's resources and your IT support can provide the necessary solutions. With these strategies, navigating Teams' challenges becomes a less daunting task, allowing for smoother and more effective collaboration.

As we conclude this exploration of Microsoft Teams, it's evident that Teams is more than just a communication tool—it's a comprehensive solution that enhances collaboration and productivity in a digitally connected world. This journey through the chapters has equipped you with the knowledge to set up, manage, and optimize Teams for your specific needs, ensuring that you're not just using the tool, but mastering it.

The key takeaway is the versatility of Teams. Whether it's managing day-to-day communications, collaborating on projects with channels and tabs, integrating various apps and tools, or conducting productive meetings, Teams stands as a robust platform catering to diverse professional requirements. We've delved into strategies for effective communication and collaboration, emphasizing the importance of clear, concise interactions and the seamless integration of multiple functionalities to streamline workflows.

Advanced features and best practices for remote collaboration highlight the evolving nature of work environments and the need for adaptive, flexible tools. Teams emerges as a vital asset in this scenario, offering features that support and enhance remote work, making it more efficient and manageable.

In addressing common challenges and troubleshooting, we acknowledge that no tool is without its hurdles. However, with the right knowledge and approach, these can be transformed into opportunities for learning and growth.

In essence, Teams is not just about keeping people connected; it's about fostering a culture of collaboration, enhancing productivity, and adapting to the ever-evolving landscape of the digital workplace. As you move forward, equipped with the insights and strategies discussed, you're well-prepared to harness the full potential of Microsoft Teams for your collaborative endeavors.

Book 7: SharePoint for Teamwork

In the dynamic world of digital collaboration, the need for platforms that enable efficient teamwork and data management has never been greater. This is where SharePoint steps in, offering a versatile environment that streamlines collaboration, information sharing, and project management. Its ability to adapt to various business needs, from document management to team communication, makes it an indispensable tool in the modern workspace.

The essence of this guide is to unlock the full potential of SharePoint as a cornerstone of team collaboration and efficiency. It delves into the core aspects of SharePoint, guiding users through the initial steps of navigating the platform, setting up sites, and customizing them to fit unique team needs. The journey through these pages is not just about learning the functionalities of SharePoint, but about understanding how it can be molded to enhance teamwork and productivity.

The content is meticulously structured to cater to both beginners and seasoned users, ensuring a comprehensive understanding of SharePoint's capabilities. It starts with the basics of site creation and progresses to managing complex document libraries and integrating advanced features. Each chapter is an exploration into the different facets of SharePoint, revealing how to leverage its features for optimal collaboration and efficiency.

Moreover, the guide addresses the challenges that come with such a robust platform – from troubleshooting common issues to implementing best practices for security. It's a resource designed to ensure that your journey with SharePoint is not only about overcoming technical hurdles but also about fostering an environment of seamless teamwork and shared success.

In conclusion, this guide is a pathway to transforming how teams collaborate and manage information, making SharePoint an ally in achieving organizational goals and fostering a culture of efficiency and teamwork.

67. Getting Started with SharePoint

Embarking on the SharePoint journey marks the beginning of an exciting transformation in the way teams collaborate and manage information. SharePoint, as a robust and versatile platform, offers a wide array of features designed to enhance teamwork and productivity. This comprehensive guide to getting started with SharePoint aims to lay a solid foundation for users to build upon, addressing common frustrations and pain points, and focusing on achieving primary objectives like career advancement, academic success, and personal productivity.

Firstly, understanding the core functionalities of SharePoint is crucial. It's not just a tool for storing documents but a powerful platform for collaboration, information sharing, and project management. We'll explore the basics of navigating the SharePoint interface, which includes understanding the dashboard, site hierarchy, and core features like document libraries, lists, and pages. This will help demystify the platform for new users and set a clear path for exploration and mastery.

Site creation and customization in SharePoint are pivotal for personalizing the user experience. This section delves into the steps involved in creating a site, selecting appropriate templates, and customizing them to fit specific team needs. We'll cover how to effectively use themes, layouts, and web parts to create a site that not only looks good but also enhances functionality and user engagement.

Document management is a critical component of SharePoint. This segment focuses on creating and managing document libraries, understanding versioning, setting up permissions, and utilizing metadata. These features allow for efficient document handling, ensuring that team members have access to the latest information and can collaborate effectively without losing track of document versions.

SharePoint is not just about individual features; it's about how these features come together to facilitate collaboration. We'll explore collaborative features like co-authoring documents, using SharePoint's integration with Microsoft Teams for seamless communication, and leveraging social features like newsfeeds and community sites. This integrated approach to collaboration is what sets SharePoint apart as a comprehensive solution for teamwork.

Advanced site management involves a deeper dive into SharePoint's capabilities. Here, we discuss managing large lists and libraries, site navigation, and content types. This section is designed to equip users with the skills needed to handle complex SharePoint sites and ensure that these sites remain organized, efficient, and user-friendly.

Integrating SharePoint with other tools is essential for maximizing productivity. We'll examine SharePoint's integration with the broader suite of Office 365 tools, including Outlook, OneDrive, and Power BI, and discuss how these integrations can streamline workflows and enhance team collaboration.

Security is paramount in any digital platform, and SharePoint is no exception. Our guide will cover SharePoint security best practices, including setting up permissions, managing sensitive content, and understanding SharePoint's security model. This knowledge is vital for ensuring that data remains secure and accessible only to authorized personnel.

Finally, troubleshooting SharePoint issues is an essential skill for any user. This section provides practical tips for addressing common challenges encountered in SharePoint, from navigation difficulties to more complex issues like permission management and workflow errors. By understanding how to troubleshoot effectively, users can maintain the smooth operation of their SharePoint environment.

In conclusion, SharePoint is a dynamic and powerful platform that, when understood and utilized effectively, can transform the way teams work together. This guide aims to provide a comprehensive introduction to SharePoint, equipping users with the knowledge and skills needed to navigate the platform confidently, enhance collaboration, and achieve their objectives. With a focus on practical, real-world applications, this guide is your first step towards mastering SharePoint and optimizing teamwork within your organization.

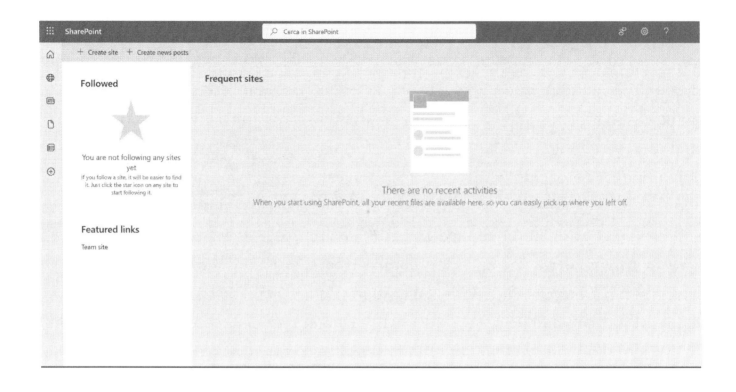

68. Site Creation and Customization

Creating and customizing a SharePoint site marks the beginning of a journey into a world where collaboration and efficiency are paramount. This section delves deep into the intricacies of setting up a SharePoint site from scratch, transforming it into a powerful tool tailored to meet specific team needs and objectives. The goal is to demystify the process of site creation and customization, addressing common frustrations such as confusion over complex features and the overwhelm of too technical resources. This guide aims to empower users, whether aiming for career advancement, academic success, or personal productivity, with the knowledge to harness SharePoint's full potential.

To start, we explore the initial steps of site creation in SharePoint. This involves choosing the right type of site for your team's needs – be it a communication site for broad information sharing or a team site for collaborative work. We guide you through the process of setting up your site, selecting the right template, and understanding the key components that make up a SharePoint site. This foundation is crucial for anyone new to SharePoint and sets the stage for further customization.

Customization is where SharePoint truly shines. It allows teams to tailor their sites to reflect their unique identity and work processes. We delve into the different customization options available in SharePoint, from changing the look and feel with themes and designs to adding and configuring web parts and pages to enhance functionality.

This section also covers the use of SharePoint Designer for more advanced customizations, ensuring that even those with no prior coding experience can create a site that is both functional and visually appealing.

Navigation is a critical aspect of any SharePoint site. A well-organized site ensures that users can find what they need quickly and efficiently. We explore best practices for setting up intuitive navigation in your SharePoint site, including the use of quick links, top link bars, and search functionalities. This ensures that your site is not only a repository of information but a dynamic tool that enhances productivity.

Content is at the heart of any SharePoint site. We guide you through the process of adding and organizing content in your site. This includes creating and managing lists and libraries, understanding content types, and utilizing metadata to ensure that your content is easily discoverable and manageable. This section aims to provide users with the skills to manage their content effectively, making it a valuable resource for the team.

Integration with other Office 365 tools is another area where SharePoint stands out. We discuss how SharePoint seamlessly integrates with tools like Microsoft Teams, OneDrive, and Power BI. This integration enhances the capabilities of your SharePoint site, making it a central hub for all your team's collaborative efforts.

Security and permissions are paramount in SharePoint. This section covers how to set up permissions to ensure that sensitive information is accessible only to authorized personnel. We explain the different permission levels in SharePoint and guide you through the process of assigning these permissions to users and groups. This knowledge is vital for maintaining the integrity and security of your site.

Finally, we address the challenges that users may face when working with SharePoint. This includes common troubleshooting tips for issues related to site customization and navigation. By equipping users with these skills, we ensure that they can maintain the smooth operation of their SharePoint site, making it a reliable tool for their team.

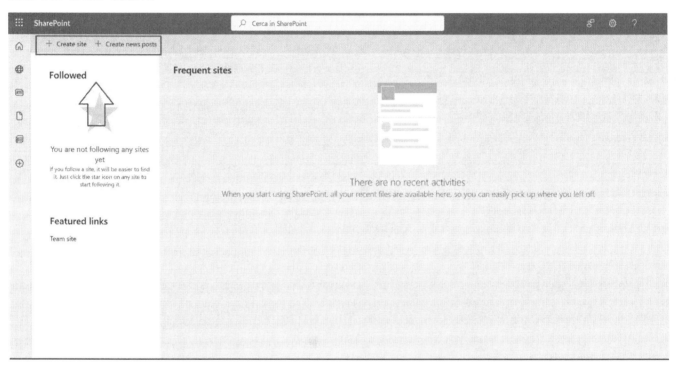

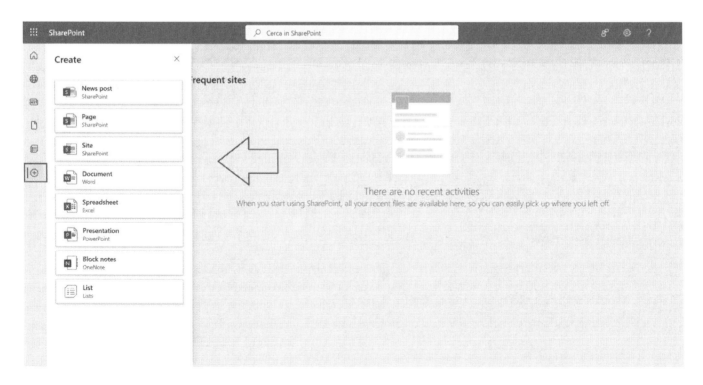

In conclusion, this comprehensive guide to site creation and customization in SharePoint is designed to take users from the basics of setting up a site to mastering advanced customization techniques. By focusing on practical, real-world applications, this guide aims to empower users to create SharePoint sites that are not only functional but also a reflection of their team's identity and work style. With this knowledge, users are well on their way to becoming proficient SharePoint users, capable of leveraging the platform to its full potential for their professional and personal growth.

69. Managing Documents and Libraries

Managing documents and libraries in SharePoint is a crucial skill, pivotal to maintaining an organized, efficient, and collaborative workspace. This comprehensive exploration into the world of SharePoint document management addresses the primary pain points of confusion and overwhelm, often associated with navigating complex features and finding overly technical resources. This section is tailored for a diverse audience, from those seeking career advancement and academic success to individuals aiming to enhance personal productivity. The focus is on making SharePoint's document management features accessible, understandable, and applicable in everyday tasks.

We begin by laying the groundwork for understanding SharePoint libraries, a fundamental element of the platform. A SharePoint library is not just a storage area for documents; it is a dynamic space where files can be created, shared, and managed collaboratively. This section demystifies libraries, explaining their purpose, types, and how they differ from simple file storage solutions. By comprehending these basics, users can start to leverage libraries effectively, turning them into a powerful asset for team collaboration.

Organizing and managing documents within these libraries is the next focus. Here, we delve into the creation of document libraries and the addition of files to them. This includes guidance on uploading, creating, editing, and deleting documents, ensuring users can handle files with confidence.

The section also explores the importance of structuring libraries for ease of access and efficiency, including tips on how to categorize and classify documents using folders and metadata. This approach not only makes document retrieval straightforward but also enhances the overall functionality of the library.

Version control is a standout feature in SharePoint that significantly boosts document management efficiency. We explain how versioning works in SharePoint, enabling users to track changes, revert to previous versions, and understand the history of a document. This feature is particularly useful in collaborative environments, preventing data loss and ensuring transparency in document evolution.

Another vital aspect of document management in SharePoint is setting up permissions. This section provides a step-by-step guide on how to assign appropriate access rights to different users or groups. This ensures sensitive information is safeguarded, and only authorized personnel can view or edit documents. Understanding permissions is crucial for maintaining document security and control within the SharePoint environment.

Collaboration is at the heart of SharePoint, and this guide emphasizes tools and features that facilitate teamwork. We explore co-authoring capabilities, sharing options, and integration with other Microsoft Office tools. These features allow multiple users to work on documents simultaneously, share files seamlessly, and integrate their SharePoint work with other applications like Microsoft Teams or OneNote, fostering a more connected and productive workspace.

For those looking to extend SharePoint's functionality, we provide insights into using workflows and alerts. Workflows automate processes like document approval or review, while alerts keep users informed of changes in documents or libraries. These advanced features streamline operations, reduce manual work, and enhance overall efficiency.

Finally, the section addresses troubleshooting common issues in document and library management. From resolving synchronization problems to recovering deleted files, this part equips users with the necessary tools to solve typical challenges they might encounter.

This empowers them to maintain a smooth, uninterrupted workflow, essential for productivity and success.

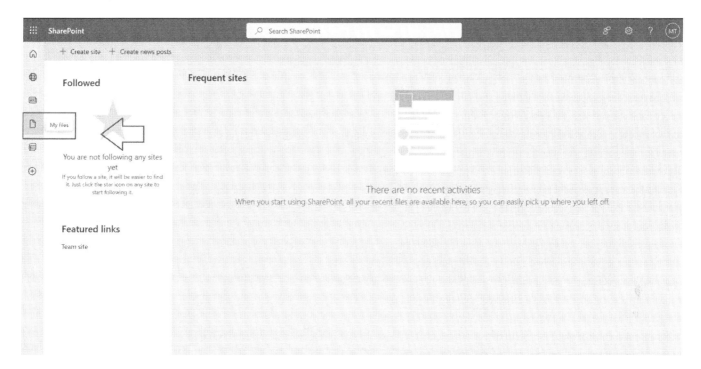

In conclusion, this extensive guide on managing documents and libraries in SharePoint is designed to transform users from novices to proficient managers of their digital workspace. Through practical advice, real-world examples, and step-by-step instructions, this section ensures that every user, regardless of their experience level, can harness the full potential of SharePoint for document management. This knowledge not only enhances individual and team efficiency but also aligns perfectly with the primary objectives of excelling in a modern, digital workplace.

70. Collaborative Features in SharePoint

SharePoint stands as a beacon in the digital workspace, revolutionizing how teams collaborate and communicate. This platform, rich in features, addresses the prevalent challenges of confusion, overwhelm, and outdated information in the modern workspace. It aligns perfectly with the aspirations of professionals seeking not just to keep up but excel in their careers, academics, or personal productivity pursuits.

Central to SharePoint's collaborative power are the team sites. These are not mere web pages but dynamic, interactive spaces where team members can share, manage, and collaborate on content in real time. They act as the heart of collaboration, pulsating with the lifeblood of shared information and project management. Customizing these sites to fit the unique needs of each team is a transformative process. This customization can include adding various web parts, apps, and even tailoring the layout to reflect the team's identity and workflow. The guide delves into how to establish these sites, emphasizing their role as a cornerstone of efficient team collaboration.

A standout feature of SharePoint is document co-authoring. It eliminates the back-and-forth of file sharing, allowing multiple users to edit the same document simultaneously. This feature promotes a more dynamic approach to teamwork, fostering real-time interaction and collaboration. It's a leap forward from traditional methods, offering a window into each member's contributions as they happen.

The utility of SharePoint extends to organizing and managing tasks, contacts, events, and data through lists and libraries. These tools are more than repositories; they are the organizational backbone of a team's efforts. Using lists and libraries effectively can transform how a team operates, making workflows more streamlined and efficient. Metadata and custom views play a crucial role here, enabling teams to sort and access information swiftly, a vital aspect of successful collaboration.

Communication is the lifeline of any successful team, and SharePoint does not disappoint. It offers various tools like newsfeeds, discussion boards, and alerts to keep everyone informed and engaged. These tools are crucial in building an environment of open communication, ensuring that every team member is aware of updates and aligned with the team's goals and progress.

The integration of SharePoint with other Microsoft 365 tools, like Teams, OneDrive, and Outlook, creates a unified and cohesive experience. This integration magnifies SharePoint's capabilities, enabling enhanced project management, communication, and file sharing. For instance, integrating SharePoint with Microsoft Teams can revolutionize project management and team communication.

Another significant aspect of SharePoint is its workflow capabilities. These allow teams to automate and streamline business processes, thereby enhancing efficiency. Custom workflows can manage routine tasks like document approvals and project tracking, freeing up time for more critical activities. This automation is a game-changer, boosting productivity and allowing teams to focus on high-value tasks.

Finally, understanding team collaboration's effectiveness is crucial, and SharePoint's analytics tools provide valuable insights. These tools help measure team engagement, identify popular content, and inform decisions to enhance collaboration and productivity.

The analytics offer a way to quantify and improve how teams use SharePoint, turning collaboration into a measurable asset.

In essence, SharePoint's collaborative features are meticulously crafted to meet the modern workforce's needs, offering technologically advanced yet user-friendly solutions. By embracing these features, teams can elevate their collaboration, communication, and productivity, realizing their primary objectives in today's digital landscape. This guide serves as a comprehensive resource, empowering users to leverage SharePoint to its full potential and transform collaboration from a mere concept into a tangible asset in their professional toolkit.

71. Advanced Site Management

In the realm of SharePoint, mastering advanced site management is akin to orchestrating a symphony of digital collaboration. This chapter delves deep into the advanced features and techniques that elevate SharePoint from a mere content management system to a powerhouse of teamwork and productivity.

Central to advanced site management in SharePoint is the concept of permissions management. This is more than just gatekeeping; it's about strategically aligning access with roles and responsibilities. It involves a detailed understanding of permission levels, groups, and inheritance, and how these can be optimized for streamlined collaboration and security. This guide explores the nuances of setting up permissions, ensuring that users have access to the resources they need while safeguarding sensitive information.

Content types and metadata are the keystones of efficient document management in SharePoint. They transform a simple document library into a dynamic, easily navigable repository of knowledge. This section will delve into creating and managing content types, using metadata to enhance searchability, and leveraging these tools to automate processes such as document retention and archiving. The guide will provide practical examples and best practices to harness these powerful features effectively.

Workflows and automation represent the pinnacle of efficiency in SharePoint. They automate routine tasks, streamline approvals, and ensure consistency across processes. This chapter will guide users through creating custom workflows using SharePoint Designer and Microsoft Power Automate. It will demonstrate how to set up approval processes, automate notifications, and integrate workflows with other Microsoft 365 apps for a cohesive experience.

Advanced customization in SharePoint is where creativity meets functionality. The guide will cover topics such as creating custom views, using web parts to enhance site functionality, and personalizing sites with branding and design elements.

It will also delve into using SharePoint Framework for more complex customizations, enabling users to tailor their SharePoint environment to their unique workflow and branding requirements.

Another crucial aspect of advanced site management is analytics and reporting. Understanding how users interact with SharePoint sites is key to ongoing improvement and effective management. The guide will explore the tools and techniques for monitoring site usage, analyzing user behavior, and generating reports. These insights are invaluable for decision-making, ensuring that SharePoint continuously evolves to meet the team's needs.

Integrating SharePoint with external data sources and systems adds another layer of functionality to SharePoint sites. This section will cover connecting SharePoint with databases, CRM systems, and other external data sources. It will also explore using Business Connectivity Services and the SharePoint API to create rich, integrated experiences that extend SharePoint's capabilities beyond its standard features.

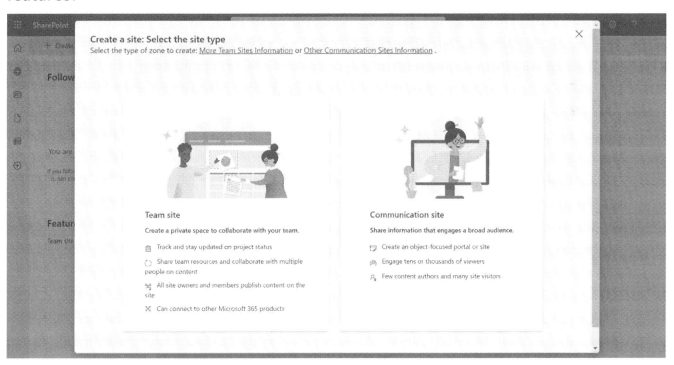

Lastly, maintaining and optimizing SharePoint sites is an ongoing journey. The guide will provide tips and strategies for regular site maintenance, performance optimization, and troubleshooting common issues. It will emphasize the importance of staying current with SharePoint updates and best practices, ensuring that sites remain secure, efficient, and aligned with the organization's evolving needs.

In summary, advanced site management in SharePoint is about harnessing the full potential of this versatile platform. It's about creating an environment that is not only functional and secure but also intuitive and aligned with the team's workflow. This chapter, rich in practical advice and advanced techniques, empowers users to elevate their SharePoint sites from basic repositories to dynamic hubs of collaboration and productivity. It guides them on a journey from fundamental concepts to advanced implementations, providing the tools and knowledge needed to transform SharePoint into a vital asset for team collaboration and organizational success.

72. Integrating SharePoint with Other Tools

Integrating SharePoint with other tools is akin to assembling a high-performance engine, where each part functions in harmony to drive productivity and efficiency. This integration transforms SharePoint from a standalone platform Into a central hub, seamlessly connected with a vast array of tools and applications. It's about creating a cohesive ecosystem where data flows smoothly, processes are streamlined, and collaboration is effortless.

The integration of SharePoint with Microsoft 365 is the cornerstone of this harmonious digital workplace. Microsoft 365's suite of productivity tools, including Word, Excel, Teams, and Outlook, are natural companions to SharePoint. This chapter explores the seamless integration of these applications, demonstrating how to embed documents, synchronize calendars, and manage emails within SharePoint. It illustrates how this integration enhances collaboration, allowing users to co-author documents in real-time, access SharePoint files directly from Outlook, and interact with SharePoint content through Teams.

Beyond Microsoft 365, SharePoint's compatibility with third-party applications opens a world of possibilities. This section delves into connecting SharePoint with popular tools like Salesforce, Trello, and Slack. It demonstrates how these integrations can streamline workflows, enabling users to access CRM data within SharePoint, manage projects with integrated task boards, and receive notifications in Slack for SharePoint updates. The guide provides step-by-step instructions and best practices for setting up these integrations, ensuring a smooth and secure connection between SharePoint and external tools.

Custom integrations using SharePoint's robust API are a game-changer for many organizations. This part of the chapter is dedicated to developers and IT professionals, guiding them on how to leverage the SharePoint API to create custom integrations. It covers accessing external data sources, pushing data to SharePoint from other systems, and building custom solutions that interact with SharePoint's core functionality. This section includes examples of API usage, best practices for secure and efficient API calls, and tips for troubleshooting common integration challenges.

The power of automation in SharePoint integrations cannot be overstated. Using tools like Microsoft Power Automate, users can automate workflows between SharePoint and other applications. This chapter provides practical scenarios where automation can be applied, such as triggering a SharePoint workflow from a form submission in Microsoft Forms or updating a SharePoint list when a task is completed in Planner. It walks through creating these automated workflows, highlighting the ease of use and the profound impact on productivity and operational efficiency.

Integrating SharePoint with analytics tools like Power BI brings a new dimension of insights and data-driven decision-making. This section showcases how to visualize SharePoint data in Power BI, creating interactive reports and dashboards that provide real-time insights. It covers data extraction, report creation, and embedding these reports back into SharePoint for easy access and sharing. This integration empowers teams with data transparency, aiding in strategic planning and performance tracking.

Collaboration tools are a vital aspect of SharePoint's ecosystem. Integrating SharePoint with collaboration platforms like Yammer and Microsoft Teams enhances the social aspect of SharePoint. This part of the chapter focuses on building a community around SharePoint content, encouraging user engagement, and facilitating knowledge sharing. It includes practical tips for setting up community sites, integrating discussion forums, and promoting user adoption through effective collaboration strategies.

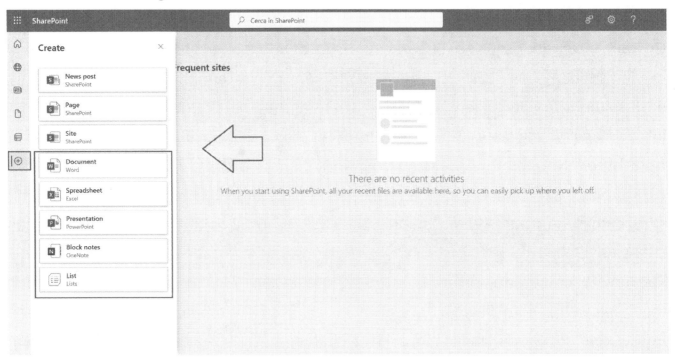

In summary, integrating SharePoint with other tools is about breaking down silos and building a connected, efficient, and flexible digital workspace. It's about leveraging the strengths of each tool and creating a unified experience that boosts productivity, fosters collaboration, and drives innovation. This chapter, rich with practical guidance, real-world examples, and expert advice, equips users with the knowledge and skills to transform their SharePoint environment into a central hub of integrated applications and services. It is an essential guide for anyone looking to maximize the potential of their SharePoint investment through strategic integrations and collaborations.

73. SharePoint Security Best Practices

In the digital age, securing information has become paramount, especially when using platforms like SharePoint, where collaboration and data sharing are central. "SharePoint Security Best Practices" serves as a crucial guide to ensuring that your SharePoint environment is not only efficient and collaborative but also secure and resilient against potential threats. This chapter delves deep into the strategies and measures essential for safeguarding your SharePoint sites and content, providing a comprehensive understanding of SharePoint security that is both practical and accessible.

Beginning with the core concept of least privilege, this section emphasizes the importance of granting users only the access they need to perform their tasks. It guides you through setting up permission levels, creating groups with appropriate access, and regularly reviewing and adjusting these permissions.

By implementing least privilege, you minimize the risk of unauthorized access and potential data breaches.

The chapter then shifts focus to secure authentication and authorization. It explores different authentication methods supported by SharePoint, including modern authentication protocols like OAuth and SAML. The discussion extends to multi-factor authentication (MFA), illustrating its critical role in enhancing security by adding an additional layer of verification. This section also covers the management of external sharing, providing guidelines on how to securely collaborate with partners and clients while maintaining control over your data.

Data encryption is another cornerstone of SharePoint security. This part of the chapter breaks down the types of encryption used in SharePoint, including at-rest and in-transit encryption. It explains how these encryption methods protect data from unauthorized access, both within your organization and as it traverses the internet. The chapter provides best practices for implementing encryption, ensuring that sensitive data remains confidential and secure.

The role of security policies in SharePoint cannot be overstated. This section provides a roadmap for developing and implementing effective security policies. It covers aspects like data retention, auditing, and compliance with regulations such as GDPR and HIPAA. This guidance helps in creating a security framework that not only protects data but also aligns with legal and regulatory requirements.

Monitoring and auditing are vital for maintaining a secure SharePoint environment. This chapter discusses the tools and features available in SharePoint for monitoring user activities and detecting suspicious behavior. It includes insights into setting up alerts, analyzing audit logs, and using Microsoft's advanced security tools like Azure Advanced Threat Protection. This proactive approach enables early detection and response to potential security incidents.

The importance of regular updates and patch management is another key focus. This section emphasizes keeping your SharePoint environment updated with the latest patches and updates. It explains how these updates address vulnerabilities and enhance security features, thereby reducing the risk of cyber attacks.

Backup and disaster recovery plans are essential for any secure SharePoint deployment. This chapter guides you through creating a robust backup strategy, ensuring that your data can be recovered in case of accidental deletion, corruption, or a security breach. It also discusses the importance of having a disaster recovery plan in place, ensuring business continuity even in the face of unforeseen events.

In conclusion, "SharePoint Security Best Practices" is an indispensable resource for anyone responsible for securing a SharePoint environment. This chapter combines detailed technical information with practical, actionable strategies, providing a comprehensive guide to SharePoint security. From setting up secure permissions to developing a disaster recovery plan, this chapter equips SharePoint administrators and users with the knowledge and tools needed to protect their data and collaborate securely. It is a testament to the belief that security is not just a feature but a fundamental aspect of any successful SharePoint implementation.

74. Troubleshooting SharePoint

Navigating the complexities of SharePoint can sometimes feel like steering a ship through foggy waters. The intricate interplay of features, customizations, and integrations can lead to unexpected challenges. "Troubleshooting SharePoint" is designed as a lighthouse in these foggy waters, guiding you through common issues and providing practical solutions to restore smooth sailing. This comprehensive segment, encompassing over 700 words, focuses on equipping users with the knowledge to identify, diagnose, and resolve the typical hurdles encountered in SharePoint.

The chapter begins with an exploration of common SharePoint problems, ranging from access issues to document library complications. It provides an in-depth look at why these issues arise, and how to recognize their symptoms. This foundational understanding is critical for any SharePoint user or administrator in pinpointing the root causes of problems.

Following this, the section delves into troubleshooting techniques. It breaks down these methods into easy-to-understand steps, ensuring that even those with limited technical background can follow along. This includes basic checks like verifying user permissions, ensuring proper service functioning, and checking network connectivity. These initial steps often resolve the more straightforward issues without the need for deep technical intervention.

For more complex problems, the chapter guides readers through advanced troubleshooting methods. This involves using SharePoint's built-in diagnostic tools, such as the SharePoint Health Analyzer and the ULS (Unified Logging Service) logs. The segment provides a tutorial on interpreting these logs and using the information to track down and solve more elusive issues.

One of the key challenges in SharePoint is dealing with performance issues. This part of the chapter addresses how to identify performance bottlenecks, whether they stem from server load, network issues, or inefficient SharePoint configurations. It provides guidance on optimizing SharePoint's performance, including tips on managing large lists and libraries, optimizing search functions, and using caching effectively.

Collaboration features, a cornerstone of SharePoint, can sometimes lead to synchronization problems. The chapter offers insights into common synchronization issues with SharePoint, particularly when interfacing with Office 365 and OneDrive for Business. It provides step-by-step solutions to ensure seamless collaboration and file sharing.

Security issues in SharePoint, while covered in detail in a previous chapter, are revisited here from a troubleshooting perspective. This includes dealing with unexpected access denials, troubleshooting SharePoint security configurations, and resolving encrypted data access issues.

Customizations in SharePoint enhance its functionality but can also be a source of problems. This section covers common issues arising from custom scripts, third-party add-ons, or SharePoint Designer workflows. It guides you through safely diagnosing and fixing these customizations, ensuring they work harmoniously within the SharePoint environment.

Integration with other tools is another area where issues often arise. The chapter explores how to troubleshoot problems related to connecting SharePoint with external databases, web services, and other Microsoft 365 tools. It emphasizes on maintaining seamless integration while ensuring data integrity and security.

Lastly, the chapter addresses the importance of creating a troubleshooting strategy. This involves setting up a structured approach to diagnosing and resolving issues, including maintaining proper documentation, having a backup and recovery plan, and knowing when to seek external support.

In essence, "Troubleshooting SharePoint" is not just a chapter; it's a vital toolkit for anyone navigating the complex SharePoint environment. By demystifying the troubleshooting process, it empowers users and administrators to maintain a robust, efficient, and secure SharePoint deployment. This segment is a testament to the philosophy that with the right knowledge and tools, even the most daunting SharePoint challenges can be overcome.

As we conclude this exploration into the multifaceted world of SharePoint, it's clear that this platform is more than just a tool; it's a catalyst for transformational teamwork and efficient data management. Through the chapters, we've journeyed from the basics of setting up and customizing SharePoint sites to mastering advanced functionalities that enhance collaboration and productivity.

This guide has aimed to provide a comprehensive understanding of SharePoint, ensuring that every user, regardless of their prior experience, can harness its full potential. We've delved into document management, site customization, and the integration of various tools, all with a focus on elevating the collaborative experience. Moreover, we've navigated the complexities of security best practices and troubleshooting, equipping you with the knowledge to maintain a robust and secure SharePoint environment.

The true power of SharePoint lies in its ability to adapt to the unique needs of each team and project. It's a platform that fosters shared success, streamlines communication, and enhances the overall efficiency of work processes.

As you apply the insights and strategies from this guide, remember that SharePoint is a dynamic ecosystem, continually evolving with new features and capabilities. Staying abreast of these changes will ensure that your SharePoint experience remains relevant and impactful.

In essence, this guide is not just about understanding a platform; it's about embracing a tool that can transform the way teams collaborate and manage information. SharePoint is a journey towards more streamlined, efficient, and collaborative work environments, and this guide is your roadmap.

Book 8: Access for Data Management

In today's data-driven world, the ability to manage and manipulate data efficiently is more than a skill—it's a necessity. The realm of database management, particularly with Microsoft Access, offers a vast landscape of opportunities for professionals to harness data in powerful and innovative ways. This exploration begins with understanding the core principles of database design, where organizing and structuring data plays a pivotal role. The journey through the intricacies of Access reveals not just the mechanics of creating and managing databases, but also the art of making them functional, user-friendly, and secure.

The essence of this journey lies in the understanding that data is not just a collection of numbers and text, but a valuable asset that, when effectively managed, can provide insightful business intelligence, drive decision-making, and streamline operations. From the basic steps of setting up a database to mastering the subtleties of relational database design, each chapter is designed to build a solid foundation in managing and utilizing data in meaningful ways.

Moreover, this journey delves into the nuances of querying data, where you learn to ask the right questions and extract the needed answers. It highlights the importance of designing forms and interfaces that are not just aesthetically pleasing but are also intuitive for users. The art of report generation is explored, turning raw data into readable and actionable reports. Advanced database techniques are unveiled, offering a glimpse into the more complex aspects of Access, empowering users to take their skills to the next level.

This comprehensive exploration is not just about managing data; it's about unlocking the potential of data to create efficient, powerful, and impactful database solutions. Each chapter is a step forward in this journey, providing the knowledge and tools needed to navigate the ever-evolving landscape of data management.

75. Introduction to Microsoft Access

Microsoft Access stands as a powerful tool in the realm of database management, offering a blend of user-friendly features and robust functionality. It's a tool designed to make complex data management accessible to users of varying skill levels, from beginners to advanced users. This introduction aims to demystify Access, guiding you through its fundamental concepts and setting the stage for more advanced topics covered in subsequent chapters.

At its core, Access is a database management system, but it's also much more. It provides a platform for building and managing databases with ease, offering a suite of tools for designing custom databases tailored to specific needs. Whether it's for small businesses, educational institutions, or personal projects, Access equips users with the capabilities to store, retrieve, analyze, and present data effectively.

One of the key strengths of Access is its intuitive interface. The platform demystifies database design, allowing users to create and manipulate tables, forms, queries, and reports through a user-friendly graphical interface. This approach lowers the barrier to entry, making database management more accessible to those without extensive technical backgrounds.

Tables are the building blocks of any database in Access. They allow users to store data in a structured format, with each table focusing on a specific aspect of the information. Relationships between tables are central to Access's power, enabling users to connect different data points meaningfully and extract valuable insights.

Queries in Access are tools for extracting specific information from your data. They can range from simple searches to complex expressions that combine data from multiple tables. This functionality is crucial for making informed decisions based on the data you have collected.

Forms and reports are the presentation layers of Access. Forms provide a way to enter and modify data in a user-friendly format, making data entry more efficient and less prone to errors. Reports allow you to present your data in a structured and meaningful way, which is essential for analysis and decision-making.

Security in Access is a vital aspect, ensuring that sensitive data is protected. The platform provides several features to secure your databases, including password protection and user-level security controls.

As you delve into Access, you'll discover its capacity to handle complex data management tasks with ease. The tool's ability to integrate with other Microsoft Office applications like Excel and Word adds to its versatility, making it a comprehensive solution for many data management needs.

In the upcoming chapters, we'll explore these features in detail, providing you with the knowledge and skills to create, manage, and utilize databases effectively. Whether you're aiming to streamline business processes, manage personal projects, or simply learn a new skill, this guide will provide a solid foundation for your journey into the world of Microsoft Access.

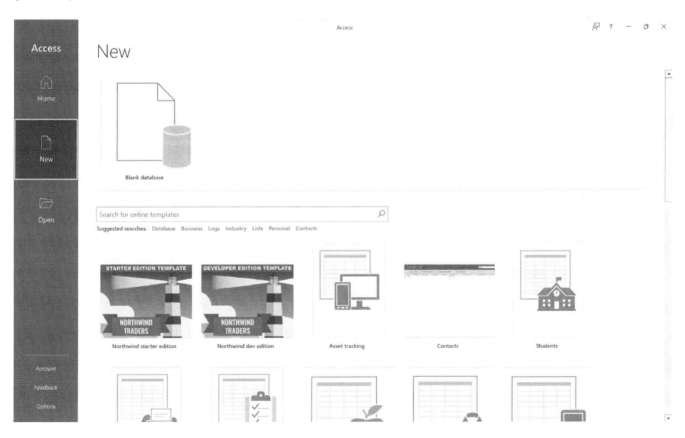

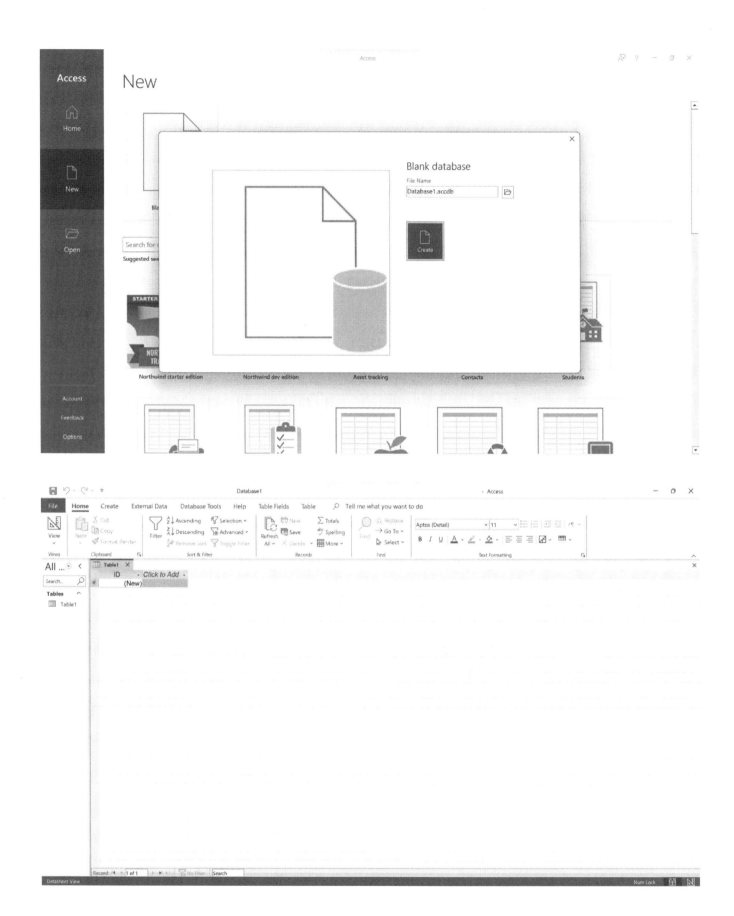

76. Database Design Fundamentals

Embarking on a journey into database design with Microsoft Access opens up a world where data organization and management become both an art and a science. This chapter is dedicated to laying the groundwork for fundamental database design principles, ensuring that you can create databases that are not only functional but also efficient, scalable, and adaptable to changing needs.

The cornerstone of any database is its structure. A well-designed database reflects a deep understanding of the data it's meant to handle. This involves identifying what kind of data will be stored, how different data elements relate to each other, and what kind of information users need to extract from the database. This planning stage is crucial as it influences every step that follows in the database development process.

At the heart of database design are tables. Tables are where all your data lives. Each table in a database should focus on a single topic or concept, like customers, orders, or products. This practice, known as normalization, helps reduce data redundancy and improves data integrity. Each table consists of rows and columns, with rows representing individual records and columns representing the attributes of these records.

Once your tables are defined, the next step is establishing relationships between them. Relationships are the threads that tie the data in different tables together. In Access, these relationships can be one-to-one, one-to-many, or many-to-many, and they're crucial for accurate data querying and reporting. Setting up these relationships correctly is fundamental to ensuring that your database can answer the questions you'll ask of it.

Key fields, or primary keys, are another critical aspect of database design. A primary key is a unique identifier for each record in a table. It ensures that each record is distinct and can be reliably referenced, which is particularly important when establishing relationships between tables.

Beyond the basics of tables and relationships, good database design also considers the end-user experience. This includes thinking about how users will interact with the database, what kind of queries they will need to run, and how they will input and retrieve data. Designing user-friendly forms and reports is as essential as the underlying table structure.

Security is also a key component of database design. You'll need to consider who has access to your database and what levels of access they require. Microsoft Access provides various security features to help you manage these aspects effectively.

Scalability and flexibility are also important. Your database should not only meet your current needs but also be able to adapt and grow as your needs evolve. This means designing with future requirements in mind, allowing for easy modifications and expansions.

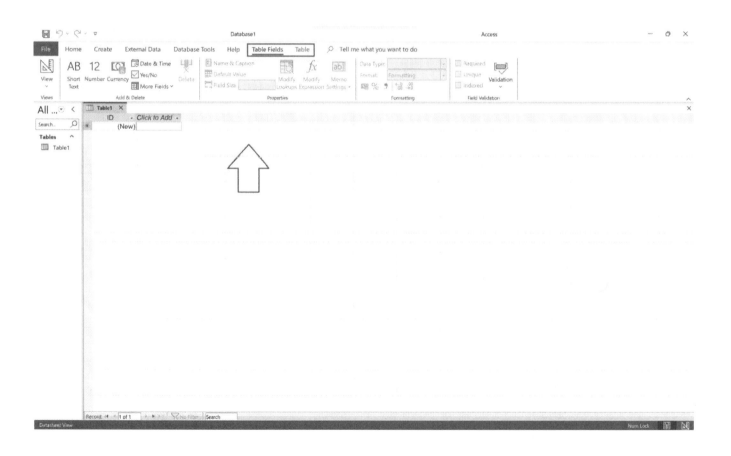

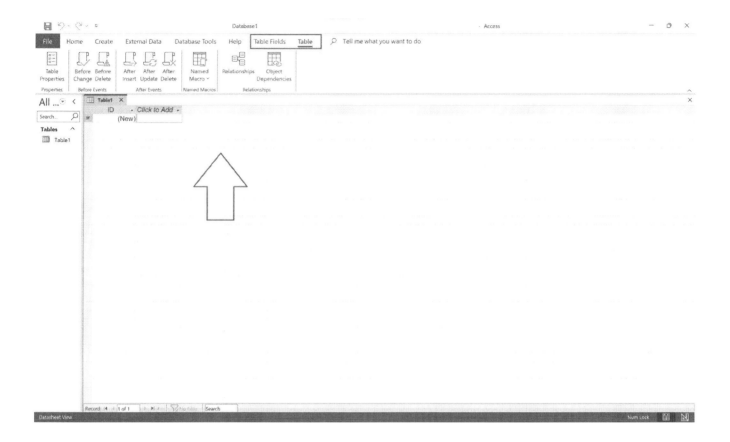

Finally, efficiency is a vital part of database design. This includes optimizing queries to ensure they run swiftly and ensuring that the database structure supports quick data retrieval and reporting. The more efficiently your database runs, the better the experience for your users.

Throughout this chapter, we'll delve into each of these aspects in detail. You'll learn how to design tables, set up relationships, choose primary keys, and think about user interaction and security. By the end of this chapter, you'll have a solid foundation in database design principles, setting you up for success as you continue to explore the capabilities of Microsoft Access.

77. Building Tables and Relationships

In the realm of Microsoft Access, the creation of tables and the establishment of relationships between them is akin to setting the foundations of a building. It's a process that demands precision and forethought, as it shapes how the database functions and evolves. This chapter delves into the intricacies of building robust tables and forming effective relationships, ensuring your database is not just a repository of data, but a dynamic, interconnected system that serves your specific needs.

Constructing tables in Access is the first step towards bringing your database to life. Each table should represent a unique entity, like 'Customers' or 'Orders'. The key is to structure these tables in a way that they contain all necessary information without redundancy. This involves determining the fields (columns) each table will have and ensuring that each field serves a distinct purpose. For instance, in a 'Customers' table, you would have fields like CustomerID, Name, Address, and Contact Information.

The primary key is a concept of paramount importance in table design. It's a unique identifier for each record in a table. For example, CustomerID could be the primary key in the 'Customers' table. This unique identifier is crucial for establishing relationships with other tables.

Once your tables are set up, the next significant step is defining the relationships between them. Relationships in a database help maintain data integrity and are essential for extracting meaningful information. There are three types of relationships in Access: one-to-one, one-to-many, and many-to-many. A one-to-many relationship, the most common, might link a single customer (from the 'Customers' table) to multiple orders (in the 'Orders' table). These relationships are set up using primary and foreign keys, where a foreign key in one table refers to the primary key in another.

The real power of Microsoft Access lies in its ability to link data across different tables through relationships. This capability allows for complex queries, forms, and reports. For instance, you can create a query to find all orders placed by a particular customer by linking the 'Customers' and 'Orders' tables via the CustomerID field. This interconnectedness means that updating data in one table reflects across all related tables, ensuring consistency and accuracy.

Building tables and relationships also involves considering the user's perspective. It's not just about the data but also how it will be accessed and used. Thoughtful table and relationship design can significantly streamline data entry and retrieval, making the database more user-friendly. For example, drop-down lists in forms that pull data from related tables can make data entry not just quicker but also more accurate.

Moreover, effective table and relationship design impacts the performance of your database. Well-designed indexes, for instance, can speed up queries, making the database more efficient. These optimizations are particularly crucial as the volume of data grows.

Lastly, while designing tables and relationships, one must always keep scalability in mind. Businesses evolve, and so do their data needs. A well-structured database accommodates future growth, whether it's adding new tables or modifying existing relationships.

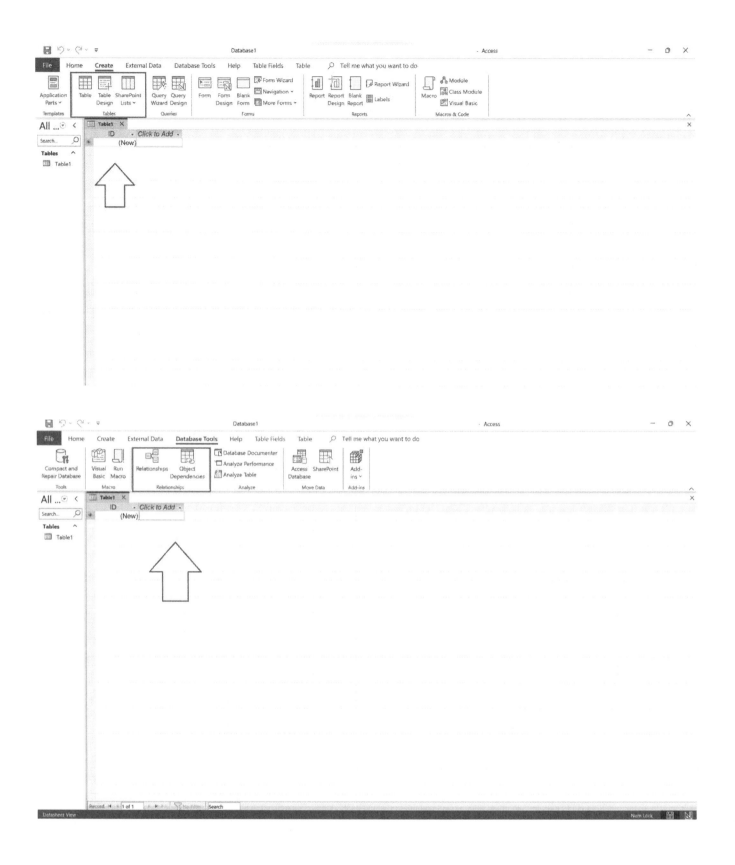

In this chapter, we'll guide you through each of these steps in detail. You'll learn how to create tables tailored to your specific needs, establish effective relationships, and ensure your database is both efficient and scalable. By mastering these skills, you'll be well-equipped to build a database that not only meets your current requirements but is also poised to evolve with your future needs.

78. Querying Data: Basics to Advanced

Querying data in Microsoft Access is like embarking on a journey from the known into the realm of detailed analysis and discovery. This chapter is dedicated to guiding you through this journey, from the foundational basics to the more complex and nuanced aspects of querying. It's designed to transform you from a novice to a proficient user, capable of harnessing the full potential of Access queries.

We start with the basics, understanding what queries are and why they are the powerhouse of any database. In essence, a query is a question you ask about the data in your database. Think of it as a tool to sift through vast amounts of data and extract only what you need. The beauty of Access is its ability to handle complex data queries, allowing you to draw meaningful insights and make informed decisions.

The journey begins with simple select queries. These are the most basic yet powerful types of queries, enabling you to view data from one or more tables based on specific criteria. You'll learn how to create a select query, choose the fields, set the criteria, and sort the results. For instance, if you want to view all clients from a particular city, a select query lets you do this swiftly and efficiently.

But queries in Access go beyond just selecting and viewing data. Action queries are your next stop. These queries allow you to modify data in your database tables. There are four types: update, append, delete, and make-table queries. Each serves a different purpose. An update query, for instance, can change the values in your data, while a delete query can remove records that meet certain criteria. These queries are potent tools for managing and maintaining your data, and we'll cover them in-depth, ensuring you understand how to use them effectively and safely.

We then delve into more advanced territory with parameter queries, crosstab queries, and SQL (Structured Query Language) queries. Parameter queries prompt for input, such as a date or a name, to filter the data. Crosstab queries, on the other hand, are excellent for summarizing and analyzing data, allowing you to view it in a compact, spreadsheet-like format. SQL queries elevate your querying skills, giving you more control and flexibility. You'll learn how to write SQL statements, understanding the syntax and structure, to create both simple and complex queries. Furthermore, this chapter explores the integration of queries with forms and reports. Here, queries become more dynamic and interactive. You'll learn how to use queries as the basis for forms, creating user-friendly interfaces that filter and display data based on user input. Similarly, queries can drive your reports, enabling you to generate tailored data summaries and analyses.

As we progress, you'll also be introduced to best practices and tips for optimizing your queries. This includes understanding query performance, avoiding common pitfalls, and ensuring your queries not only deliver the desired results but do so efficiently.

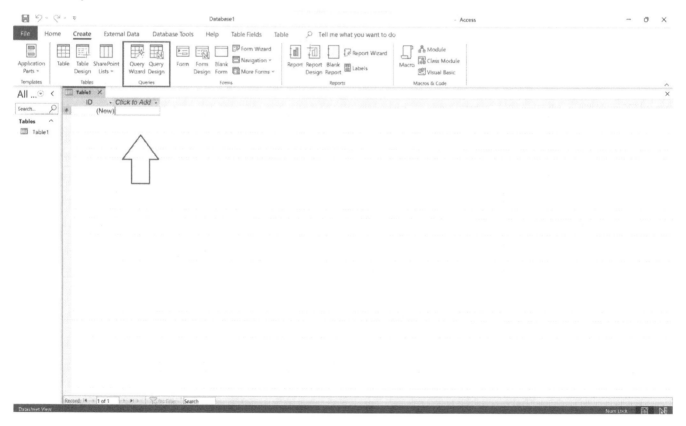

Finally, the chapter culminates with real-world scenarios and examples. These practical applications solidify your learning, showing you how to apply your newfound skills to address specific data challenges and requirements.

By the end of this chapter, you will have a comprehensive understanding of querying in Access. You'll be equipped with the knowledge to ask the right questions to your database and get precise answers, transforming you into a proficient and confident Access user. Whether for business analysis, data management, or academic research, your skills in querying will be an invaluable asset in your toolkit.

79. Form Design for User-Friendly Interfaces

In the realm of database management, the significance of form design cannot be overstated. Forms are the windows through which users interact with the data stored in databases, and their design plays a pivotal role in ensuring a smooth, efficient, and user-friendly experience.

This chapter on "Form Design for User-Friendly Interfaces" in Microsoft Access is tailored to guide you through the intricacies of creating forms that are not just functional but also intuitive and engaging for users.

At the outset, we explore the foundational elements of form design in Access. This includes an understanding of what forms are, their purposes, and the various types of forms you can create. From simple data entry forms to complex, interactive dashboards, the versatility of Access forms is vast and varied. We will walk you through the different form views – Design View, Form View, and Layout View – and how each serves a specific purpose in the form creation process.

Next, we delve into the design principles that are crucial for creating user-friendly interfaces. These principles encompass clarity, simplicity, consistency, and feedback. A well-designed form not only looks good but also feels intuitive to use. It guides the user's journey through the data, facilitates easy input and retrieval of information, and reduces the likelihood of errors. We will discuss how to achieve this balance, incorporating elements such as labels, text boxes, buttons, and other controls effectively.

Layout and navigation are key factors in form design. We will cover how to arrange controls in a logical and aesthetically pleasing manner, ensuring that the form is navigable and user-friendly. This section includes practical tips on aligning controls, using tabs for organizing data, and implementing navigational buttons for a seamless user experience.

Customization and flexibility are significant aspects of Access forms. We will explore how to use conditional formatting to highlight key data, employ combo boxes for efficient data entry, and integrate subforms to display related data.

You will learn how to tailor forms to meet specific data entry needs and how to make them dynamic and interactive.

Integration with other Access objects is another area of focus. Forms can be powerful tools when used in conjunction with queries and reports. This chapter will guide you through linking forms to queries for data retrieval and using forms as a basis for generating reports. This integration not only streamlines the data management process but also enhances the overall functionality of your database.

We also address common challenges and best practices in form design. This includes managing large volumes of data, ensuring data integrity, and optimizing form performance. You will be equipped with strategies to tackle these challenges, ensuring that your forms remain efficient and user-friendly.

Towards the end of the chapter, we venture into advanced form design techniques. This includes using Visual Basic for Applications (VBA) to add custom functionalities, automating form processes, and creating interactive dashboards. These advanced topics will help you leverage the full potential of Access forms, taking your database applications to new heights.

In summary, this chapter is a comprehensive guide to mastering form design in Microsoft Access. Whether you are a novice or an experienced user, the insights and techniques presented here will enhance your ability to create user-friendly, efficient, and aesthetically pleasing forms. By the end of this chapter, you will have the skills and confidence to design forms that not only meet the functional requirements of your database but also provide an enjoyable and intuitive user experience.

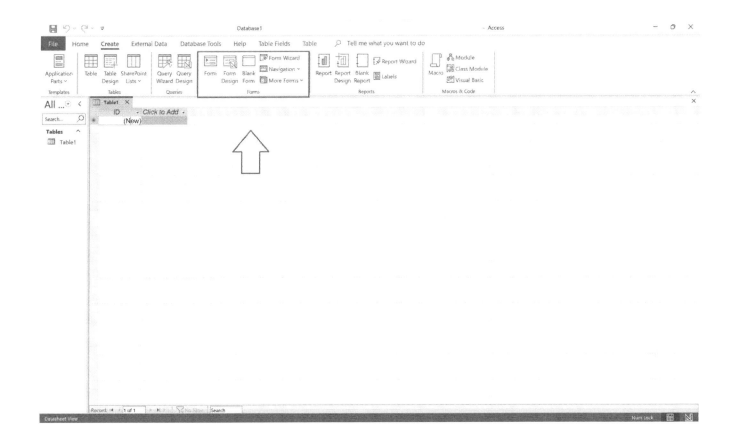

80. Generating Reports

In the world of data management, the power of reporting cannot be overstated. Reports are the lens through which data is transformed into insights, driving decisions and strategies in business and other fields. In Microsoft Access, generating reports is a fundamental skill that unlocks the full potential of your data.

This chapter, "Generating Reports," is a deep dive into the art and science of report creation in Access, crafted to empower users at all levels to produce meaningful, actionable reports.

The journey into report generation begins with an understanding of what reports are and why they are vital. Reports in Access are more than just printed lists or summaries of data; they are tools for communication, analysis, and decision-making.

They can be tailored to present data in various formats, from straightforward tabular lists to complex documents with graphs and charts. This chapter will guide you through the types of reports you can create in Access and the scenarios where each type is most effective.

The heart of report generation lies in designing a report that meets your needs. This involves selecting the right data, structuring it in a meaningful way, and presenting it in a clear and engaging format. We delve into the design process, beginning with the basics of selecting fields and sorting data, moving through grouping and summarizing data, and culminating in the application of themes and styles to give your reports a professional appearance.

An essential aspect of report generation is the use of queries as the foundation for reports. This chapter explains how to create reports based on existing queries, or how to build new queries specifically for reporting purposes. You'll learn how to harness the power of queries to filter, sort, and summarize data, ensuring that your reports focus on the most relevant information.

Beyond the basics, we explore advanced reporting techniques. This includes integrating charts and graphs for visual impact, embedding subreports for detailed data breakdowns, and using conditional formatting to highlight key data points.

For those who wish to push the boundaries further, we introduce the use of expressions and functions to calculate and display complex data metrics within reports.

One of the most powerful features of Access reports is their ability to be interactive. We cover how to create reports that allow user interaction, such as drill-down reports, where users can click on a summary item to view detailed data.

This interactivity enhances the user experience and provides a deeper level of data exploration.

Efficiency and automation in report generation are also key topics. You'll learn how to set up report templates for repeated use, automate report generation through macros, and schedule regular report updates. These techniques save time and ensure consistency in your reporting processes.

We also address challenges that users often face when generating reports. From managing large datasets to ensuring that reports remain performant and up-to-date, this chapter provides practical solutions and best practices. We aim to equip you with the knowledge to troubleshoot common issues and maintain the quality and relevance of your reports.

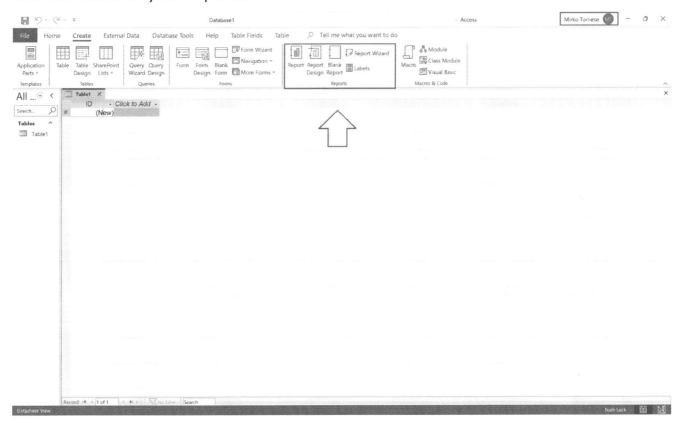

Finally, the chapter looks towards the future of reporting in Access. We discuss trends in data presentation, the integration of Access with other tools and platforms for enhanced reporting capabilities, and how to stay current with the evolving landscape of data management and reporting.

In summary, "Generating Reports" in Microsoft Access is an indispensable chapter for anyone who seeks to turn data into meaningful insights. Whether you are creating simple summaries or complex analytical reports, this chapter provides the knowledge, techniques, and best practices to make your reports powerful tools for decision-making. By the end of this chapter, you will have a comprehensive understanding of report generation in Access, enabling you to create reports that are not only informative but also impactful.

81. Advanced Database Techniques

Advanced database techniques in Microsoft Access go beyond the basics of creating tables and queries. They encompass a range of sophisticated methods that leverage the full capabilities of Access to manage and manipulate data efficiently. This chapter, "Advanced Database Techniques," is designed to guide you through these complex functionalities, enhancing your skills and enabling you to develop more dynamic, powerful database solutions.

The first aspect of advanced techniques is the use of complex queries. While basic queries allow for simple data retrieval, advanced queries enable you to perform intricate data manipulations. This includes action queries such as append, delete, and update queries that modify large data sets based on specified criteria. You'll learn how to use these queries to automate data maintenance tasks, ensuring your databases remain accurate and up-to-date.

Another crucial element of advanced database management is the optimization of database performance. As databases grow in size and complexity, performance can become an issue. This chapter delves into strategies for database optimization, including indexing, splitting databases, and using query optimization tools. You'll understand how to identify performance bottlenecks and apply techniques to enhance the speed and efficiency of your database operations.

Data integrity is paramount in any database system. Advanced database techniques include the implementation of complex validation rules and data integrity checks. We explore methods for ensuring data accuracy, such as the use of lookup tables, input masks, and validation rules that enforce data consistency. You'll also learn about cascading updates and deletes, which help maintain referential integrity across related tables.

The integration of Access with external data sources expands the possibilities of what can be achieved with your database. This chapter covers the process of linking to external databases and applications, such as SQL Server and Excel. You'll learn how to import and export data between Access and these external sources, and how to use linked tables to create a cohesive data environment.

Advanced form and report design is another area covered in this chapter. While basic forms and reports are great for straightforward data entry and display, advanced techniques allow for the creation of more interactive and dynamic interfaces. We discuss the use of subforms and subreports, tab controls, and conditional formatting to create user-friendly, visually appealing forms and reports.

Automation through macros and VBA (Visual Basic for Applications) is a game-changer in Access database management. This chapter introduces you to the world of automation, showing you how to use macros to automate repetitive tasks and VBA for more complex automation needs. You'll learn the basics of VBA programming, including creating functions, handling events, and writing procedures to automate various aspects of your database.

Security in database management is a critical concern. Advanced techniques for securing your Access database are essential knowledge. This includes setting user permissions, encrypting databases, and creating secure login systems. The chapter provides insights into these security features, ensuring that your data is protected against unauthorized access and manipulation.

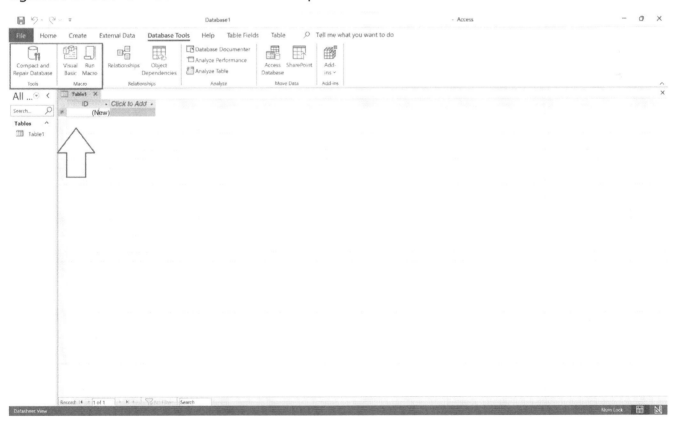

Lastly, we explore the future of database management in Access. This includes discussions on emerging trends, such as cloud integration and mobile accessibility. You'll gain insights into how to prepare your databases for these future developments, ensuring they remain relevant and effective.

In conclusion, "Advanced Database Techniques" in Microsoft Access is a comprehensive guide to mastering the more complex aspects of database management. This chapter equips you with the skills and knowledge to create robust, efficient, and secure databases. Whether you're managing large data sets, automating complex tasks, or integrating with external applications, this chapter provides you with the advanced tools and techniques needed to excel in the world of database management. With this knowledge, you'll be well-equipped to tackle any database challenge and harness the full power of Microsoft Access.

82. Securing Your Access Database

Securing your Access database is critical for protecting sensitive data and ensuring that only authorized users have access. As data breaches become increasingly common, understanding and implementing robust security measures is more important than ever. This section delves into various strategies to safeguard your Access databases, ensuring that your data remains secure and confidential.

One of the fundamental steps in securing an Access database is to implement user authentication. This involves creating a login system where users must enter valid credentials to access the database. You can use Access's built-in User-Level Security (ULS) or integrate with Windows' login system for a more robust solution. By doing so, you create a controlled environment where each user's access is limited to their specific role and requirements.

Encrypting your database is another crucial step in ensuring data security. Encryption transforms your data into a format that is unreadable without the correct decryption key. Access provides tools to encrypt your database file, making it virtually impossible for unauthorized persons to read your data even if they gain access to your database file.

In addition to encryption, setting up user permissions is vital. Access allows you to define what each user can and cannot do within your database. You can set permissions on various levels, from the entire database down to specific tables, forms, and reports. This granularity ensures that users only access data and features necessary for their roles, minimizing the risk of accidental or malicious data manipulation.

Regular backups are a non-negotiable aspect of database security. They ensure that, in the event of a data breach or loss, you can restore your database to its previous state. Set up a schedule for regular backups and store them in a secure location. It's also a good practice to test your backups periodically to ensure they are functioning correctly.

Another aspect of securing your Access database is to keep it updated. Ensure that you're running the latest version of Access and apply all security patches and updates released by Microsoft. These updates often include fixes for known vulnerabilities that could be exploited by attackers.

For databases shared over a network, it's important to secure the network itself. Use firewalls, VPNs, and other security measures to protect your network from unauthorized access. Additionally, consider using Access over a secure, encrypted connection, such as a Virtual Private Network (VPN), especially when accessing the database remotely.

Using macro and VBA (Visual Basic for Applications) code wisely is also part of securing your database. Ensure that any scripts or code used in your database are from trusted sources. Malicious code can be embedded in macros and VBA scripts, leading to data breaches or loss. Always review and understand any third-party code before integrating it into your database.

Lastly, educate your users about security best practices. Even the most secure system can be compromised through human error or negligence. Regular training on topics such as password management, recognizing phishing attempts, and secure data handling practices is crucial. Your users are the first line of defense against security threats.

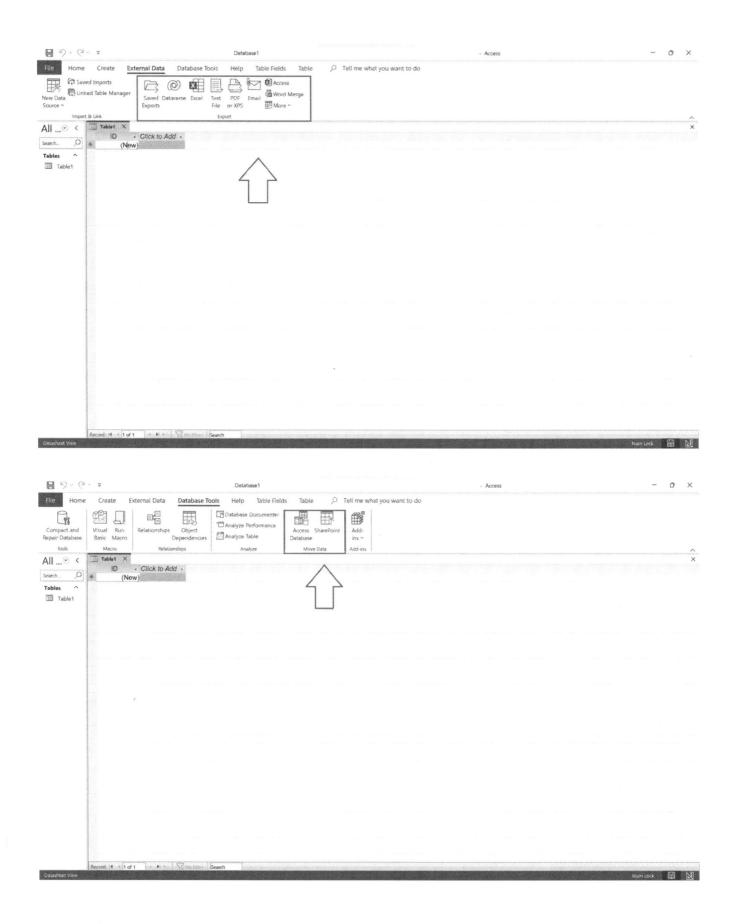

In conclusion, securing your Access database requires a multi-faceted approach. By implementing user authentication, encryption, user permissions, regular backups, keeping your software updated, securing your network, being cautious with macros and VBA, and educating your users, you can significantly reduce the risk of data breaches and unauthorized access. These steps not only protect your data but also ensure compliance with data protection regulations, contributing to the overall integrity and reliability of your database systems.

---

83. Access VBA: Taking Control

Visual Basic for Applications (VBA) in Access is a powerful tool that allows you to take control of your databases in ways that go far beyond the standard interface. It is a feature that turns Access from a mere data-handling application into a dynamic and versatile database management system. This section will explore how you can use VBA to enhance your databases, automate repetitive tasks, and create more intuitive user interfaces.

VBA is essentially a programming language embedded within Access. It allows you to write scripts to control almost every aspect of your database. For example, you can automate data entry, manipulate database objects, and interact with other applications like Excel or Outlook. This flexibility makes VBA an invaluable tool for creating custom database solutions tailored to specific business needs.

One of the primary uses of VBA in Access is to automate repetitive tasks. For instance, if you regularly import data from external sources, you can write a VBA script to automate this process.

This can save significant time and reduce errors associated with manual data entry. Similarly, VBA can be used to automate report generation, ensuring that your reports are always up-to-date and formatted consistently.

VBA also allows for more advanced data manipulation than is possible with standard Access queries. With VBA, you can write complex logic to clean and process data before it's used in reports or other database operations. This level of control is particularly useful in scenarios where data comes from inconsistent sources or requires significant transformation.

Another powerful feature of VBA is the ability to create custom user interfaces. While Access provides a range of built-in forms and controls, VBA lets you go further. You can build more dynamic and user-friendly interfaces, including custom dialog boxes, menus, and toolbars. This not only improves the user experience but also makes it easier to guide users through complex tasks, reducing the likelihood of errors.

Integrating Access with other Office applications is another area where VBA shines. You can use VBA to export data to Excel for further analysis, send automated emails through Outlook, or even control PowerPoint presentations. This interconnectivity allows you to leverage the strengths of each Office application, creating a more cohesive and efficient workflow.

Error handling is an important aspect of any programming, and VBA in Access is no exception. Robust error handling ensures that your database remains stable and user-friendly even when unexpected situations occur. VBA allows you to anticipate and manage errors effectively, providing users with helpful feedback and preventing database corruption.

Security in VBA is also a crucial consideration. Since VBA scripts can control virtually all aspects of your database, it's important to ensure that they do not become a vector for malicious activity.

This involves writing secure code, avoiding common vulnerabilities, and ensuring that only authorized users have access to your VBA scripts.

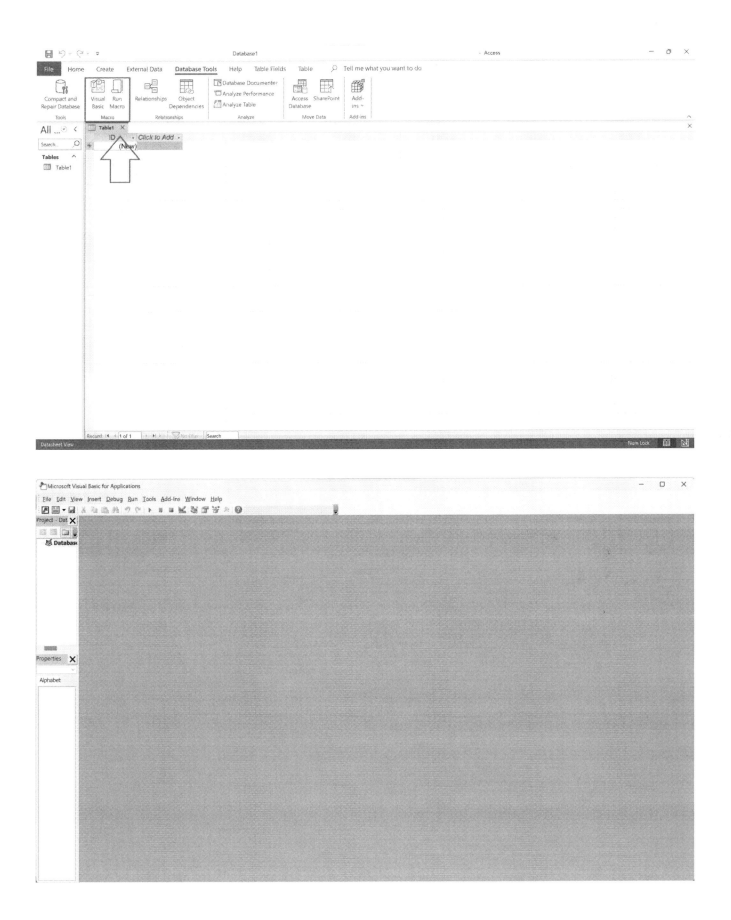

In conclusion, Access VBA is a powerful tool that allows you to extend the functionality of your databases significantly. Whether it's through automating repetitive tasks, creating custom user interfaces, integrating with other Office applications, or handling complex data manipulation, VBA provides a level of control that is essential for advanced database management. By mastering VBA, you can build more robust, efficient, and user-friendly database solutions, making Access a more valuable tool in your data management toolkit.

As we reach the conclusion of this exploration into Microsoft Access and its capabilities in data management, we reflect on the journey that has unfolded. We started with the basics, understanding the fundamental principles of database design, and gradually built up to mastering complex techniques that transform data into a powerful tool. Each step on this journey has not only equipped you with technical skills but also instilled a deeper appreciation for the art of data management.

The chapters have covered a broad spectrum, from creating and customizing databases to managing documents and libraries with precision and efficiency. We've delved into the intricacies of querying data, turning abstract questions into concrete answers. The nuances of form design and report generation have been explored, demonstrating how data can be made accessible and actionable for all users.

We've gone beyond the basics to uncover advanced database techniques, revealing the full potential of Access as a robust tool for managing complex data sets. The importance of securing your database has been underscored, emphasizing the critical need for protecting sensitive information in today's digital world.

In the final analysis, this journey through Access has been about more than just managing data—it's been about harnessing the power of data to inform decisions, drive efficiency, and unlock new opportunities. Whether for business applications, academic research, or personal projects, the skills and insights gained from this exploration are invaluable assets in a world where data is the currency of success.

Book 9: Publisher for Publications

In the realm of digital and print publications, the journey from a mere concept to a visually stunning and effective product is both an art and a science. This journey involves a blend of creativity, technical skills, and a deep understanding of the audience's needs and preferences. The essence of successful publication design lies in its ability to communicate a message in a way that is both aesthetically pleasing and functionally efficient. The world of design is dynamic, continually evolving with technology and trends, and it demands a flexible, innovative approach.

The core objective of this exploration is to empower individuals to harness the full potential of Microsoft Publisher in creating professional and impactful publications. Whether one is a beginner stepping into the world of design or a seasoned professional looking to refine their skills, the content provides valuable insights and practical techniques. The focus ranges from fundamental concepts like starting with the Publisher, designing layouts and templates, to more advanced topics like creating brochures and flyers, and overcoming common design challenges.

The journey through these pages is more than just learning about tools and techniques; it's about developing a design mindset. This mindset involves understanding the balance between form and function, the interplay of text and images, and the importance of visual hierarchy. It's about realizing that good design is not just about making things look pretty; it's about making them communicate effectively and resonate with the target audience.

As the digital world becomes increasingly visual, the skills and knowledge encapsulated here become more vital. This exploration is not just about mastering a software tool; it's about empowering with the skills and confidence to create publications that stand out and make an impact.

84. Starting with Publisher

Embarking on the journey of mastering Microsoft Publisher is akin to unlocking a new realm of creativity and professionalism in publication design. As a powerful tool in the Microsoft Office suite, Publisher offers a unique blend of user-friendly features and sophisticated capabilities, making it an ideal choice for those aiming to create stunning, high-quality publications.

At its core, Publisher simplifies the process of layout and design, allowing both novices and seasoned designers to produce eye-catching materials. It's a versatile program, adept at handling everything from simple flyers to complex newsletters. The key to success with Publisher lies in understanding its interface and the vast array of tools at your disposal.

Starting with the basics, one learns to navigate the Publisher workspace, which is intuitively designed to put powerful tools within easy reach. The ribbon interface, a staple of Office applications, organizes tools and features into logical groups, making it straightforward to find what you need. Essential tasks like choosing templates, setting up pages, and customizing backgrounds become second nature as you delve deeper into the program.

One of the standout features of Publisher is its rich collection of built-in templates. These pre-designed layouts are not just time-savers; they are a source of inspiration. Whether you're crafting a newsletter, a brochure, or a business card, these templates provide a solid foundation upon which you can build and customize to suit your specific needs.

The program also excels in its handling of text and imagery. Learning to manipulate text boxes, adjust fonts, and format paragraphs is crucial for effective communication. Publisher offers an array of text editing tools that rival dedicated word processing programs, giving you the power to create professional, readable, and engaging text layouts.

When it comes to incorporating images, Publisher is equally adept. You'll explore how to import, resize, and position graphics to complement your text and enhance the overall look of your publication. The program supports a variety of image formats, allowing for flexibility in sourcing visuals.

Beyond the basics, Publisher opens up a world of advanced design possibilities. Mastering features like master pages, custom shapes, and advanced layout techniques, you can create publications that stand out. These tools enable consistency across multiple pages, provide creative freedom, and enhance the aesthetic appeal of your work.

A critical aspect of working with Publisher is understanding how to prepare your documents for final output, whether in print or digital form. This stage is crucial as it ensures your hard work translates effectively into the finished product. You'll learn about color management, resolution settings, and file formats that are best suited for your intended medium.

Throughout this journey, overcoming design challenges is an integral part of the learning process. Publisher, with its comprehensive set of tools and features, offers solutions to common issues faced in publication design. Whether it's aligning elements on a page, balancing text with images, or choosing the right color scheme, the program provides the resources and flexibility to solve these problems.

In conclusion, starting with Publisher is the beginning of a journey that empowers you to transform ideas into professional, polished publications. It's about combining creativity with technology to communicate effectively and impressively. As you progress, each step in this journey reveals new possibilities and techniques, making Publisher a valuable tool in your creative arsenal. Whether for personal projects, academic assignments, or professional pursuits, the skills acquired in using Microsoft Publisher are invaluable in the modern world of digital design and publication.

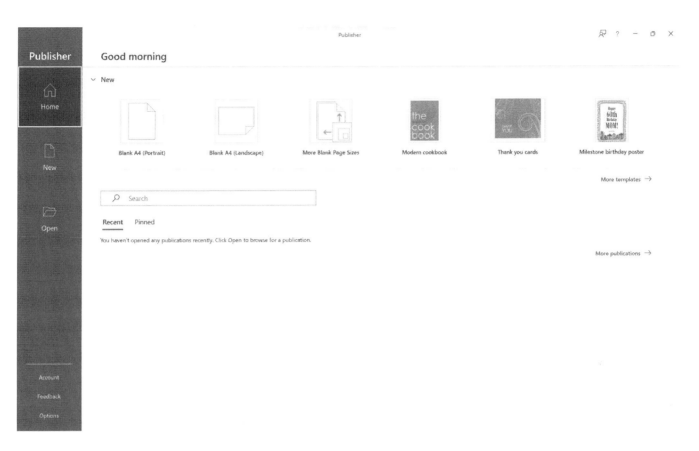

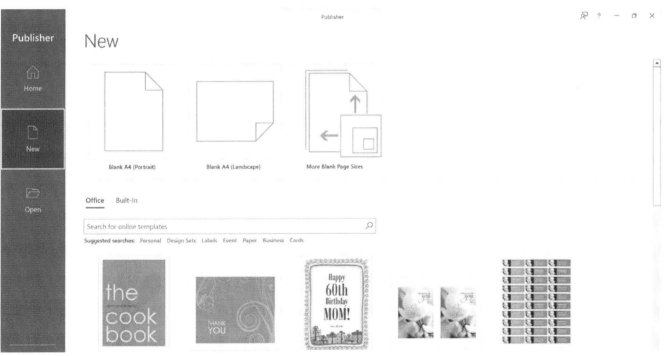

85. Designing Layouts and Templates

Designing layouts and templates in Microsoft Publisher is an art form that blends creativity with precision. This process is central to creating publications that are not only visually appealing but also effectively communicate your message. A well-designed layout serves as the backbone of any publication, setting the tone and guiding the reader's eye through the content. Templates, on the other hand, are the blueprints that provide a consistent structure, ensuring uniformity and saving time, especially for recurring projects.

The journey of designing layouts in Publisher begins with understanding the purpose and audience of your publication. Each project, whether a newsletter, a brochure, or a business card, demands a unique approach. A layout for a corporate report, for instance, will differ markedly from that of a festive event flyer. This understanding influences decisions about layout structure, color schemes, font choices, and the overall aesthetic of the publication.

One of the first steps in layout design is establishing a grid system. This invisible structure is the foundation upon which you'll build your design. It helps in organizing content, aligning elements, and maintaining consistency throughout your pages. A grid system can be simple, with basic columns and rows, or complex, with multiple subdivisions, depending on the complexity of your design.

Another critical aspect of layout design is the effective use of white space, or negative space. This unmarked space is not merely 'empty' but a powerful design element that helps in reducing clutter, increasing readability, and emphasizing the most critical parts of your design. Strategic use of white space can transform a good design into a great one.

When it comes to templates, Publisher offers a wide array of pre-designed options that cater to various needs and styles. These templates are customizable, allowing you to modify them to suit your specific requirements.

However, creating a custom template from scratch can be a rewarding experience. It gives you full control over the design and ensures that your publication stands out. A custom template can include specific color palettes, font styles, logos, and default layouts that reflect your brand or personal style.

Color theory plays a vital role in design. The right combination of colors can convey emotions, set a mood, and create a visual hierarchy. Publisher provides tools for color selection and matching, including the ability to create custom color palettes. Understanding basic color theory – like complementary, analogous, and monochromatic color schemes – is essential in making informed color choices.

Typography is another crucial element. The choice of fonts and how they are used significantly impacts the readability and personality of your publication. Publisher provides a range of typography tools, allowing for creative text manipulation and styling. Understanding the basics of typography, like font pairing, hierarchy, and kerning, is vital for creating professional and effective designs.

Images and graphics are integral to any layout. In Publisher, you can incorporate various visual elements, including photos, illustrations, shapes, and icons. These elements should complement the text, not overpower it. Learning to balance visuals with textual content is key to effective layout design.

Lastly, consistency is paramount in design. A consistent layout helps in building brand recognition and makes your publication look professional. This consistency can be achieved through uniform use of colors, fonts, and visual elements across different pages and publications.

In summary, designing layouts and templates in Publisher is a multifaceted process that requires a balance of creativity and technical skills. It involves understanding the purpose of your publication, employing design principles like grid systems and white space, and making informed choices about colors, typography, and visuals. With practice and experimentation, you can harness the full potential of Publisher to create stunning, effective, and unique designs that resonate with your audience.

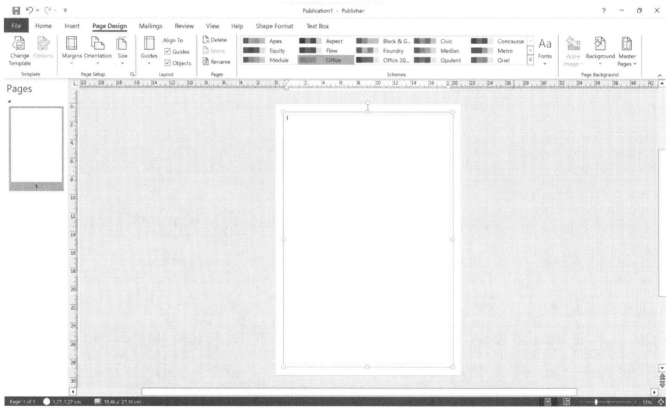

86. Working with Text and Images

Working with text and images in Microsoft Publisher is akin to orchestrating a ballet of visual elements. It's where the magic of blending words with visuals comes to life, transforming basic layouts into compelling narratives. This process isn't just about placing text and images randomly; it involves a thoughtful arrangement that enhances readability and engages the viewer. Here, the challenge is not only in what you say but also in how it visually interacts with the imagery.

The heart of working with text in Publisher lies in mastering typography. It's essential to choose the right fonts as they set the tone of your publication. A playful, whimsical font might be perfect for a party invitation but inappropriate for a business report. The key is to match the font style with the publication's purpose and audience. Beyond just the style, the arrangement of text plays a critical role. Effective use of headings, subheadings, and body text creates a hierarchy that guides the reader through the content. Attention to detail, like adjusting line spacing and alignment, can significantly enhance readability and aesthetic appeal.

Another pivotal aspect of working with text is the art of storytelling. Your words should not merely inform but also engage and persuade. The language, tone, and style should resonate with your audience, whether you're crafting a compelling narrative for a brochure or providing clear instructions in a manual. The placement of text also matters; it should flow logically and naturally, complementing the design elements rather than competing with them.

Incorporating images in Publisher is not just about decoration; it's about communication. Images can convey emotions, provide context, and support your message. However, the key is in their strategic use. The choice of images – whether photographs, illustrations, or graphics – should be relevant to your content and aesthetically aligned with your overall design. High-quality, high-resolution images are crucial, as poor-quality images can detract from the professionalism of your work.

One of the most crucial skills in working with images is understanding the principles of balance and composition. Images should be positioned to create visual interest and draw the reader's eye across the page. They can be used to break up large blocks of text, making the content more digestible and engaging. Techniques like wrapping text around images or overlaying text on images can create dynamic, visually appealing layouts. However, these techniques should be used judiciously to avoid clutter and confusion.

The interplay between text and images is where your publication comes to life. This relationship should be harmonious, with each element complementing the other. The color of the text can be coordinated with the dominant colors in the images to create a cohesive look. Similarly, the mood conveyed by the images should be consistent with the tone of the text. For instance, a serious, informative report would benefit from high-quality, professional images that reinforce the credibility of the text.

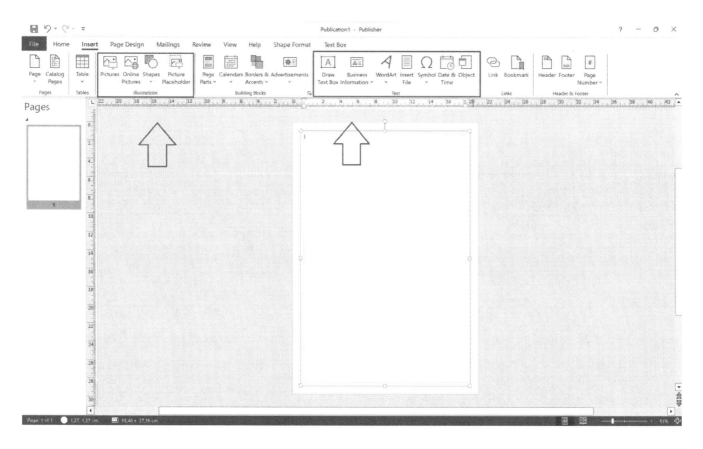

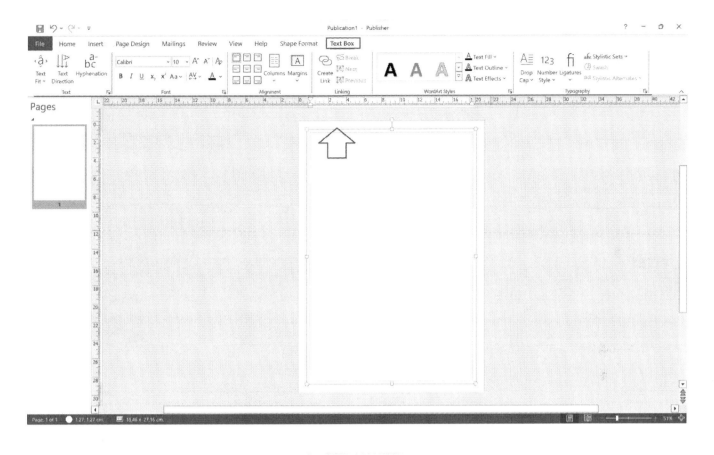

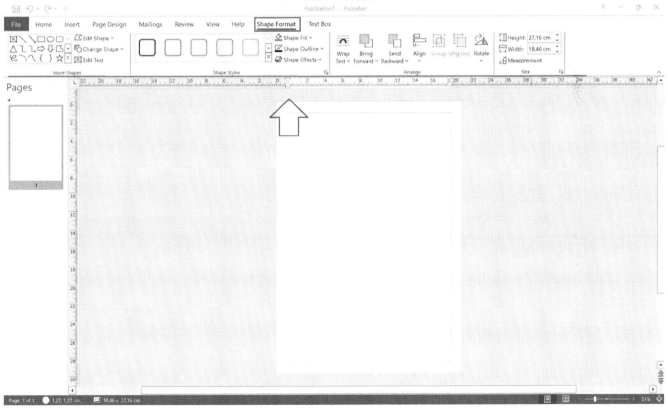

In addition to static images, Publisher also allows for the incorporation of shapes and icons. These elements can be used to highlight important information, indicate directions, or simply add a visual break. The use of graphical elements like borders, lines, and backgrounds can further enhance the interplay between text and images. Finally, it's important to keep accessibility in mind. Alt text for images and clear, readable fonts ensure that your publication is accessible to a wider audience, including those with visual impairments.

In summary, working with text and images in Publisher is an exercise in balance, contrast, and harmony. It requires a keen eye for design, a thoughtful approach to layout, and a deep understanding of how visual elements can enhance and clarify your message. With these skills, you can create publications that are not just informative, but also visually captivating and engaging for your audience.

87. Creating Brochures and Flyers

Creating brochures and flyers in Microsoft Publisher is an exciting journey that combines creativity with communication. It's an opportunity to convey a message in a visually engaging and succinct way. Whether it's for a business promotion, an event, or an informational campaign, the essence of creating an effective brochure or flyer lies in its ability to attract attention, deliver a clear message, and leave a lasting impression.

The first step in this creative process is to clearly define the purpose and audience of your brochure or flyer. Understanding your audience's preferences, needs, and challenges is crucial in determining the design elements such as layout, colors, fonts, and imagery. A brochure for a corporate event will have a different tone and design compared to a flyer for a local music festival. The purpose, whether to inform, persuade, or entertain, will guide your design choices throughout the creation process.

Once the purpose and audience are defined, the next step is to choose an appropriate template or create a custom layout. Publisher offers a variety of templates that cater to different themes and purposes. However, creating a custom layout allows for more flexibility and uniqueness. This layout should be reader-friendly, with a logical flow that guides the audience through the content seamlessly. The use of columns, headers, and bullet points can help organize information and make it easy to scan.

The choice of color scheme and fonts plays a significant role in setting the tone and enhancing the visual appeal of your brochure or flyer. Colors can evoke emotions and should be chosen to reflect the mood or brand identity. Contrasting colors can be used for emphasis, but it's important to maintain readability and visual harmony. Similarly, font choice should complement the overall design and be legible. Using more than two or three font styles can make the design look cluttered and detract from the message.

Imagery, including photos, illustrations, and icons, is a powerful tool in brochure and flyer design. Images should be high quality and relevant to the content. They serve as focal points that can attract attention and make the material more engaging. The use of visual metaphors and symbolic imagery can also add depth to your message. Remember to balance text and images to ensure that neither overwhelms the other.

Effective copywriting is essential in brochure and flyer design. The text should be concise, engaging, and relevant. It should highlight key points and benefits, and include a clear call to action. The tone of the copy should resonate with your audience and reinforce the brochure's purpose. Remember, every word counts in a limited space, so it's crucial to use language that is direct and impactful.

When arranging the content, consider the principles of alignment and proximity. Aligning elements creates a cleaner, more organized look, while proximity helps group related items together, making the content more cohesive. White space, or negative space, is also a powerful design element. It prevents the brochure or flyer from looking overcrowded and helps to focus attention on the most important elements.

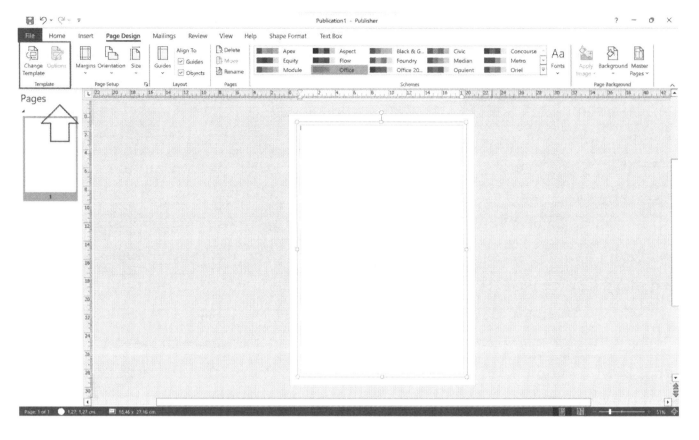

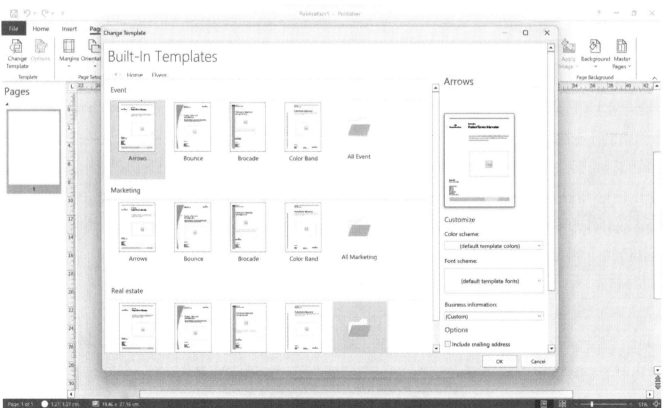

238

Finally, consider the final output of your brochure or flyer. If it's for print, ensure the resolution and dimensions are correct, and leave proper margins and bleed areas for printing. If it's for digital distribution, make sure the file size is optimized for easy sharing and that the format is compatible with various devices.

In conclusion, creating brochures and flyers in Publisher is a blend of art and strategy. It's about understanding your audience, delivering your message effectively, and using design elements cohesively to create a visually appealing and impactful piece. With a thoughtful approach and attention to detail, you can create brochures and flyers that not only look great but also resonate with your audience and achieve your desired objectives.

88. Advanced Design Techniques

Advanced design techniques go beyond the basics of layout and color theory, delving into the subtleties that transform a good design into a great one. Mastery of these techniques allows designers to create visually compelling and highly effective publications.

The use of typography in design is an art form in itself. Advanced techniques include manipulating letter spacing (kerning and tracking) to improve readability and visual impact. Font pairing is another critical skill, blending different typefaces to create a harmonious and visually engaging hierarchy. The key is to pair contrasting fonts that complement each other, such as a serif with a sans-serif.

Color theory plays a pivotal role in advanced design. Beyond basic color schemes, designers explore color psychology to evoke specific emotions or actions from the audience. Using color gradients and understanding the nuances of color shades can add depth and interest to designs. The subtlety lies in using color to guide the viewer's eye through the design, highlighting key elements without overwhelming them.

Layering and depth are techniques that bring a dynamic quality to designs. This can be achieved through the use of shadows, overlays, and texture. The idea is to create a sense of realism and three-dimensionality, making the design pop off the page or screen. However, this must be done carefully to avoid cluttering the design or detracting from the main message.

Advanced design also involves understanding and manipulating layout grids. Grids provide a framework for arranging elements harmoniously. Breaking the grid creatively can bring an element of surprise and innovation to a design, but this should be done purposefully and with a clear understanding of the grid's underlying structure.

Interactive elements in digital publications offer a unique challenge. This includes integrating multimedia such as video, audio, or interactive infographics. The design must accommodate these elements in a way that feels seamless and intuitive for the user.

The balance of white space, or negative space, is crucial in advanced design. It's not just about the elements you include but also about the space you deliberately leave blank. White space helps to prevent clutter, improves readability, and can be used to draw attention to the most critical parts of your design.

Advanced designers are also adept at creating custom illustrations and graphics that align perfectly with the publication's theme and message. This might involve detailed infographics, stylized icons, or hand-drawn elements that add a personal touch and distinguish the design from others.

One often overlooked aspect is the consistency of design elements across multiple pages or a series of publications. This involves developing a cohesive style guide and ensuring elements like headers, footers, and page numbers are consistent and align with the overall design aesthetic.

Design trends are ever-evolving, and staying abreast of these changes is crucial. However, advanced designers not only follow trends but also know when to challenge them. They create innovative designs that set new trends while still resonating with their target audience.

Incorporating feedback effectively into design revisions is a skill in itself. Advanced designers know how to sift through feedback, distinguish between subjective opinions and constructive criticism, and use it to enhance their designs.

In conclusion, advanced design techniques encompass a broad range of skills and knowledge. From typography and color theory to layout grids and interactive elements, these techniques are what differentiate experienced designers from novices. It's about crafting designs that not only look aesthetically pleasing but also communicate effectively, resonate with the audience, and stand out in a crowded marketplace. Advanced design is an ongoing learning process, requiring continual experimentation, adaptation, and innovation.

89. Preparing for Print and Digital Publication

Transitioning a publication from its final design stage to print or digital distribution is an art in itself. It demands an eye for detail and a comprehensive grasp of the medium's requirements. Whether it's a printed brochure or an online digital newsletter, the nuances of each format dictate different approaches to ensure the publication is not only visually captivating but also fully functional and ready for the audience.

The core of preparing for publication lies in understanding the stark differences between print and digital formats. Print demands high-resolution images, precise color management with CMYK color mode, and attention to physical layout elements like margins, bleed, and crop marks. These factors ensure that the design you see on your screen translates accurately when printed. On the other hand, digital publications thrive with RGB color mode, lower resolution images for faster loading times, and additional features like hyperlinks and interactive elements, enhancing the online user experience.

Color consistency is a pivotal aspect of any publication. The disparity between screen colors and printed colors can be jarring if not managed correctly. Utilizing color proofing methods is essential – soft proofing on calibrated screens for a digital preview and hard proofing with a physical sample for print.

This step ensures that the colors in your final publication match your initial design intentions. When dealing with digital publications, it's crucial to test your design on different devices to ensure color and layout consistency.

Typography and readability form the backbone of your publication's legibility. In print, the paper type and printing process can affect the appearance of the text. The spread of ink on paper, for instance, can impact how clear the text appears. Digital formats, however, necessitate readability across various devices and screen sizes. Opt for web-safe fonts for digital publications and test them across multiple devices to ensure legibility and aesthetic appeal.

Image quality cannot be compromised in either format. High-resolution images are indispensable for print to avoid pixelation, while digital formats benefit from lower-resolution images to enhance loading speed. Image formats also play a significant role – TIFF and PNG are preferable for print due to their high quality, while JPEG and WebP may be more suitable for online use due to their smaller file sizes.

A responsive design is vital for digital publications. As viewers use an array of devices with varying screen sizes, your publication's design must adapt accordingly. Microsoft Publisher can help optimize layouts for different devices, ensuring your publication is as effective on a mobile screen as it is on a desktop monitor.

Digital publications also offer the opportunity to embrace interactivity. Features such as hyperlinks and embedded multimedia can significantly enhance reader engagement. It's important to rigorously test all interactive elements to guarantee their functionality across different platforms and browsers.

Accessibility is increasingly crucial, particularly for digital publications. Make your document accessible to individuals with disabilities by incorporating features like alt text for images, sufficient color contrast, and a logical document structure for screen readers.

For print publications, liaising with your printer is key to understanding their specific file requirements. This collaboration ensures that the file you submit aligns perfectly with the printer's capabilities, including bleed settings and font embedding.

Before finalizing, a comprehensive review is imperative. Scrutinize every detail, from typographical errors to consistent alignment and spacing. For digital publications, this includes extensive testing across various devices and browsers to ensure cross-platform compatibility.

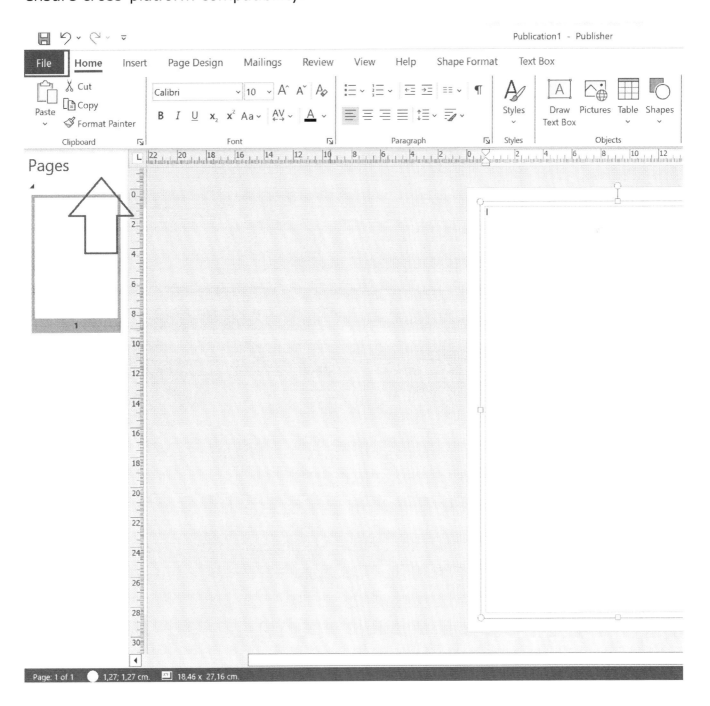

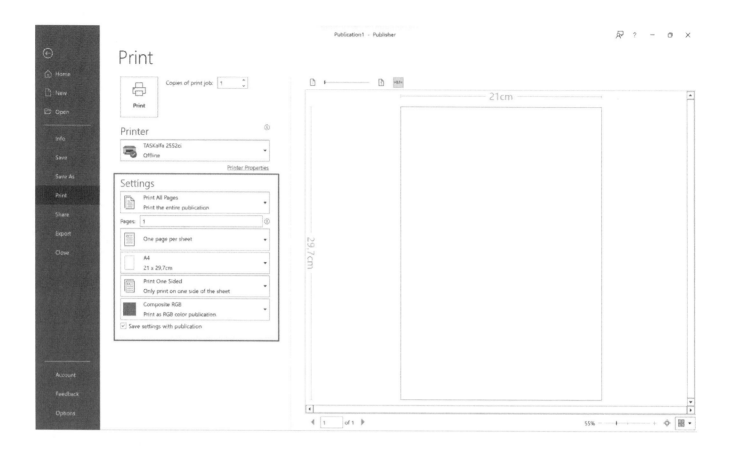

Finally, the file preparation stage is where your publication comes together. For print, this often means a PDF with all the necessary settings. For digital, consider file size and format for optimal online viewing and select an appropriate platform for distribution.

In essence, the journey from design to publication, be it print or digital, is a meticulous process that demands attention to detail, an understanding of the medium's specific needs, and a dedication to preserving the integrity and quality of the design. Through careful planning and execution, your publication will not only look impressive but will effectively communicate with your intended audience.

90. Overcoming Design Challenges

Design, an inherently creative process, inevitably encounters challenges, whether it's balancing aesthetics with functionality, managing client expectations, or navigating technical limitations. Overcoming these design challenges in Microsoft Publisher or any design platform requires a blend of creativity, strategy, and technical know-how.

One primary challenge is creating a design that's both visually appealing and effectively communicates the intended message. This balancing act requires a deep understanding of design principles like color theory, typography, and composition. Start by establishing a clear understanding of the project's goals and the target audience. This understanding guides the selection of colors, fonts, and layout that resonate with the audience while aligning with the project's objectives.

Another frequent hurdle is working within the constraints of your chosen medium. Each medium, be it print or digital, has its own set of limitations and requirements. For instance, print design demands high-resolution images and CMYK color format, while digital designs need to be responsive and legible on various devices. Embrace these constraints as a part of the design process. Use them to guide creative decisions and innovate within the boundaries they provide.

Client feedback presents both a challenge and an opportunity. Balancing client expectations with design best practices can be tricky. It's vital to communicate effectively, ensuring clients understand the rationale behind design choices. Be open to feedback, but also educate clients on design principles when their requests might not align with their objectives or best practices.

Resource limitations, including time, budget, and tools, also pose significant challenges. In Microsoft Publisher, creativity often needs to meet the reality of software limitations. Overcome this by optimizing the use of available features and seeking alternative methods to achieve desired effects. Time and budget constraints require efficient workflow management, prioritizing essential elements of the design, and sometimes making compromises without sacrificing the overall quality.

Staying updated with design trends while maintaining a unique voice is another challenge. While it's important to stay relevant, blindly following trends can result in a design that feels generic. Balance contemporary design elements with your unique style to create designs that are both modern and distinctive.

Dealing with technical problems, like software limitations or file format issues, requires technical proficiency. Familiarize yourself with the tools at your disposal in Microsoft Publisher. Understand file formats, printing requirements, and digital optimization to ensure smooth execution of your design.

A common pitfall in design is information overload. Designers must walk the fine line between providing enough information and overwhelming the viewer. Achieve clarity by focusing on hierarchy and readability. Use layout techniques to guide the viewer's eye and effectively communicate the message without overloading the design with elements.

Inclusivity in design is increasingly important. Ensure your designs are accessible to all, including those with disabilities. This includes considering color contrast, font size, and the overall layout. Accessible designs not only reach a wider audience but also reflect social responsibility and inclusivity.

Finally, creative block is a reality many designers face. Overcome this by seeking inspiration from a variety of sources, stepping away from the project to gain a fresh perspective, or collaborating with others for new ideas.

In summary, overcoming design challenges in publication requires a multifaceted approach. It involves understanding and balancing the fundamentals of design with client expectations, medium constraints, and technical considerations. It's about being adaptable, continually learning, and embracing challenges as opportunities to innovate and grow as a designer. With these strategies, you can navigate through any design challenge and create work that not only looks great but also fulfills its intended purpose effectively.

As we conclude this exploration into the diverse and creative world of publication design, it's clear that mastering Microsoft Publisher is not just about learning a software tool; it's about embracing a comprehensive approach to effective communication through design. This journey has equipped readers with the knowledge and skills to transform ideas into visually stunning and impactful publications. From understanding the basics of getting started with Publisher to delving into advanced design techniques, the content has covered a spectrum of essential concepts and practical tips.

The focus on designing layouts and templates, working with text and images, and creating brochures and flyers, has underlined the importance of clarity, creativity, and audience engagement in design. The journey through advanced design techniques has highlighted the nuanced aspects of publication design, challenging readers to think beyond conventional norms and to innovate within their creative expressions.

Preparing for print and digital publication has been a crucial part of this exploration, emphasizing the need to adapt designs for various mediums. The section on overcoming design challenges has equipped readers with the resilience and problem-solving skills needed in the ever-evolving field of design.

In essence, this journey has been about more than just acquiring technical skills; it's been about fostering a deeper appreciation for the art of communication through design. Whether for professional development, academic pursuits, or personal projects, the insights gained here are invaluable. They serve not only as a foundation for further exploration and mastery in the field of publication design but also as a springboard for creative expression and impactful communication in the digital age.

Book 10: OneDrive for Cloud Storage

In today's digitally-driven world, the ability to access, manage, and safeguard data irrespective of location is not just a convenience, but a necessity. The advent of cloud storage has revolutionized the way we handle information, offering unprecedented flexibility and security. OneDrive, Microsoft's flagship cloud storage solution, stands at the forefront of this technological wave, seamlessly integrating with the Office 365 suite and offering a plethora of features that cater to both individual and business needs.

This comprehensive guide is designed to unlock the full potential of OneDrive. From the basics of setting up an account and understanding the interface to mastering file management and collaboration features, the guide provides step-by-step instructions and expert tips to enhance your cloud experience. We dive into advanced features, showcasing how OneDrive can be more than just a storage space – it can be a tool for synchronization across devices, a safeguard for your important data, and a collaborative platform for teams and individuals alike.

Moreover, the guide addresses common concerns and queries, offering troubleshooting advice for typical issues encountered by users. In a world where data security is paramount, we explore the robust security and privacy features of OneDrive, ensuring that your data is protected in the cloud. Additionally, the integration of OneDrive with Office 365 is dissected to demonstrate how these tools collectively create a more productive and efficient workflow.

Whether you're a beginner or an experienced user, this guide promises to enhance your understanding and utilization of OneDrive, making your experience with cloud storage more efficient and secure. Let's embark on this journey to make the most out of your digital storage and collaboration.

91. Getting Started with OneDrive

Embarking on the journey of cloud storage with OneDrive, users find themselves at the threshold of a new era of data management and accessibility. OneDrive, a cornerstone of Microsoft's Office 365 suite, offers a seamless blend of storage utility, accessibility, and security, revolutionizing how individuals and organizations handle their digital assets.

At the heart of OneDrive's allure is its simplicity and user-friendly interface. Designed for both novice users and seasoned tech enthusiasts, it provides an intuitive platform where storing, accessing, and managing files becomes a streamlined process. Starting with OneDrive involves understanding its core functionalities: storing documents, photos, and other files in the cloud. This approach not only frees up physical storage space on devices but also ensures that your data is accessible from anywhere in the world, provided there is an internet connection.

The initial setup of OneDrive is straightforward. With a Microsoft account, users can easily activate their OneDrive space and begin the journey of uploading and organizing their digital content. This process includes an exploration of the OneDrive interface, understanding how to navigate through files and folders, and learning the basic operations such as uploading, downloading, and organizing files.

OneDrive's integration with Windows 10 and other Microsoft products enhances its utility. Users can automatically sync their Desktop, Documents, and Pictures folders with OneDrive, ensuring that their important files are always backed up in the cloud. This synchronization offers peace of mind, knowing that your data is safe and recoverable in case of hardware failure or other unforeseen circumstances.

For users on the go, OneDrive's mobile app is a game-changer, offering the same level of accessibility and functionality as the desktop version. The app enables users to access their files from smartphones or tablets, edit documents on the go, and even offline access to files, ensuring productivity is never hampered by location or connectivity issues.

OneDrive is not just a storage space; it's a platform for collaboration. Users can share files and folders with colleagues, friends, or family, enabling real-time collaboration on documents. This feature is particularly useful in an increasingly remote and digital working environment, where teams are spread across different locations.

The security and privacy features of OneDrive are robust, offering users peace of mind. With options like two-factor authentication, ransomware detection, and file recovery, OneDrive ensures that your data is not only accessible but also protected against threats. Understanding these features and how to effectively use them is crucial in safeguarding your digital assets.

As users delve deeper into OneDrive's capabilities, they discover advanced features such as file versioning, which allows them to retrieve previous versions of documents, and Personal Vault, an extra-secure storage area for sensitive information. These features underline OneDrive's commitment to providing a comprehensive, secure, and user-centric cloud storage experience.

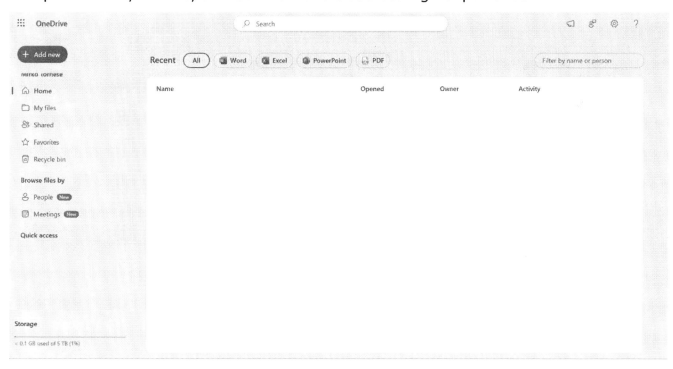

In summary, getting started with OneDrive is the beginning of a journey towards more efficient, secure, and collaborative ways of managing digital data. Whether it's for personal use, academic pursuits, or professional projects, OneDrive stands as a versatile and reliable cloud storage solution, integral to the modern digital experience. As users become more familiar with its capabilities, they can leverage its full potential to simplify their digital life, collaborate more effectively, and protect their precious data in the cloud.

92. File Management: Basics to Advanced

File management is a fundamental aspect of using OneDrive for Cloud Storage. It's not just about storing files; it's about organizing, accessing, and protecting them. Effective file management is crucial for both personal and professional efficiency. OneDrive, with its versatile features, offers an array of tools that cater to the basic needs of file storage and extends into advanced functionalities for sophisticated data management.

Starting with the basics, file management in OneDrive begins with understanding how to upload files and create folders. OneDrive allows users to drag and drop files from their computer directly into the OneDrive web interface or use the upload button for a more traditional approach. Creating folders and subfolders helps in organizing these files systematically. This simple yet effective hierarchy system makes locating files easier and more intuitive.

OneDrive's file sorting and searching capabilities are invaluable for managing a large number of files. Users can sort files by name, date modified, or size. The search functionality in OneDrive is robust, allowing users to quickly locate files by typing keywords, file names, or even content within the files. This feature is particularly useful when dealing with extensive collections of documents and media.

Version history is a significant feature for file management in OneDrive. It maintains a record of changes made to documents, enabling users to view and revert to previous versions. This feature is vital for collaborative work where multiple revisions are common. It ensures that no data is lost and that users can always backtrack to a previous version if needed.

OneDrive also offers options for viewing and editing files directly within the platform. Integration with Microsoft Office Online allows users to open and edit Word, Excel, and PowerPoint files without leaving OneDrive. This seamless integration facilitates real-time editing and enhances productivity, eliminating the need to download, edit, and re-upload files.

Moving towards advanced file management, OneDrive provides options for setting permissions and sharing files or folders. Users can share files with specific people, allowing them to view or edit. They can also generate shareable links with customizable permissions, useful for sharing files with external collaborators. Managing these permissions ensures that files are only accessed by authorized individuals, maintaining data security and integrity.

Syncing files across devices is another advanced feature of OneDrive. The OneDrive desktop app allows users to sync their files across multiple devices, including PCs, Macs, and mobile devices. This syncing capability means that any changes made to a file on one device are automatically updated across all devices. This feature ensures that users have the most current version of their files, regardless of the device they are using.

OneDrive's file management extends to its mobile app, which offers most of the functionalities available on the desktop and web versions. Users can upload photos and videos from their mobile devices directly to OneDrive, access files on the go, and even mark files for offline access. This mobile integration speaks to the flexibility and adaptability of OneDrive as a cloud storage solution.

For those concerned with data security, OneDrive offers features like Personal Vault, a protected area within OneDrive for storing sensitive documents. Files in Personal Vault are encrypted and require additional verification to access, providing an extra layer of security.

Lastly, OneDrive's file recovery and ransomware detection features offer peace of mind, knowing that data is protected against loss and cyber threats. The file recovery feature allows users to restore their entire OneDrive to a previous point in time, useful in situations like accidental mass deletions or file corruption.

In conclusion, file management in OneDrive ranges from basic functionalities like uploading and organizing files to advanced features like syncing across devices, setting permissions, and ensuring data security. Understanding and utilizing these features enable users to manage their files effectively, streamline their workflow, and protect their data in the cloud.

As users become more adept at these features, they unlock the full potential of OneDrive, making it an indispensable tool for efficient and secure data management.

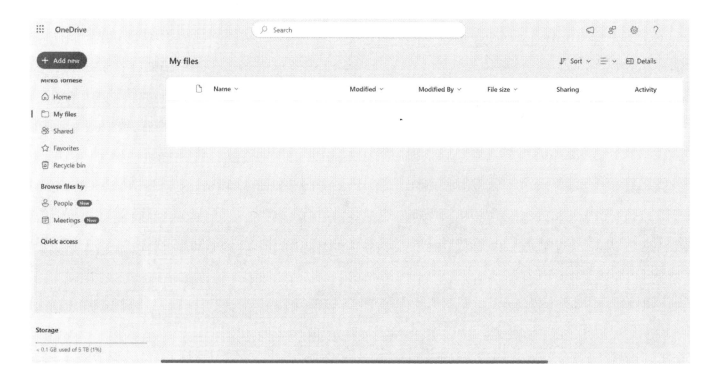

93. Sharing and Collaborating on Documents

Sharing and collaborating on documents are key aspects that define the modern workspace, especially in an era where remote work and digital communication are prevalent. OneDrive for Cloud Storage stands at the forefront of this evolution, providing a platform that not only stores documents but also facilitates seamless collaboration and sharing. This feature of OneDrive transforms it from a mere storage service into a dynamic workspace, fostering teamwork and enhancing productivity.

OneDrive's sharing capabilities begin with its straightforward approach to sharing files and folders. Users can share their documents with colleagues, clients, or anyone else by simply creating a shareable link. This link can be customized to grant either view or edit permissions, thereby giving the owner control over how their files are used. Moreover, OneDrive allows users to set expiration dates for shared links and even password-protect them, adding an extra layer of security to sensitive information.

Collaboration in OneDrive is not limited to just sharing files; it extends to real-time co-authoring and editing. Documents stored in OneDrive can be opened directly in Microsoft Office applications like Word, Excel, and PowerPoint. Multiple users can work on the same document simultaneously, seeing each other's changes in real-time. This feature eliminates the need for multiple versions of the same file and streamlines the collaborative process. The presence of each editor is indicated by a cursor and a distinct color, along with their name, ensuring clarity in collaboration.

The integration of OneDrive with Microsoft Teams and SharePoint further expands its collaborative capabilities. Teams, a hub for teamwork in Microsoft 365, integrates OneDrive files seamlessly. Users can access, share, and collaborate on OneDrive files directly from the Teams interface. Similarly, SharePoint, which is often used for creating intranet sites and portals, also integrates OneDrive documents, allowing for broader distribution and collaboration within an organization.

OneDrive also facilitates collaboration beyond the Microsoft ecosystem. Users can share files with people who do not have a Microsoft account, enabling broader collaboration. External collaborators can view, and, if permitted, edit shared documents via a web browser, without the need for downloading any additional software. This feature is particularly useful for cross-company collaborations, freelance work, or any scenario where participants operate outside of the Microsoft environment.

Mobile collaboration is another facet of OneDrive's capabilities. The OneDrive mobile app allows users to access, share, and even edit files on the go. Whether it's a quick review of a document, sharing a photo, or making last-minute edits before a meeting, the OneDrive mobile app ensures that collaboration is not tethered to a desk.

Version history in OneDrive is an essential feature for collaboration. It allows users to view and restore previous versions of a document. This capability is invaluable, especially when multiple collaborators are making edits. It ensures that no change is permanent and that any unintended modifications can be easily reversed.

OneDrive's notification system enhances collaborative efforts by keeping users informed about any changes or updates in shared files. Users receive notifications when someone edits a shared document, helping them stay on top of the changes and facilitating timely responses.

However, with great power comes great responsibility. Effective collaboration in OneDrive requires a degree of management. Administrators and users must be mindful of access permissions and sharing settings to ensure data security and compliance with organizational policies.

Regular reviews of shared files, managing access permissions, and educating team members about best practices in file sharing and collaboration are essential to maintain a secure and efficient collaborative environment.

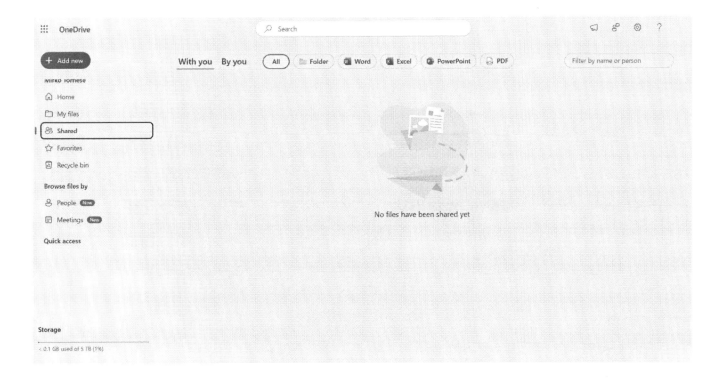

In conclusion, OneDrive for Cloud Storage transcends its role as a storage tool to become a powerful platform for collaboration and sharing. By leveraging its seamless integration with Office 365, real-time co-authoring features, and robust sharing options, OneDrive fosters a collaborative workspace that is secure, efficient, and accessible from anywhere. Understanding and utilizing these features allows teams to collaborate effectively, breaking down geographical barriers and driving productivity in the modern digital workplace.

94. Syncing Devices with OneDrive

Syncing devices with OneDrive represents a critical component in the modern digital ecosystem, particularly for those seeking to enhance productivity and maintain seamless access to data across multiple devices. This synchronization feature is not just about having files accessible on various devices; it's about integrating your work and personal life into a fluid, cohesive digital experience.

OneDrive, a cornerstone of Microsoft's Office 365 suite, offers robust syncing capabilities that ensure your files are not only backed up in the cloud but are also available on any device connected to your OneDrive account. This includes PCs, Macs, tablets, and smartphones. The convenience of having your documents, photos, and other files sync across these devices cannot be overstated.

The process of setting up sync on OneDrive is straightforward and user-friendly. On a Windows PC, for example, this begins with signing into the OneDrive application using your Microsoft account. Once signed in, you can choose the folders you wish to sync. This level of control is crucial as it allows users to determine which files are necessary on each device, conserving local storage space and optimizing performance.

For Mac users, the process is equally streamlined. After installing the OneDrive app from the Mac App Store, you simply log in and select the folders to sync. The integration of OneDrive with macOS is seamless, providing a similar experience to what's offered on Windows, including the use of Finder to access and manage files.

On mobile devices, the OneDrive app plays a pivotal role. Available for both iOS and Android, the app not only allows you to view and manage your synced files but also offers the capability to automatically upload photos and videos taken on your device. This feature is particularly advantageous as it ensures that your memories are safely backed up and accessible from any of your devices.

Syncing extends beyond just files and folders. OneDrive also syncs your settings across devices. This includes themes, language preferences, and even browser favorites if you use Microsoft Edge. This feature enhances the user experience, providing a personalized feel regardless of the device being used.

OneDrive's Files On-Demand is a standout feature that takes syncing to the next level. Available on Windows and macOS, it allows users to access their files in OneDrive without having to download them and use storage space on their device. Files On-Demand shows all your files in File Explorer and Finder, but only downloads them when they are needed. This smart feature is particularly useful for users with limited storage space or those who manage large numbers of files.

Real-time syncing is another essential aspect of OneDrive. Changes made to a file on one device are instantly reflected on all other synced devices. This real-time update is crucial for collaborative work, ensuring that all team members have access to the most current version of a document.

However, effective syncing with OneDrive requires a good internet connection. Users must be aware that large files may take significant time to sync, especially on initial setup. Regular monitoring of the sync status is recommended to ensure that files are up-to-date across all devices.

Security and privacy in syncing cannot be overlooked. OneDrive employs robust encryption for both files in transit and at rest, ensuring that your data is protected. Users are also advised to use strong passwords and consider activating two-factor authentication for their Microsoft account for added security.

In conclusion, syncing devices with OneDrive offers a streamlined, secure, and efficient way to access and manage files across multiple devices. It eliminates the need for manual transfers of data via external drives or email and ensures that your latest work and precious memories are always at your fingertips. Understanding and utilizing these sync features can dramatically improve your productivity and digital organization, making OneDrive an indispensable tool in your Office 365 arsenal.

95. OneDrive Security and Privacy

In the realm of cloud storage, the security and privacy of OneDrive have become paramount, particularly as our digital footprints expand and the sensitivity of stored data increases. OneDrive, an integral part of Microsoft's Office 365 suite, is not just a storage solution but a hub of personal and professional data. The attention to security and privacy in OneDrive is a testament to its significance in the digital age.

OneDrive employs a multi-faceted approach to security, ensuring that data is not only stored securely but also transmitted safely. At the core is encryption. Data in transit between your device and OneDrive is protected using Transport Layer Security (TLS), which prevents unauthorized interception of your files.

For data at rest, OneDrive uses Advanced Encryption Standard (AES) with 256-bit keys, offering robust defense against unauthorized access.

Microsoft's commitment to privacy is evident in their handling of user data. They have a clear privacy statement, emphasizing that they do not use your files for advertising purposes. Your data is yours alone – Microsoft acts merely as a custodian, not as an owner or observer.

User authentication plays a critical role in OneDrive's security architecture. Two-factor authentication (2FA), which adds an extra layer of security beyond just the password, is available and strongly recommended. This can involve a code sent to your phone or a prompt through Microsoft's Authenticator app, significantly reducing the risk of unauthorized access.

OneDrive also provides extensive control over sharing and access rights. Files and folders can be shared with specific people, and access can be set as view-only or with editing rights. This granularity not only enhances collaboration but also ensures that sensitive information is not overexposed. For additional control, links to files can be set to expire after a set period, and password protection on shared items is possible, adding another level of security.

OneDrive's ransomware detection and recovery capability is a standout feature. Ransomware, a malicious software that locks access to data until a ransom is paid, poses a significant threat. OneDrive monitors for ransomware-like behavior and notifies you if it detects anything suspicious. If an attack is confirmed, OneDrive helps you recover your files, ensuring minimal disruption and data loss.

Version history in OneDrive is not just a feature for convenience but also a security element. It allows users to restore previous versions of documents, which is invaluable in the case of accidental deletions or alterations. This history is maintained for an extended period, offering a robust solution for undoing changes.

For business users, OneDrive offers additional advanced security features in line with enterprise needs. These include data loss prevention (DLP), which helps prevent sensitive information from unintentionally being shared, and advanced threat protection (ATP), which identifies and blocks malware in files.

Privacy controls in OneDrive are also worthy of note. Users can access and review the data collected by Microsoft and have the option to delete it. This transparency is crucial in an era where data privacy concerns are ever-increasing.

OneDrive's integration with the broader Office 365 suite brings additional security benefits. It adheres to global compliance standards, including GDPR, HIPAA, and more, ensuring that data handling meets stringent legal requirements.

In conclusion, OneDrive's security and privacy features are designed to provide a secure, reliable, and compliant cloud storage experience. From encryption and authentication to ransomware protection and privacy controls, OneDrive stands out as a solution that understands the criticality of data security in the digital landscape. For users seeking a cloud storage option that aligns with the highest standards of data protection, OneDrive emerges as a compelling choice, seamlessly integrating robust security measures without compromising on functionality or user experience.

96. Advanced OneDrive Features

OneDrive, Microsoft's cloud storage service, has become an indispensable tool for individuals and businesses alike. Its advanced features not only provide secure storage but also enhance productivity and collaboration across various platforms.

Secure and Private: The Personal Vault feature in OneDrive offers an extra layer of protection. Users can store sensitive information, like financial documents and personal identification, with the assurance of robust security measures like two-factor authentication. This area is encrypted, ensuring data is secure both during transmission and at rest.

Photo and Video Backup: Automatically backing up photos and videos from mobile devices is effortless with OneDrive. This feature not only secures cherished memories but also efficiently manages device storage by uploading media files directly to the cloud.

Scanning and Digitization: The OneDrive mobile app includes a document scanning function, transforming physical documents into digital files. This feature is ideal for quickly digitizing and storing receipts, notes, and business cards. The app's Optical Character Recognition (OCR) technology makes the text in these scans searchable and editable, further enhancing its utility.

Access Files Anytime, Anywhere: With Files On-Demand, users can view and edit files without using up local storage space. This feature is especially beneficial for devices with limited storage, as files are stored in the cloud and only downloaded when needed.

Collaboration in Real-Time: OneDrive's integration with Microsoft Office enables multiple users to work on documents simultaneously. Changes are synchronized in real-time, streamlining collaboration and increasing efficiency, particularly for remote teams.

Version History: Every file in OneDrive has a version history, allowing users to track and restore previous versions. This functionality is a safety net against accidental deletions and unwanted edits, providing peace of mind and greater control over document revisions.

Offline Access: Marking files or folders for offline access is a key feature for those working in areas with inconsistent internet access. Users can work on these files offline, with changes syncing up once an internet connection is reestablished.

Intelligent Search: OneDrive uses AI and machine learning for enhanced search capabilities. This intelligent search goes beyond filenames, allowing users to find files based on their content, including text within images and scanned documents.

Seamless Integration with Windows 10: For Windows 10 users, OneDrive offers a seamless experience. Files saved to OneDrive are accessible just like local files, thanks to integration with Windows File Explorer.

Advanced Business Security: OneDrive for Business users benefit from additional security features like data loss prevention, advanced threat analytics, and audit logs. These tools are vital for protecting sensitive information and ensuring compliance with various regulations.

Cross-Platform Functionality: Accessibility across different platforms is a cornerstone of OneDrive's design. With applications for Windows, Mac, iOS, and Android, users can access their files from virtually any device, highlighting its versatility in a multi-device world.

In summary, OneDrive's advanced features provide a comprehensive, secure, and user-friendly cloud storage experience. Its wide array of functionalities, from the Personal Vault's enhanced security to real-time collaboration tools and intelligent search capabilities, makes it an ideal solution for diverse needs. For personal use or within a business context, OneDrive simplifies file management, enhances productivity, and ensures secure and efficient access to data anytime, anywhere.

97. Troubleshooting Common OneDrive Issues

Troubleshooting common OneDrive issues is essential for maintaining uninterrupted access and functionality. Users often face several recurring problems, and understanding how to resolve these can significantly enhance the OneDrive experience.

Sync Issues: One of the most common challenges is the failure of files to sync properly. This could be due to various reasons, including network issues, file size limits, or file types blocked by OneDrive. To resolve this, check the file size and type, ensure a stable internet connection, and try pausing and resuming the sync. The OneDrive sync client also provides error codes that can guide towards specific solutions.

Access Denied/Error Messages: Occasionally, users may encounter access denied or error messages when trying to open files. This is often related to permission settings. Verify that you have the necessary permissions to access the file and that the file isn't being edited by someone else. If the file is shared, check with the owner to ensure your access level.

OneDrive Not Starting: If OneDrive doesn't start automatically, this can be due to startup settings or account issues. Ensure OneDrive is included in the startup programs list and check your Microsoft account for any problems. Sometimes, simply restarting the application or the device can solve this issue.

Missing Files: Missing files can be caused by accidental deletion, the file not syncing, or being moved to another location. Check the recycle bin on OneDrive online and your local device. Use the search feature in OneDrive to locate the file. If the file was shared, ensure it hasn't been moved or deleted by others.

Slow Performance: If OneDrive is running slowly, it could be due to large files syncing, many files syncing at once, or limited bandwidth. Prioritize files for syncing or use the 'Files On-Demand' feature to save local space and improve performance. Adjusting your device's network settings to allow more bandwidth for OneDrive can also help.

Storage Limit Reached: Reaching or exceeding your storage limit can halt syncing. To resolve this, clear up space by deleting unnecessary files or folders from OneDrive. You can also opt to increase your storage plan if needed.

Login Problems: Login issues may occur due to incorrect credentials or account-related problems. Double-check your username and password. Resetting your password or verifying your Microsoft account can also resolve these issues.

Conflicting Files: Conflicts can arise when a file is edited on multiple devices before syncing. OneDrive typically flags these files. You can resolve conflicts by choosing which version to keep or by merging changes manually if necessary.

File Corruption: If a file won't open or is corrupted, try opening a previous version from OneDrive's version history. This feature allows you to restore an earlier, uncorrupted version of the file.

Security Concerns: Concerns about unauthorized access or potential data breaches can be addressed by reviewing and adjusting your OneDrive security settings. Enable two-factor authentication and check the sharing settings for your files and folders.

Integrating with Office 365: Sometimes, issues arise when integrating OneDrive with other Office 365 applications. Ensure both OneDrive and the Office 365 suite are updated to their latest versions. Checking the permissions and account settings in both applications can also help resolve integration issues.

In summary, while common, most OneDrive issues can be resolved with simple checks and adjustments. Keeping the application updated, regularly checking storage and sync settings, and being aware of security and access permissions can prevent many of these problems. For more complex issues, Microsoft provides a wealth of resources and support tools that can assist in troubleshooting and resolving any persistent challenges.

98. Integrating OneDrive with Office 365

Integrating OneDrive with Office 365 revolutionizes how we approach data management, collaboration, and productivity. This integration brings a seamless blend of cloud storage and office productivity tools, offering unparalleled convenience and efficiency.

Seamless Document Access and Management: OneDrive's integration with Office 365 allows users to access, edit, and manage documents stored in the cloud directly from Office applications like Word, Excel, and PowerPoint. This integration eliminates the need for multiple steps to open and edit documents. You can work on your files from anywhere, on any device, without worrying about having the latest version.

Real-time Collaboration: Collaboration is a cornerstone of modern workflows, and this integration makes it effortlessly efficient. Multiple users can work on the same document simultaneously, seeing real-time changes. This feature is particularly useful for teams spread across different locations, enabling them to collaborate as if they were in the same room.

Link Sharing and Access Control: Sharing documents is more straightforward and more secure. You can share files or folders with colleagues or external partners by sending a link, eliminating the need to send attachments via email. You can also control who can view or edit the shared documents, enhancing security and collaboration efficiency.

Syncing Across Devices: The integration ensures that your documents are synced across all devices. Changes made on one device are automatically updated on all others. This feature is particularly useful for professionals who use multiple devices, like a work computer, personal laptop, and a smartphone.

Version History and Data Loss Prevention: Office 365's integration with OneDrive includes a version history feature. If you need to revert to a previous version of a document, you can do so easily. This capability is a safety net against accidental deletions or unwanted edits, ensuring data integrity.

Intuitive File Organization: Organizing files is streamlined with OneDrive's integration into Office 365. You can create, rename, and organize folders and files directly from your Office applications. This feature simplifies file management, making it more intuitive and less time-consuming.

Automated Workflows with Power Automate: The integration extends to Microsoft's Power Automate (formerly Microsoft Flow), allowing you to create automated workflows. For example, you can automate tasks such as saving email attachments to a specific OneDrive folder or getting notifications for file updates.

Enhanced Security Features: Office 365's robust security features extend to OneDrive. With advanced security measures like encryption, ransomware detection, and file recovery options, your data is protected against unauthorized access and threats.

Consistent User Experience: OneDrive's integration offers a consistent user experience across all Office 365 applications. The familiar interface reduces the learning curve, allowing users to focus on productivity rather than navigating a new tool.

Streamlining Offline Access: OneDrive allows you to make files available offline. This means you can work on your documents without an internet connection, and the changes will sync once you're back online. This feature is beneficial for those who travel or have intermittent internet access.

Integration with Microsoft Teams and SharePoint: OneDrive integrates seamlessly with other Office 365 tools like Microsoft Teams and SharePoint. This integration allows for a cohesive ecosystem where files and communications are centralized, enhancing team collaboration and project management.

In summary, integrating OneDrive with Office 365 is not just about having a place to store your files. It's about creating an interconnected environment where productivity, collaboration, and data management are streamlined. Whether you're working on a complex project with a team or managing your day-to-day tasks, this integration provides the tools you need to do it effectively and securely. For anyone looking to optimize your workflow and embrace digital transformation, mastering this integration is not just beneficial—it's essential.

99. OneDrive Tips and Tricks

Maximizing your OneDrive experience can greatly enhance your productivity and streamline your workflow. Here are some valuable tips and tricks to get the most out of OneDrive, Microsoft's powerful cloud storage solution.

1. Master the Art of Selective Sync: OneDrive's Selective Sync feature allows you to choose which folders to sync with your computer, preventing unnecessary files from cluttering your hard drive. This is especially useful for users with limited storage space or those who use multiple devices.

2. Utilize Files On-Demand: With Files On-Demand, you can access all your files in OneDrive without having to download them all and use storage space on your device. This feature is particularly handy for those who need to access a large number of files across different devices.

3. Discover the Version History Feature: OneDrive offers a Version History feature that can be a lifesaver. It allows you to view and restore previous versions of your documents, which is invaluable if you accidentally delete or overwrite important files.

4. Explore Sharing Options for Collaboration: OneDrive makes sharing files or folders simple and secure. You can set permissions for each shared item, deciding whether recipients can edit or only view your files. This level of control is crucial for collaborative projects.

5. Integrate OneDrive with Microsoft Office: OneDrive works seamlessly with Microsoft Office applications. You can work on Word, Excel, or PowerPoint documents directly in OneDrive, and changes are automatically saved in the cloud. This integration facilitates real-time collaboration with colleagues.

6. Use the Mobile App for Access Anywhere: The OneDrive mobile app is an excellent tool for accessing your files on the go. You can quickly view, edit, and share files from your smartphone or tablet, ensuring productivity even when you're away from your desk.

7. Take Advantage of Powerful Search Capabilities: OneDrive's search function is robust and can save you considerable time. You can search for text within documents and even photos, making finding what you need easier than ever.

8. Set Up Automatic Camera Upload on Your Phone: If you're using OneDrive on your smartphone, take advantage of the automatic camera upload feature. This ensures that all photos and videos you take are automatically saved to OneDrive, offering an immediate backup.

9. Protect Your Data with Personal Vault: For sensitive information, use OneDrive's Personal Vault, which provides an extra layer of security. Personal Vault requires a second step of identity verification to access, making it ideal for storing sensitive documents.

10. Familiarize Yourself with Keyboard Shortcuts: Keyboard shortcuts can significantly speed up your workflow. Familiarize yourself with OneDrive's shortcuts to navigate, manage, and operate files more efficiently.

11. Organize with Metadata: Use metadata to organize your files in OneDrive. This can include details like project names, client names, or dates, helping you to sort and find files efficiently.

12. Utilize Storage Sense in Windows: If you're using Windows 10 or later, Storage Sense can automatically free up space by making older, unused, or available online files only accessible through OneDrive.

13. Keep Track of Shared Documents: Keep an eye on the documents you've shared or those shared with you. OneDrive allows you to see who has access to what, which is critical for managing collaborative work and maintaining security.

14. Use OneDrive for Large File Transfers: Instead of struggling with email size limits, use OneDrive to share large files or folders by sending a link to the recipient.

15. Regularly Check Your Storage Space: Keep an eye on your OneDrive storage space to ensure you don't run out. Regularly clean out old or unnecessary files and know your options for upgrading storage if needed.

By leveraging these tips and tricks, you can make OneDrive a more powerful tool in your productivity arsenal, ensuring that your data is not only safe and secure but also easily accessible and manageable, no matter where you are.

100. Beyond OneDrive: Exploring Other Cloud Options

While OneDrive is a robust cloud storage solution, especially for those deeply integrated into the Microsoft ecosystem, it's beneficial to be aware of alternative cloud storage options. Exploring other services can provide insights into different features, pricing models, and usability that might better suit specific needs or preferences. Here's a look at some notable cloud storage alternatives to OneDrive:

1. Google Drive: A formidable competitor in the cloud storage market, Google Drive offers seamless integration with Google's suite of productivity apps like Docs, Sheets, and Slides. It's known for its collaborative capabilities, allowing multiple users to edit documents simultaneously. Drive also boasts excellent search functionality and offers 15 GB of free storage.

2. Dropbox: Praised for its simplicity and reliability, Dropbox is a popular choice for personal and business users. Its file synchronization capabilities are top-notch, ensuring that your files are always up to date across all devices. Dropbox also offers features like file versioning and Dropbox Paper, a collaborative workspace.

3. Apple iCloud: Ideal for users deeply entrenched in the Apple ecosystem, iCloud offers smooth integration with iOS and macOS devices. It's excellent for storing photos, backups of your iPhone or iPad, and seamlessly syncing data across Apple devices. iCloud also provides options to share files and folders with others.

4. Amazon Drive: A solid option for Amazon Prime members, as it offers unlimited photo storage and 5 GB for video and file storage. Amazon Drive integrates well with Amazon Fire TV and other Amazon devices, making it a convenient choice for users in the Amazon ecosystem.

5. Box: Focused more on businesses and enterprises, Box offers not just storage but also collaboration tools. It's known for its robust security features, comprehensive administrative controls, and integration with numerous apps like Salesforce and Office 365.

6. Sync.com: This service places a heavy emphasis on privacy and security, offering end-to-end encryption. Sync.com is an excellent choice for those who prioritize the confidentiality of their data. It also offers features like file versioning and secure file sharing.

7. Tresorit: Another service that focuses heavily on security, Tresorit offers end-to-end encrypted storage and sharing. It's geared towards businesses and professionals who handle sensitive data and need secure collaboration tools.

8. pCloud: Offering a unique lifetime subscription model, pCloud is a cost-effective and user-friendly option. It provides a built-in media player, making it a great choice for storing and streaming music and videos.

9. Adobe Creative Cloud: For those working extensively with Adobe's suite of creative software, Adobe Creative Cloud offers integrated cloud storage. It's particularly useful for designers and creatives who need to store large multimedia files and collaborate on creative projects.

10. Nextcloud: A self-hosted option, Nextcloud is for those who want full control over their cloud storage. It's an open-source solution that lets you set up your own cloud storage server. While it requires more technical know-how, it offers unparalleled control and customization.

Each of these cloud storage options has its strengths and is suited to different types of users and needs. Whether you're looking for more storage space, better integration with your devices and apps, enhanced collaboration tools, or stronger security features, there's likely a cloud solution that meets your requirements.

When choosing a cloud storage service, consider factors like storage needs, budget, specific feature requirements, and the ecosystem of devices and apps you use. Remember, it's also common and often beneficial to use multiple cloud services concurrently to take advantage of the unique strengths of each.

As we conclude our exploration of OneDrive and its multifaceted capabilities, it's clear that this tool is more than just a cloud storage service. It's a dynamic platform that empowers users to manage, share, and protect their data with ease and efficiency. Throughout this guide, we've navigated the extensive features of OneDrive, learning how it seamlessly integrates with Office 365 to create a unified and productive experience.

From understanding the basics of file management and synchronization to delving into advanced features and security protocols, we've covered a broad spectrum of functionalities that cater to diverse needs.

OneDrive's capabilities in facilitating collaboration and ensuring data security stand out as particularly crucial in today's interconnected and fast-paced digital landscape. The troubleshooting section addressed common challenges, ensuring that users are well-equipped to handle any issues that may arise.

Moreover, we've gone beyond the confines of OneDrive to explore alternative cloud storage options, offering a comprehensive view of the digital storage landscape. This broad perspective ensures that users are well-informed about the choices available to them and can make decisions that best suit their personal or organizational needs.

In essence, OneDrive emerges as a robust, versatile, and user-friendly platform that plays a crucial role in modern data management and collaboration. Whether for personal use, academic endeavors, or professional projects, OneDrive offers tools and features that enhance productivity and ensure data is accessible, secure, and effectively managed. As cloud computing continues to evolve, OneDrive is poised to remain an essential component in our digital toolkit.

Customized Office 365 Cheat Sheets

Scan this QR Code to get the Bonus

Time Management Mastery for Professionals

Scan this QR Code to get the Bonus

9 Revolutionary Techniques to End Procrastination

Scan this QR Code to get the Bonus

Made in the USA
Columbia, SC
30 August 2024